Designed by Raquel Hazell
ISBN: 978-1-939901-10-1

Published by AC Books, an imprint of the AC Institute.
www.acbooks.org // www.acinstitute.org
Printed by Maple Press in Pennsylvania
Distributed by Small Press Distribution

7DAYS

expanded edition

edited by holly crawford, ed

contents

introduction

by Holly Crawford, Editor and Director of AC Books

In the beginning God created the heavens and the earth, so goes the creation myth for Judeo-Christian culture. In the beginning there was a spark that lead to creation. Adam named things. Seven days...moments that are marked on the gregorian calendar signified by the rising and setting of the sun. Artists create and they learn to make. It is then—if they are very lucky—they will be exhibited, written about, publicized, collected, taught and conserved.

The art world and all the people that encompass it have daily lives that are structured in one way or another by art. But how is it structured? How do they see any one slice of their art life? What would a list of the different occupations in the art world look like? It all starts with the artists; it is from their work that the role collectors, curators, critics, art dealers, publishers, art teachers and art historians come into play. This would be a basic list but as you know, many in the art world hold more than one title.

I asked many people in many places to tell me about their art week. I defined this as seven days, though they didn't have to be consecutive. This edited book compiled from essays, texts and images showcases just a glimpse of their life. When I first approached people for this collaborative project some found my request odd, others did not. It did take thought and introspection. I was overjoyed by the thoughtful, poignant, humorous, creative and insightful contributions. In essence this project became another aspect of their art life. Several asked to see what others had sent me. I did not want to reveal their results and I did not. Many different approaches were taken to express or document this part of their lives. For many, art consumes most of their waking hours, me included. In the end this is art, both a document and a collaboration.

Why did I ask this question at all? I think the art world is different than other careers or professions. Artists use all kinds of mediums which requires different physical and mental processes. For instance, all painters paint but not all artists paint. People have different processes in art and, as you will see, many have different ways of seeing their life through art. I first noticed this variety in Critical Conversations in a Limo, a previous participation project of mine. I asked people as a group to talk about anything art related for one hour while riding around in a white limousine. There were conversations in NYC, Melbourne and San Francisco. No conversation was the same.

Whom is this book for? Who is its audience? It is for anyone and everyone in art who is curious enough to want to see how their fellow travelers see the world, the world they inhabit or want to inhabit. It is also for anyone interested in art and the art world and others.

I hope this edited book becomes part of your days.

I would like to thank everyone who contributed.

3

ann marie lequesne

is a London based artist who devises and documents performances that work with groups of people. She is interested in the social dynamic of groups — the ways that they become a group, form loyalties and identify with the group.

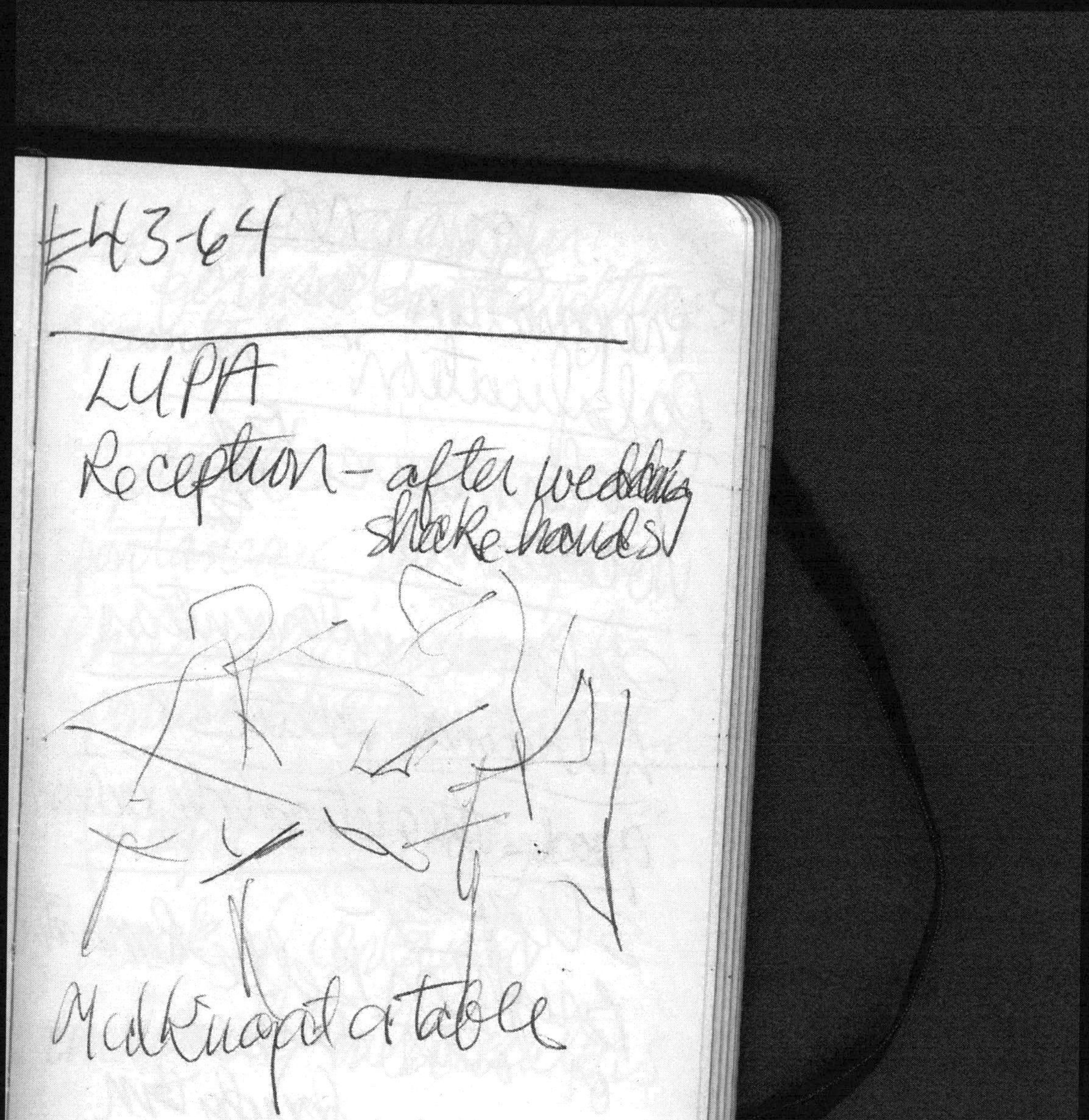
£43-64
LUPA
Reception- after wedding
shake hands

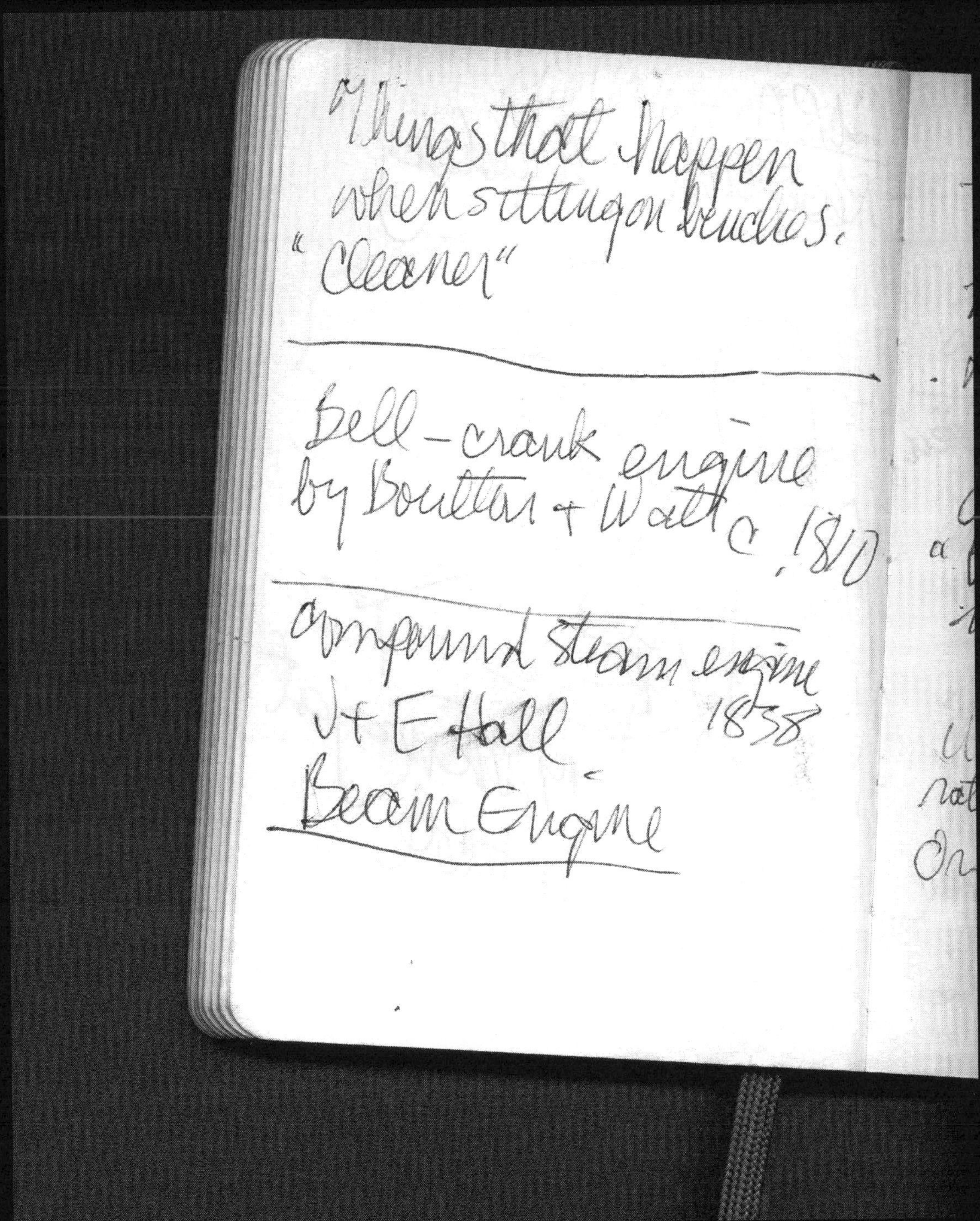
"Things that happen
when sitting on benches.
"Cleaner"
Bell-crank engine
by Boulton + Watt c. 1810
compound steam engine
J+E Hall 1838
Beam Engine

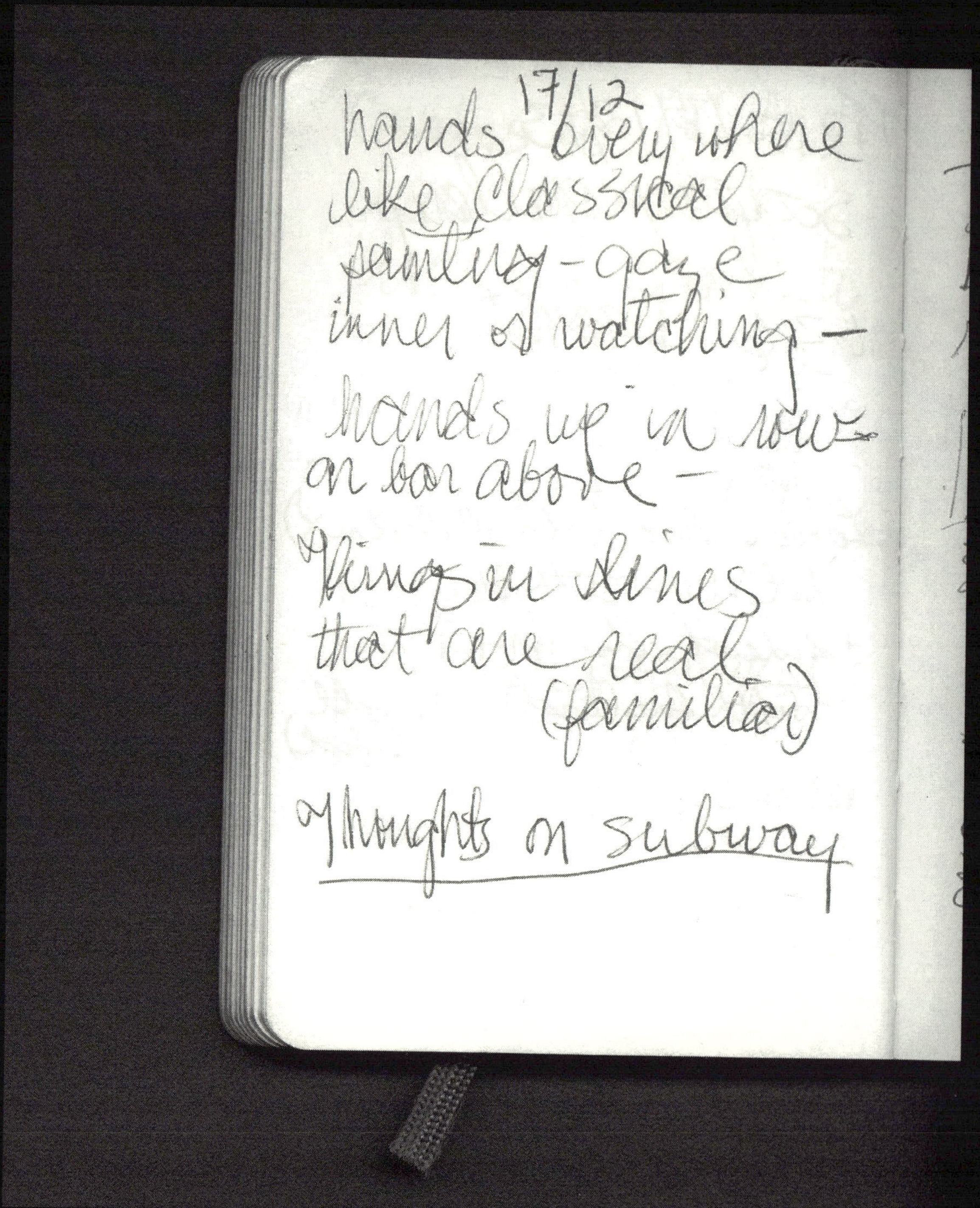
17/12
hands everywhere
like classical
painting - gaze
watching -
hands up in row
on bar above -
things in lines
that are real
(familiar)
Thoughts on subway

18/12

Banners or

Doubly supported banners

rows going by

close

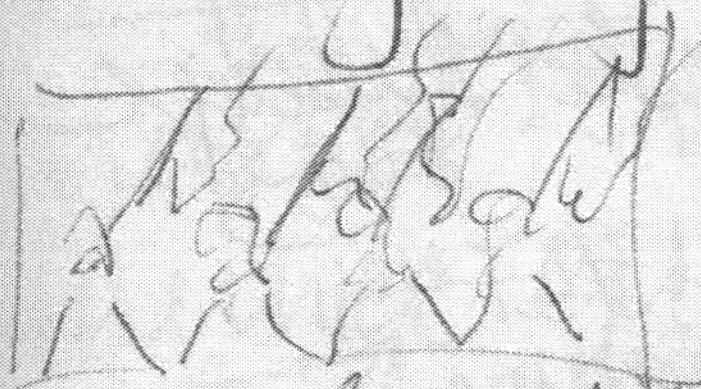

single row across st.

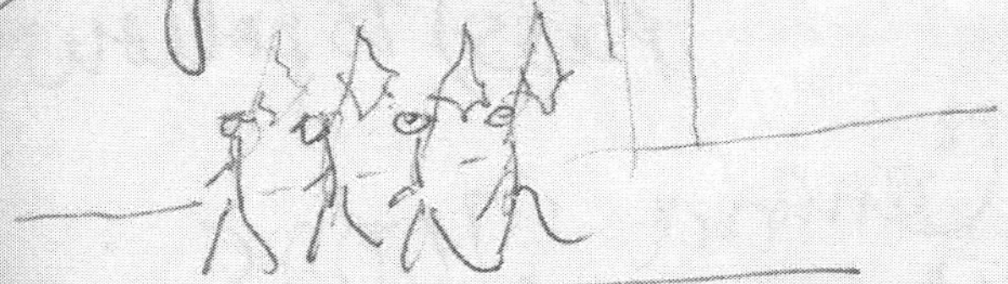

Follow procession

Film in procession

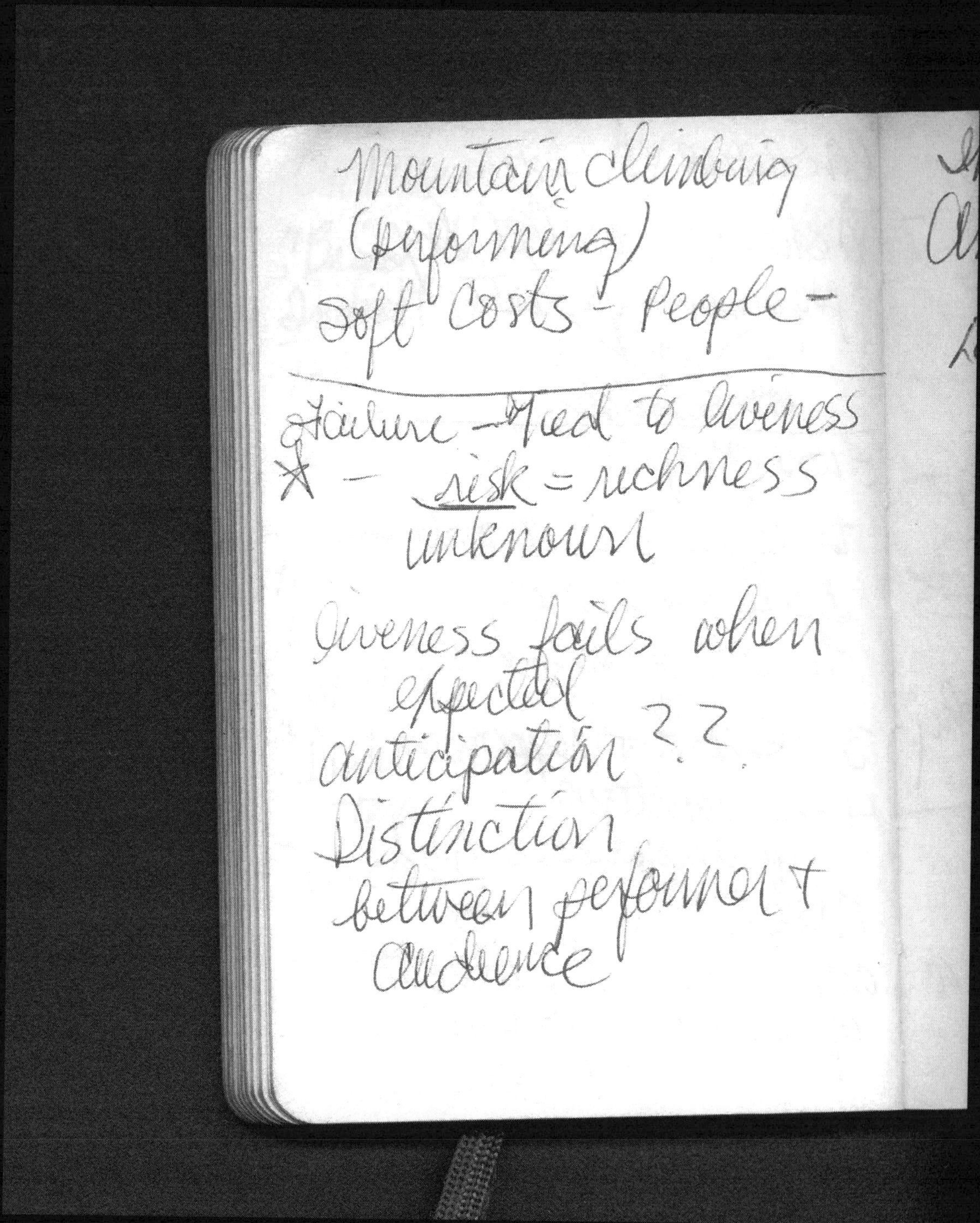

Mountain climbing
(performing)
Soft Costs - People -

Failure - Tied to liveness
✱ - risk = richness
unknown

liveness fails when
expected
anticipation ??
Distinction
between performer +
audience

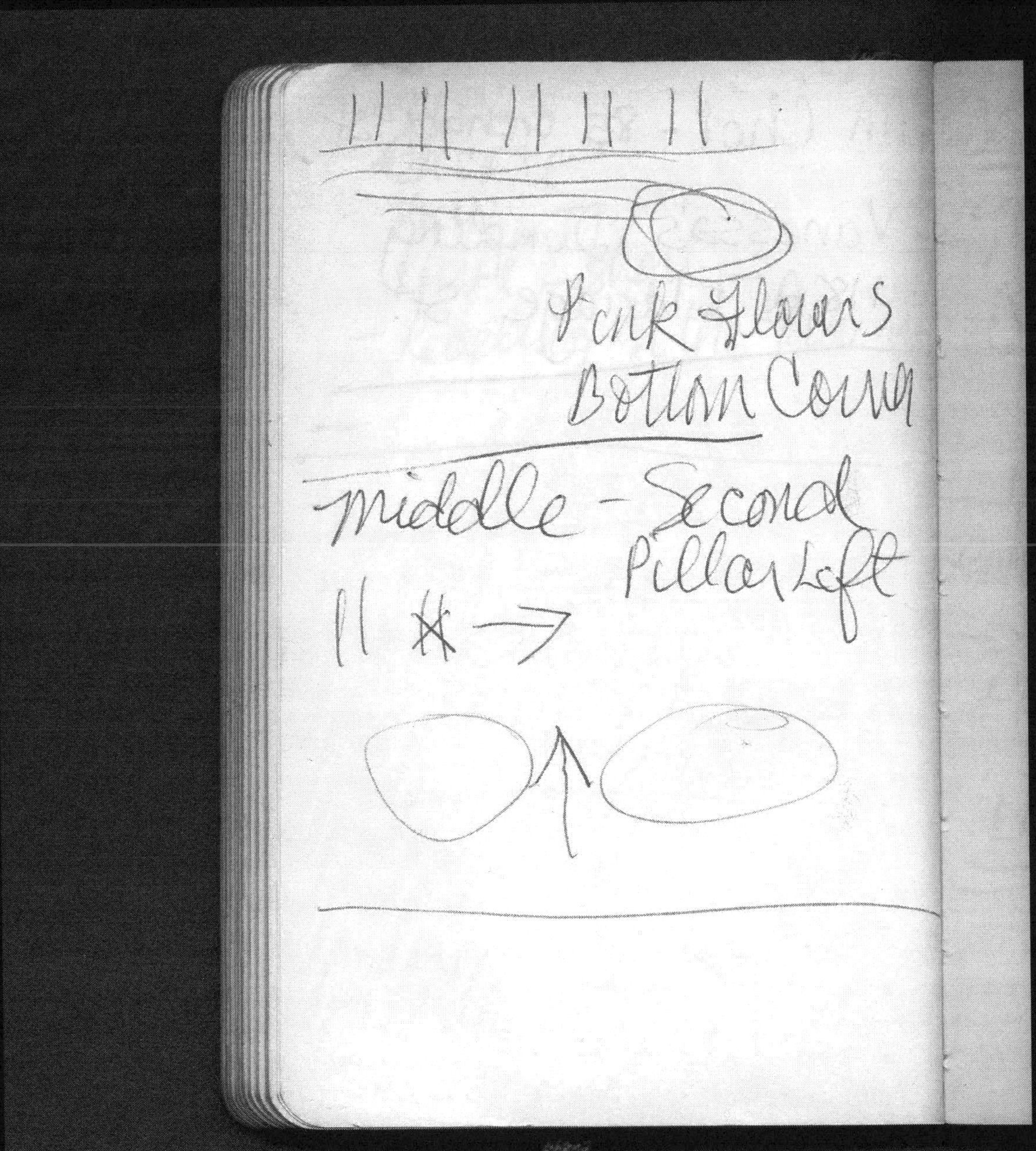
Pink Flowers
Bottom Corner
middle - Second
Pillar Left

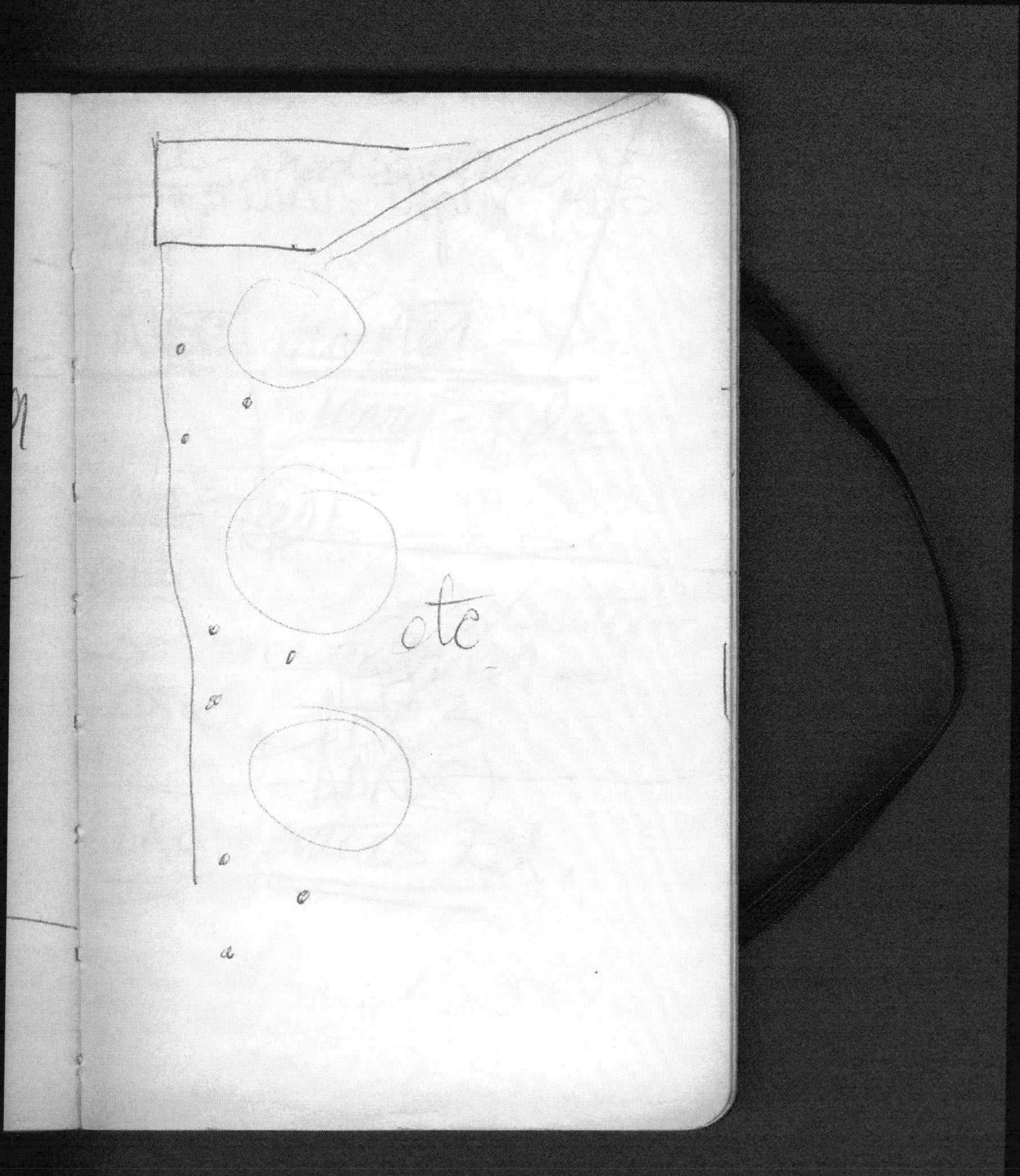

molly haslund

graduated from the Royal Academy of Fine Arts, Copenhagen (2000-2005) and Glasgow School of Art (MFA, 2003-2005). Haslund works in the intersection between sculpture, installation and performance, integrating elements from pop culture, performing arts, literature and music into a multifaceted artistic practice.

It smells of old dust and something else, I don't know what it is, wet linen or perhaps concrete paint, as I let myself into Molly's studio for the first time. The studio is located in the back building on the fourth floor in Baggesen Street, Copenhagen. I stand in the tiny kitchen. Elsewhere in the house, a band is practicing indie rock of some sort. Molly herself is attending a residency program in New York. She is going to make a new piece on an abandoned site by the Hudson River. Since her studio was already empty, she called and asked if I wanted to live there for a while.

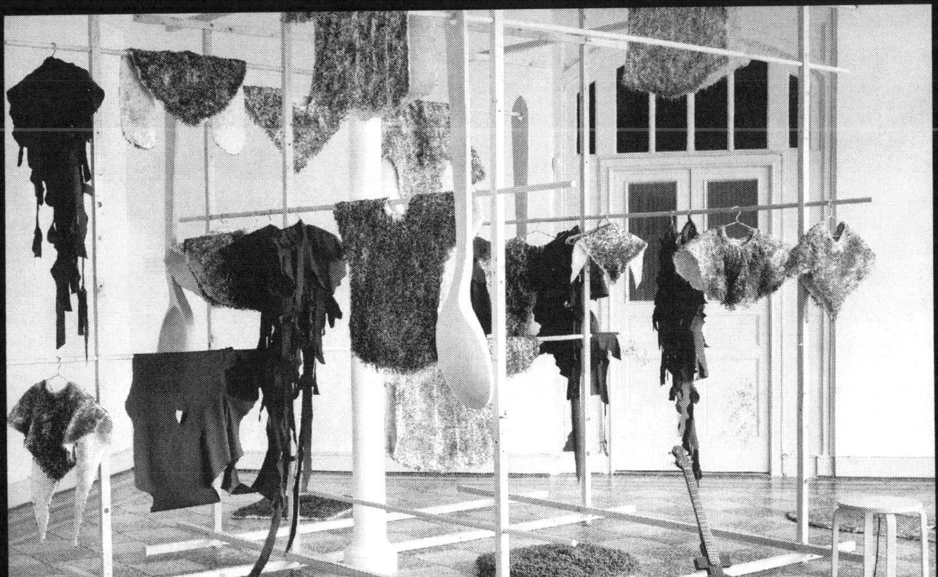

I look around the kitchen. The music has stopped. Even with the sun so strong outside there isn't much light coming in. I stand there for a while as my eyes adjust to the darkness. It looks like there hasn't been anyone here for long. By the sink are dirty cups with old dried-in coffee stain rings that someone must have left, and an orange plastic bowl. Above is a narrow window facing a yellow brick wall. Down in the yard are moving boxes containing my clothes and a few books, and my mom's Safari chair.

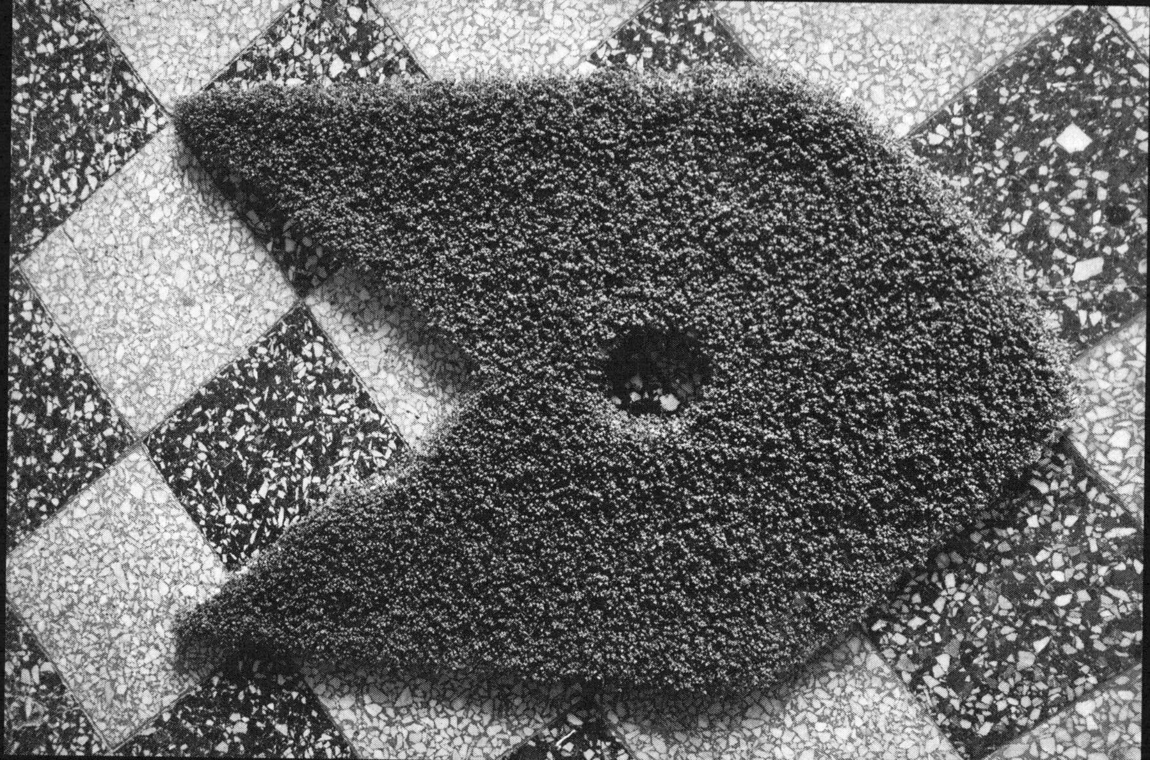

I look around the kitchen. The music has stopped. Even with the sun so strong outside there isn't much light coming in. I stand there for a while as my eyes adjust to the darkness. It looks like there hasn't been anyone here for long. By the sink are dirty cups with old dried-in coffee stain rings that someone must have left, and an orange plastic bowl. Above is a narrow window facing a yellow brick wall. Down in the yard are moving boxes containing my clothes and a few books, and my mom's Safari chair.

Molly called me from New York and said she needed someone to look after her cress-capes during the time they would be exhibited in the Art Institute. I assume Doris that told her about me. I don't know her that well. The capes are sewn out of white cotton rolls and then covered with water and cress seeds. I water them a couple of times per week while they are still lying flat on the floor. When fully grown, they are put on hangers and placed on a minimal wood structure built as a standalone room inside the huge high-ceiling exhibition space facing the canal. The adjustable modules of the structure match the measurements of her studio space. The cress patterns have different shapes. In full bloom you can wear them, put them over your shoulders as a cape or as a sort of coat or west.

Yesterday a crowd of Japanese tourists were watching while I was moving the capes around, but usually I'm alone. The sun shines through the windows and covers the mosaic floor with light square spots. I like walking in the space around and watering the cress capes. They look like huge pubic hair pieces, green and juicy when laying on the floor, or small islands floating in a blue mosaic sea. My feet are bare, the air is warm, and yet there are cooler patches of the floor that haven't been warmed up by the sun.

As the cress fades, I stop watering the capes. I hang them on metal hangers or over the wood planks in the structure as Molly told me to. The sun moves and the remaining moisture evaporates.

They dry out completely and after some days the cress-capes lose their color. They look like sealskin: stiff and grey-green.

Compared to some of the other studios Molly's is quite simple. At the far end are a couple of bookcases where she keeps props for her performances: the compasses, and the ukulele.

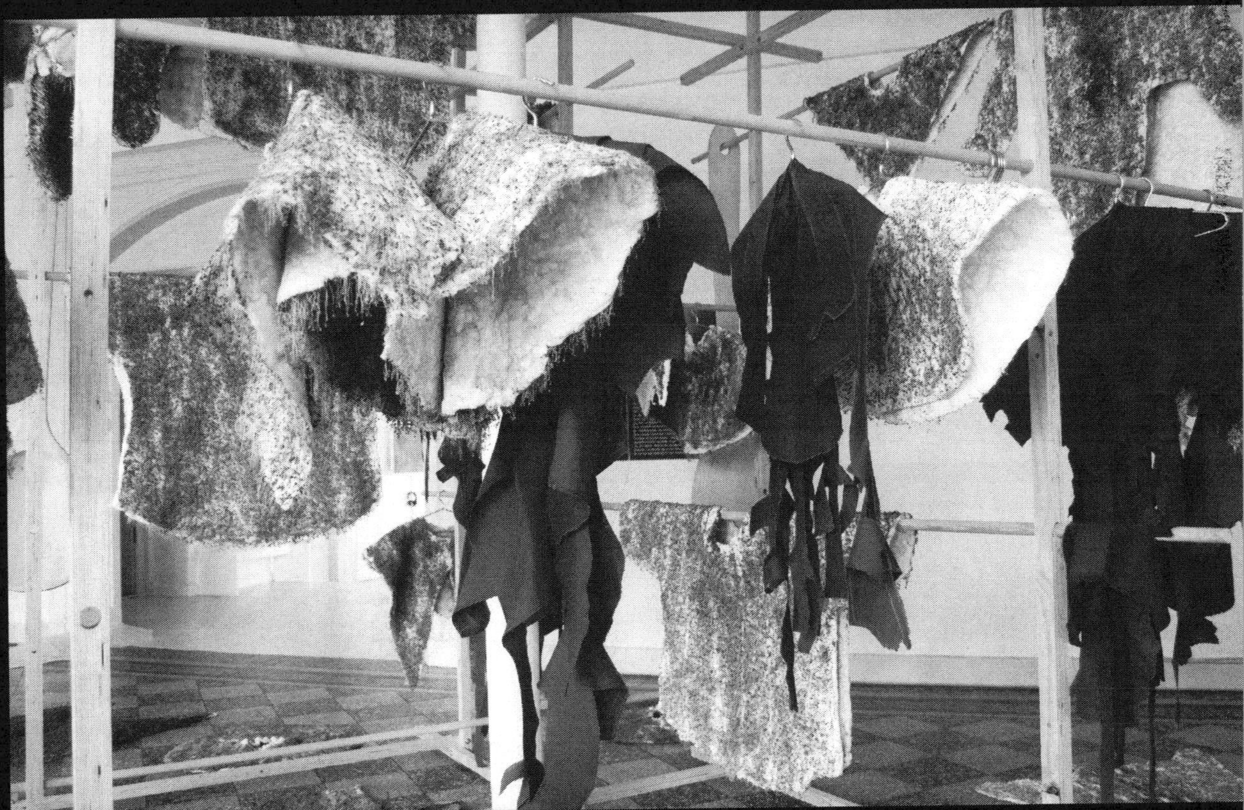

Towards the yard is a big window, and in front of it is a work table made up of two sawhorses, a table top, and an office chair. Most of my belongings are stored at my mom's. I only kept the Safari chair, which I got from her when I moved from home, my books, and some clothes. My mattress is leaning against the wall wrapped in a blue bed sheet, and in the bookcase my duvet is rolled up on a shelf. The first time I lay down on the mattress it was almost euphoric.

Alone in the sea of foam. I stretched and tried to reach the four corners of the mattress at the same time, filling it out with my entire body, trying to fulfill the intimacy of the sleep alone, not having another human next to you, not as much as a single trace from any other human that once was lying here.

I would rather that Peter had found something else as he googled my name. It's vanity, I know, but I prefer photos with me looking happy, surrounded by happy people. It could have been an

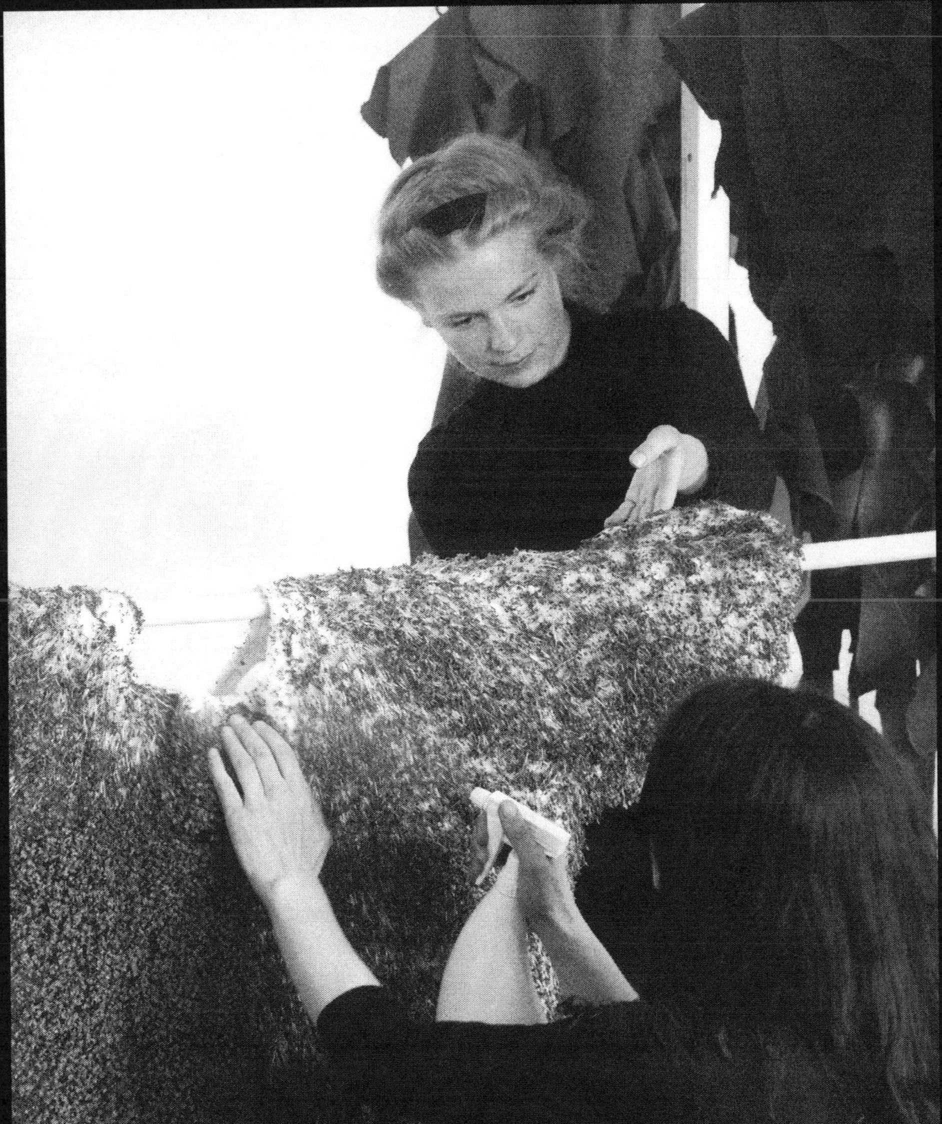

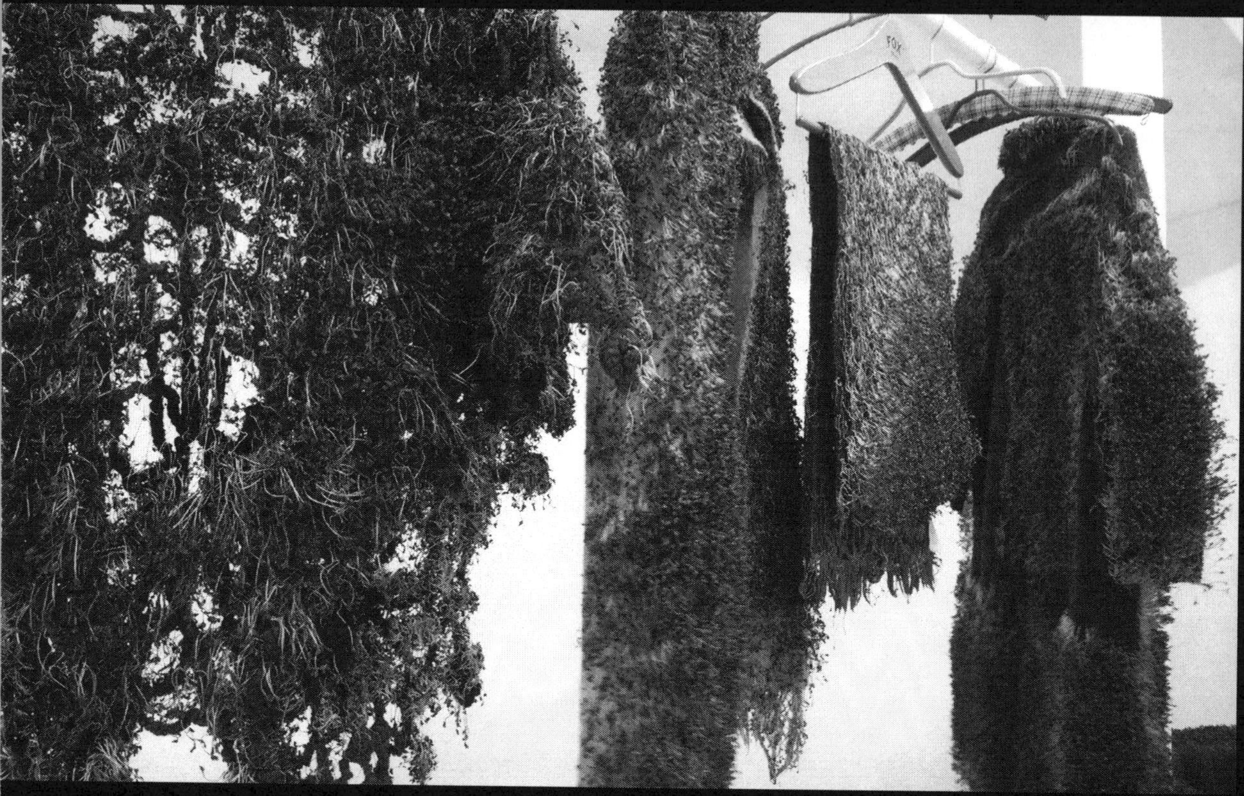

old photo of me and Doris at a Friday bar at the Literature Department. We are in our third semester, I think. We are sitting in an old sofa made of oriental textile that some students may have dragged up to the second floor. The sofa seems misplaced between the formal institutional furniture made of light beech wood. I sit in one end and look directly into the camera. A broad smile is on my face. Doris sits next to me. Her high-heel shoe is hanging loosely around her ankle wrist, and Molly sits on the arm rest dressed in black. Doris must have brought Molly along that night. This was before she began making cress–capes or performances as "I Went Into a Bar", in which she replaces the most central words with "fuck", I wanna fuck your hand, or the fucker takes it all. In the photo Molly leans towards Doris. She puts two fingers behind her head, making rabbit ears and smiling at the photographer. Doris smiles too, she doesn't know.

Silence.

I (Lola)

I am currently living in my friend's studio. Before she went to New York, she had a show in Munich, where she grew cress in second hand clothes of different materials and they are still hanging in the studio to dry. Brown shells from the seeds are everywhere. In the evenings when everyone else has gone home I find the mattress, lay on the floor and look up into the cress costumes. So when I wake up the next day I have cress seeds inside my ears.

HIM

(looks at her, a bit bemused) How does it feel, cress seeds inside your ears?

I (Lola)

Hmm, a bit like sand from the dessert, only more crisp, like fried onions..I don't know, what is it in French? Onions fried in butter and dried, I don't know...

claude closky

is a French artist working largely in the immaterial realm. He has exhibited across the world.

THURSDAY

Found objects from a profusion of cultural backgrounds were displayed equivalently and without further comment.
Then different places and incidents collapsed together.
Then bubbles and droplets recalled microcosms in seventeenth-century nature-morte painting.
Then many lives of art highlighted its ability to simultaneously uphold and destroy illusions.
Then discrete marks held their own space, emphasizing their self-contained energy.

Then viewers began to assemble a complex web of formal relations.
Then trompe l'oeil techniques in oil paint mimicked heavy sculptural stones.
Then lush and eloquent images were perfectly constructed impossibilities.
Then using a homemade bath, 8mm, 16mm and 35mm black and white film emulsion was chemically destabilized to extract the filmic image and optical sound track from the reels of celluloid.

Then interrelated bodies of work fused history, anecdote, and artefact.
Then highly distinctive techniques moved between multi-layered pictorial spaces.
Then words, phrases and doodles, were traced with a finger.
Then a mysterious palimpsest of time and space contained visual echoes of disparate details.
Then the condensation on a windowpane became the means through which the eye glimpsed the scene within.
Then graffiti took on an almost spectral presence.

Then multimedia practice investigated
the slippage between technological platforms and
ways they are consumed and decoded in the social realm.
Then abstract/semi-abstract, monochromatic forms,
simultaneously re-engaged early 20th Century black and white cinema and the tradition of the

Modernist monochrome.

Then the once duplicitous became whole.
Then boundaries were blurred by exchanges and transformations like the accuracy of radiocarbon dating continually being altered due to excess carbon entering the atmosphere from the burning of fossil fuels.

THEN FRIDAY

Then the image became less coalescent.
Then rollers and brooms were used to spread a soft palette of red, blue, green, and purple acrylic paints over unprimed canvases laid directly on the studio ground.
Then not only a potent subject matter but also a conceptual equivalent allowed to work.
Then incidental debris and textures beneath the canvas emerged as impressions during the frottage process.
Then through sculptural installations ephemeral notions of time, silence, memory, absence and dreams, resonated with imaginative tension.
Then an assemblage of plaster heads was installed like a mass of remains on the floor.

Then between homage, transgression and estrangement,
the echo of the ancient world was charged with mystery.
Then new sculptures were made from hulking industrial parts.
Then distance between subject and object, the represented and the representative was collapsed.

Then rubber mallets, dildos, bowling pins and billiard balls reminded that these works exist in the physical, as well as metaphysical, world.
Then culture took imaginative leaps forward, postulating a world of stark angles and sawtooth synthesizers.
Then retro-futuristic archeological remnants referenced human culture and the natural history of planet Earth.
Then stacked columns of polyhedra formed in MDF populated the space.
Then aesthetic impressions were created by measures of force.
Then a series of natural stones were painted to look like M&M candies.
Then the gradual process was extended with visceral abstraction.
Then actual bubblegum corresponded in some ways to the questions of painting and historical representation.

Then image, time, sound and narrative fixed onto a canvas-as-screen became a kind of "terminal projection" of a "petrified cinema." Then the visual games and enigmas that pervade Rococo and Mannerist painting were firmly rooted, formally and conceptually, within critical observations of our time

THEN SATURDAY

Then synthetic black fleeces were stained with bleach.
Then the ongoing quest for what lies at the heart of art was transformed.
Then brightly colored, stuffed textiles were manipulated to resemble overturned lit candlesticks.

Then social processes redefined fundamental parameters.
Then titles referenced aerial military surveillance and conflict areas.
Then powder, smoke and fire made shadows and imprints on paper and board.
Then the transformation of material goods endangered the specific disposition of "nature" in which human life seemed possible.
Then classical iconography and fragments of antiquity evoked the effect of ancient ruins.

Then language, movement, and interaction, constructed situations without the production of physical objects.
Then in this landscape of shadows and light, the whole universe was evoked in absentia.

Then the works revealed another sense of indeterminacy, creating a disorienting illusion of shifts between two and three dimensions.
Then photographs, videos, writings, notebooks, recordings, and publications offered a sort of empirical testing of an art that will exist post-human.
Then glass was used as an isolating container acting as a vessel for time.
Then the question was how we can produce things that are not problematic, that are more interesting.

Then rainbow saturated colored paintings revealed traces of the long forgotten individual and collective creative voices that have informed and shaped contemporary culture.

THEN SUNDAY

Then materials from local geographies traveled around the world.
Then an obsessive fight against nothingness combined references as numerous as they were eclectic: from the cinema of Billy Wilder to the rock culture of the 1960s.

Then collaborators created a singular project.
Then the human stage of the process evolved to be diachronic.
Then two sculptures referenced to Jung's theory of archetypes: the male and female qualities that we subconsciously attribute to inanimate objects.

Then an ephemeral site-specific installation included a giant high tech robot, a little bird, Michelangelo's David, a mother cradling a hybrid human-pig baby, a dinosaur, Kurt Cobain, and a young couple making love in a boat.

Then representation blurred the boundaries between past and present, film and sculpture, action and architecture.

Then a theatrical space was based on a series of tasks.
Then long stretches of time challenged distinct formal qualities again and again.
Then the inversion of acting and directing enabled viewers to be active agents in the room.
Then themes as varied as adolescence, educational structures, sexuality, religion, post-punk politics, pop psychology and repressed memory revealed unexpected connections and contradictions.
Then partially erased images, ghostly texts and disconnected symbols, reminded us that we are constructed by personal experiences, fantasies, perceptions and external events.

Then formal investigations from color, light and transparency shifted to ambitious sculptural gestures inflected by darkness and opacity.

Then this slippage between the real and the virtual, perhaps melancholic, invoked an idealized space beyond our apprehension.

Then sculptures were essentially generated by perfect equations, their flattening out into patterned surface pointed toward their origins as endlessly replicable simulations of depth and volume.

THEN MONDAY

Then preoccupation with emptiness seemed
to veer abruptly away into mere material stuff.
Then complex formal experiments with interlocking circles were constructed from appropriated swatches of traditional Japanese silks.
Then objects that have their own set of rules and criteria were assembled.
Then intrinsic structure, metaphoric on the one hand, but also utilitarian, extended the possibilities of those objects.
Then materials and processes allowed to avoid or at least minimize making the kinds of choices usually deemed "aesthetic."

Then the starting point was the self at the centre of the action.
Then a mechanized spirographic repetition captured interlocking sections.
Then the political sphere made a circular, spiral motif.
Then a series of open rooms in different cities extended the co-authorial role to anyone, to "any person arriving by chance."

Then theoretical works were conceived as instruments for developing a reflection on perception.

Then found objects crossed fluidly and fluently between varying modes of production.
Then their position in space constructed their own narrative.
Then sculptural installations focused on art, nature, and mythology.
Then works inspired from personal memory revealed the richness of imagination.
Then multidisciplinary installation-based practice combined feminist politics with literary texts, homemade crafts and 20th century avant-garde aesthetics.
Then a female figure laid sleeping, with a mechanism that simulated the movement of her breathing as she deeply slumbered.
Then this simplicity made you aware of the complexity.
Then five large-scale curled fabric elements mounted on copper hangers were devoted to the five senses.

THEN TUESDAY

Then tactile works explored a near baroque sensual experience of color.
Then something very complex was presented in a simple way.
Then a horizontal steel rod hung high on the wall.
Then the work offered a duplicitous image of its subject.
Then common objects were deprived of surreal combinations.
Then simple reductive forms exposed precarious relations.
Then a round mirror was placed adjacent to a rectangular one with a transparent round hole of the same dimensions cut out of it.

Then the provocative and aggressive emotional intensity shifted away from figuration.
Then a metal scaffold with painted iron rods was welded into a grid pattern.
Then energy and coercive charge infused abstract forms with a sense of palpable three-dimensionality.
Then overtly sexual connotations were concentrated into a profound investigation of matter.
Then creative detritus including broken body casts, chairs, wooden platforms, sex toys, buckets and other objects, were all punctuated with the viscous deep yellow of insulation foam.
Then low-fi and mass-produced materials reflected the vitality of individual and collective action for a common good.

Then smooth surfaces of geometric structures were opposed to organic forms of interior

topographies, and artificial vegetation was juxtaposed to real water.
Then visual language was enveloped in a dream-like mystery.
Then new and autonomous forms of aesthetic expression were created from the culture of hidden alternative communities.

Then the visual quality of Cy Twombly's work became a reference as did its embodiment of the existential issues of what it means to be an artist.

Then large, colorful, and spectacular photographs with a nod to Pop Art were framed in mahogany to emulate the style of boardroom furniture.
Then unexpected yet banal objects, from vacuum cleaners and inflatable flowers to novelty drink caddies and china figurines, eschewed typical standards of "good taste" in art.

THEN WEDNESDAY
Then selected texts were converted into various fonts resourced directly from the local landscape.

Then art was inseparable from the world in which it found expression.
Then commercial stock images—sunsets, rolling surf, aerial views of the city and close-up details of its vernacular architecture—were
purchased online.
Then the traditional notion of the work of art was turned inside out.
Then canvases were brushed with a clear gel medium to imbue a sense of texture and palpability.

Then there was this idea that projects are laid to rest.
Then the studio became a kind of excavation site.
Then catalysts were created between works from the past and new works.
Then fabric, cardboard, and other studio fragments were attached like mysterious satellites at the borders of indeterminate topographies.

Then a new series further developed investigation into the role of images in the construction of history.
Then political figures and events were layered with references to iconic paintings from the 20th Century.

Then wit and playfulness were
employed to seduce and engage the viewer.
Then fragments of debris metamorphosed with

the application of holographic lacquer paid homage to iconic abstractionists, from Kenneth Noland to Otto Freundlich.

Then strategies were to make art beautiful, to strive for objectivity, to give back the familiar, and to reflect—and thus empower—the viewer.
Then aspects of immediate surroundings were incorporated into the artworks as a contextual reference point.

Then the memory of the works reception fulfilled the conventions of visual art.
Then sinuous lines drawn in copper and aluminum led from floor to wall into large graphite drawings in which detailed fragments of modernist interiors and objects were collaged with partial views of urban landscapes.

b. rogers

is a self proclaimed Street Refugee, a term she coined in 2014. Her work involves creating necessities for her evolutionary advancement. On the side, she is a freelance graphic designer & social media marketer.

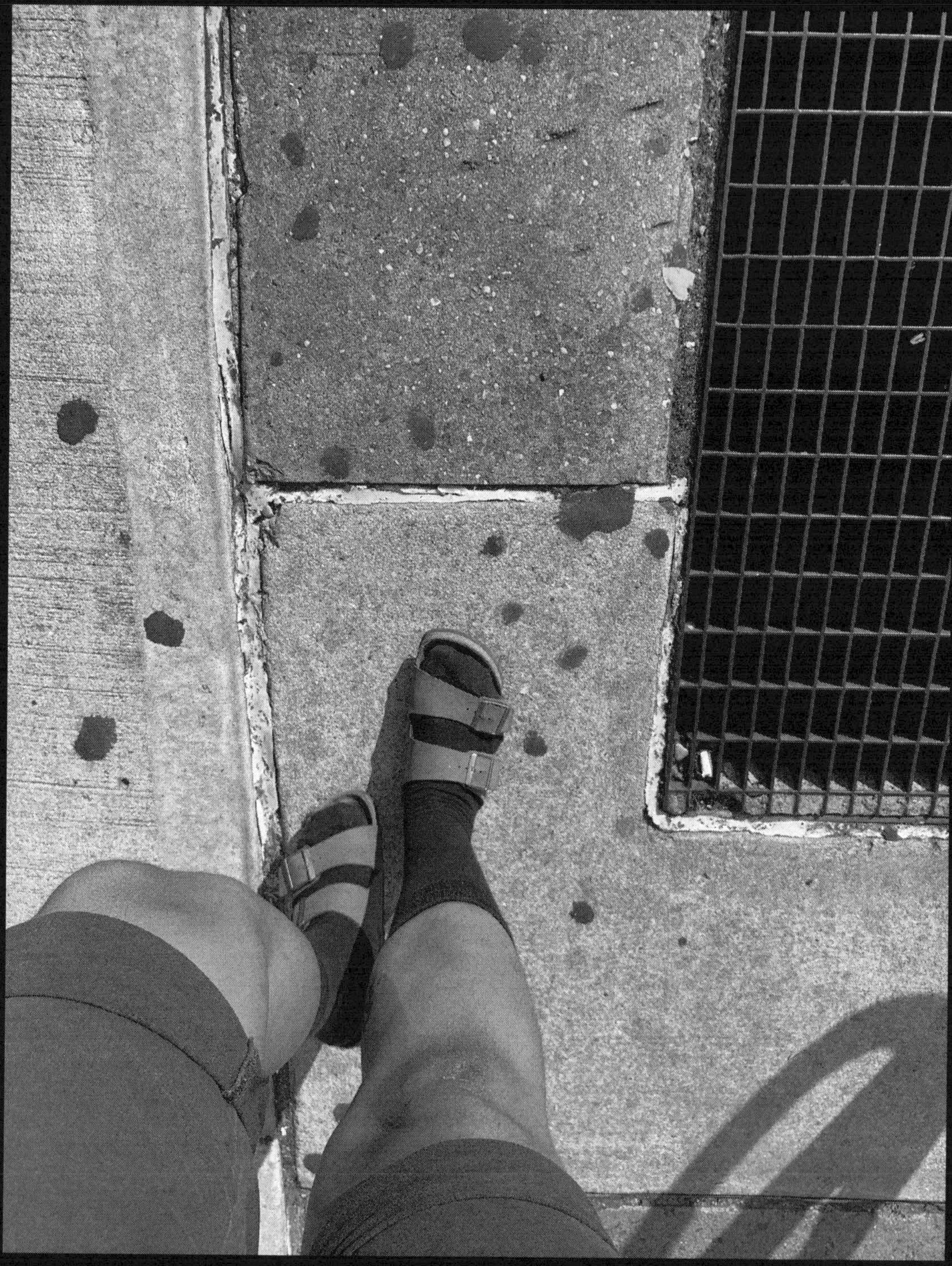

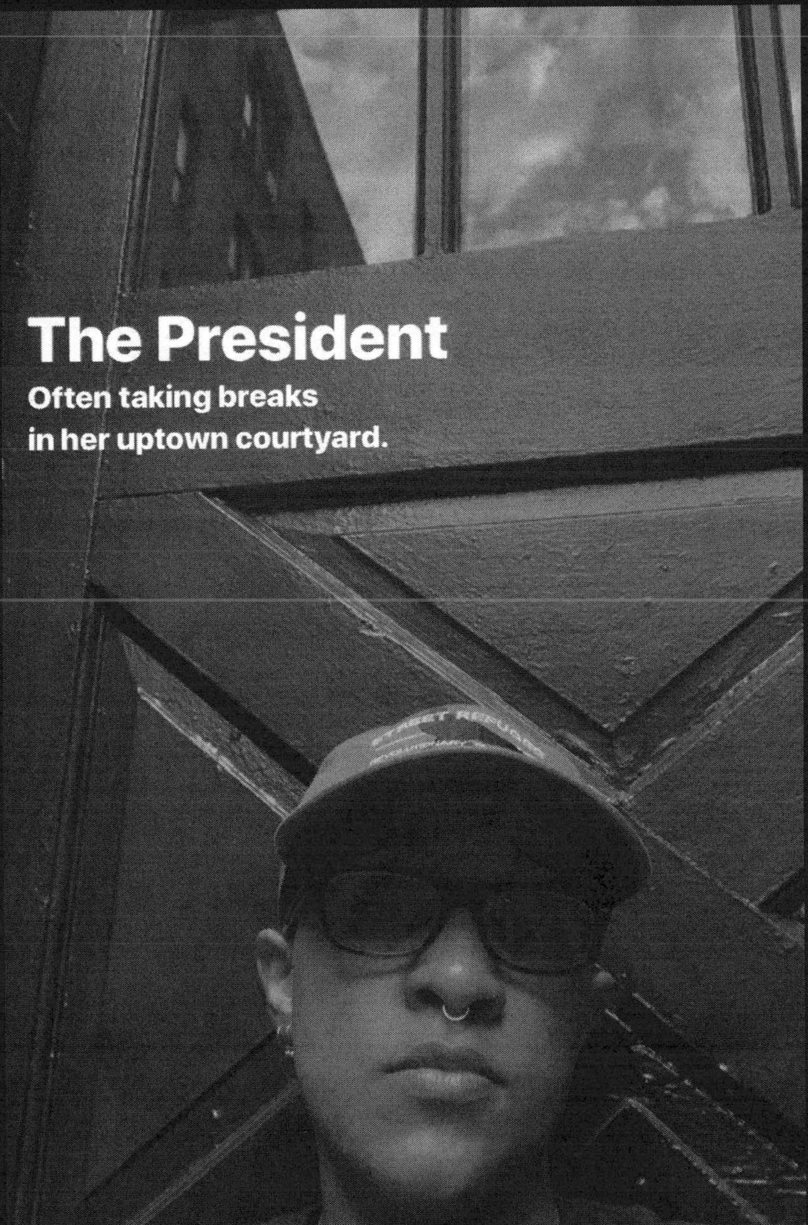

The President

Often taking breaks in her uptown courtyard.

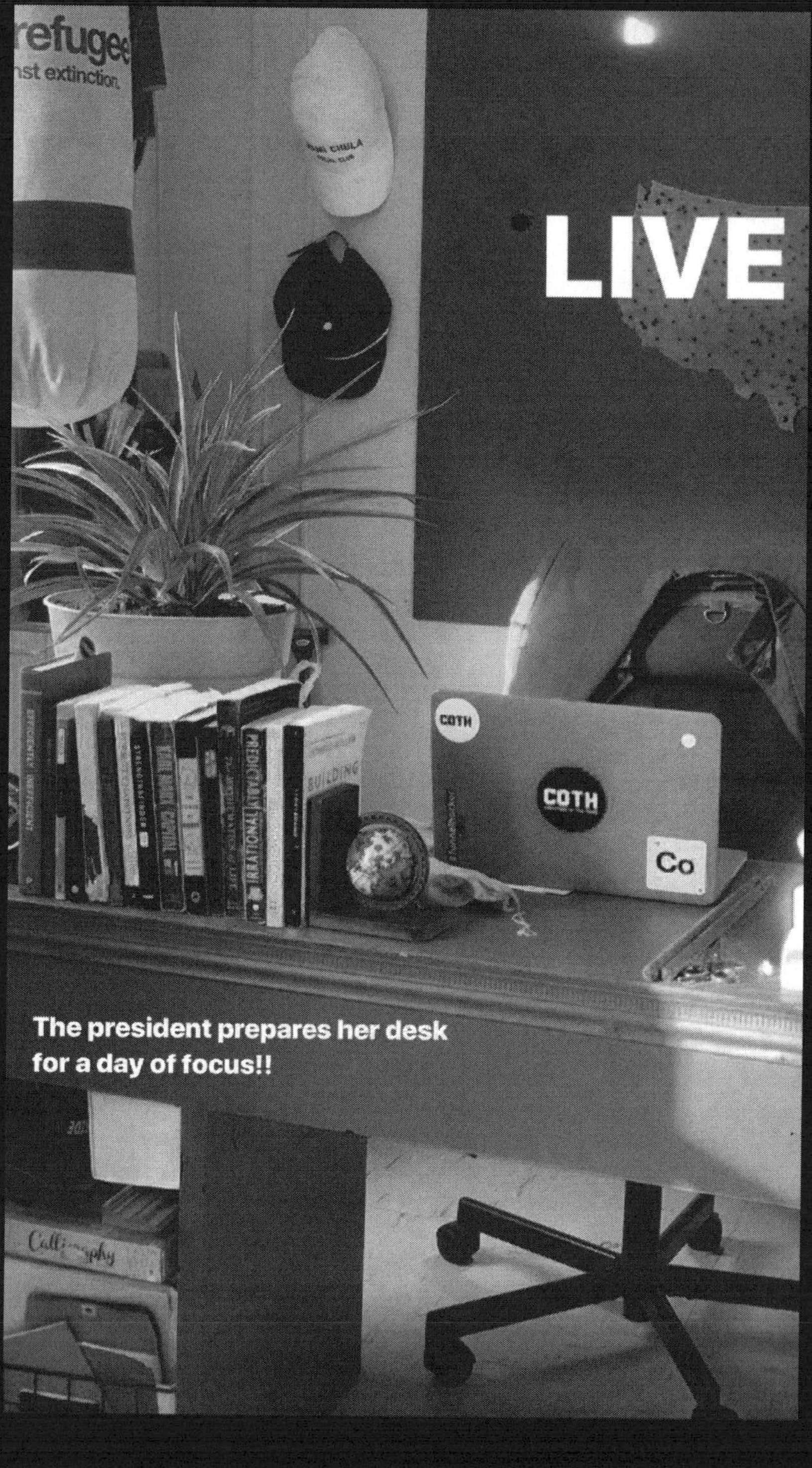

The president prepares her desk for a day of focus!!

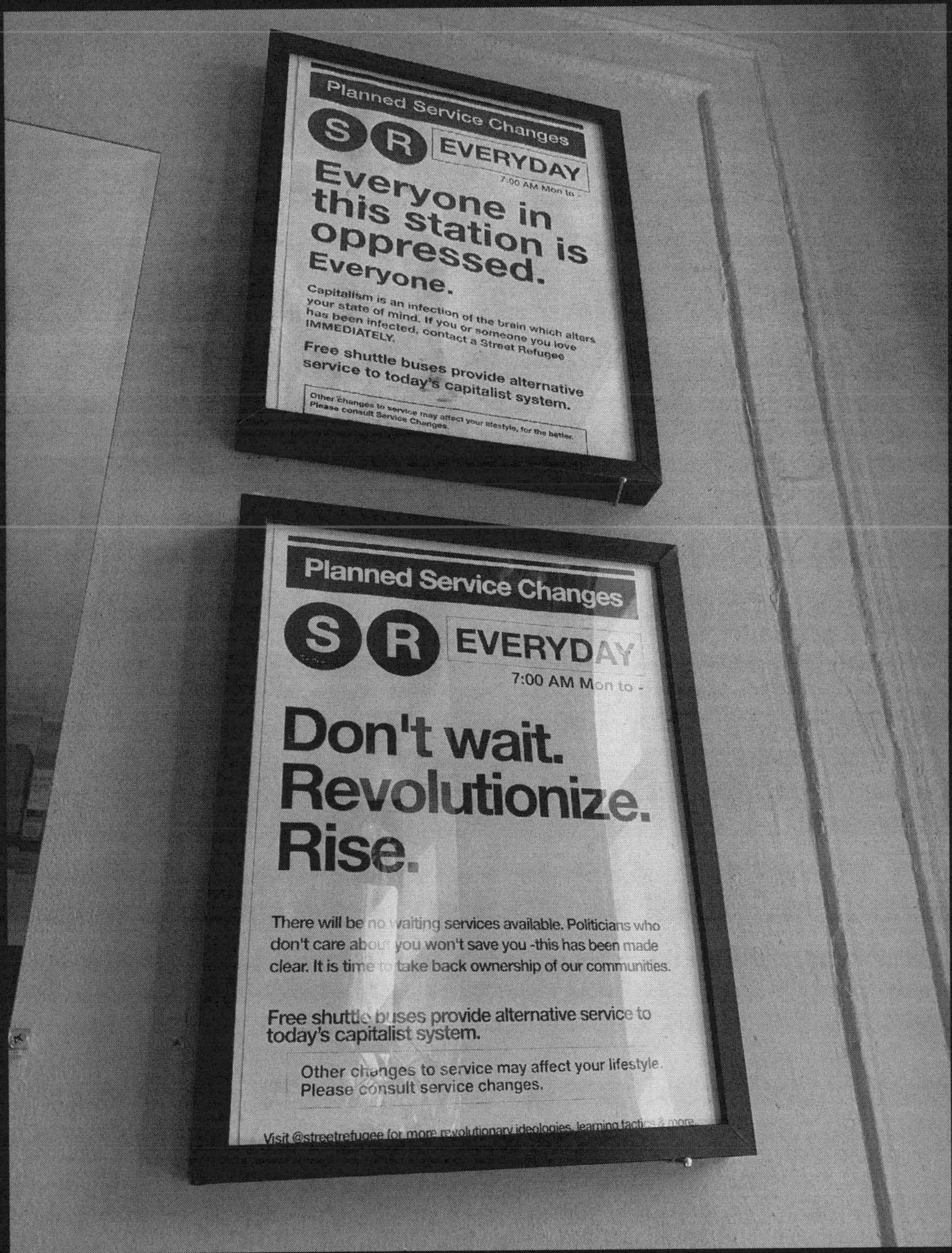
Planned Service Changes
S R
EVERYDAY
7:00 AM Mon to -
Everyone in this station is oppressed.
Everyone.
Capitalism is an infection of the brain which alters your state of mind. If you or someone you love has been infected, contact a Street Refugee IMMEDIATELY.
Free shuttle buses provide alternative service to today's capitalist system.
Other changes to service may affect your lifestyle, for the better. Please consult Service Changes.
Planned Service Changes
S R
EVERYDAY
7:00 AM Mon to -
Don't wait. Revolutionize. Rise.
There will be no waiting services available. Politicians who don't care about you won't save you -this has been made clear. It is time to take back ownership of our communities.
Free shuttle buses provide alternative service to today's capitalist system.
Other changes to service may affect your lifestyle. Please consult service changes.

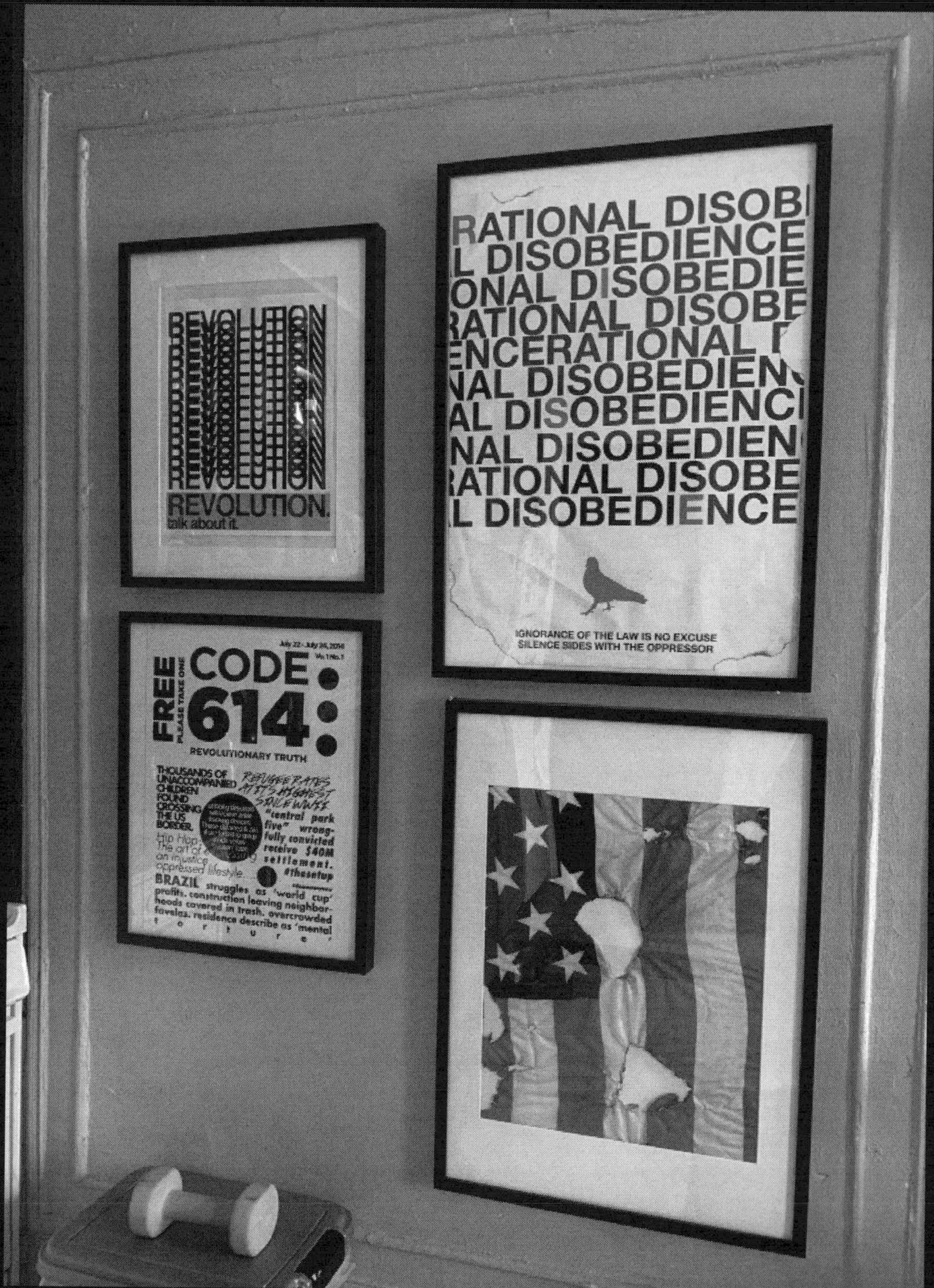
REVOLUTION.
talk about it.
IGNORANCE OF THE LAW IS NO EXCUSE
SILENCE SIDES WITH THE OPPRESSOR
FREE
PLEASE TAKE ONE
CODE
614
REVOLUTIONARY TRUTH
THOUSANDS OF UNACCOMPANIED CHILDREN FOUND CROSSING THE US BORDER.
"central park five" wrongfully convicted receive $40M settlement.
BRAZIL struggles as 'world cup' profits, construction leaving neighborhoods covered in trash, overcrowded favelas, residence describe as 'mental torture'

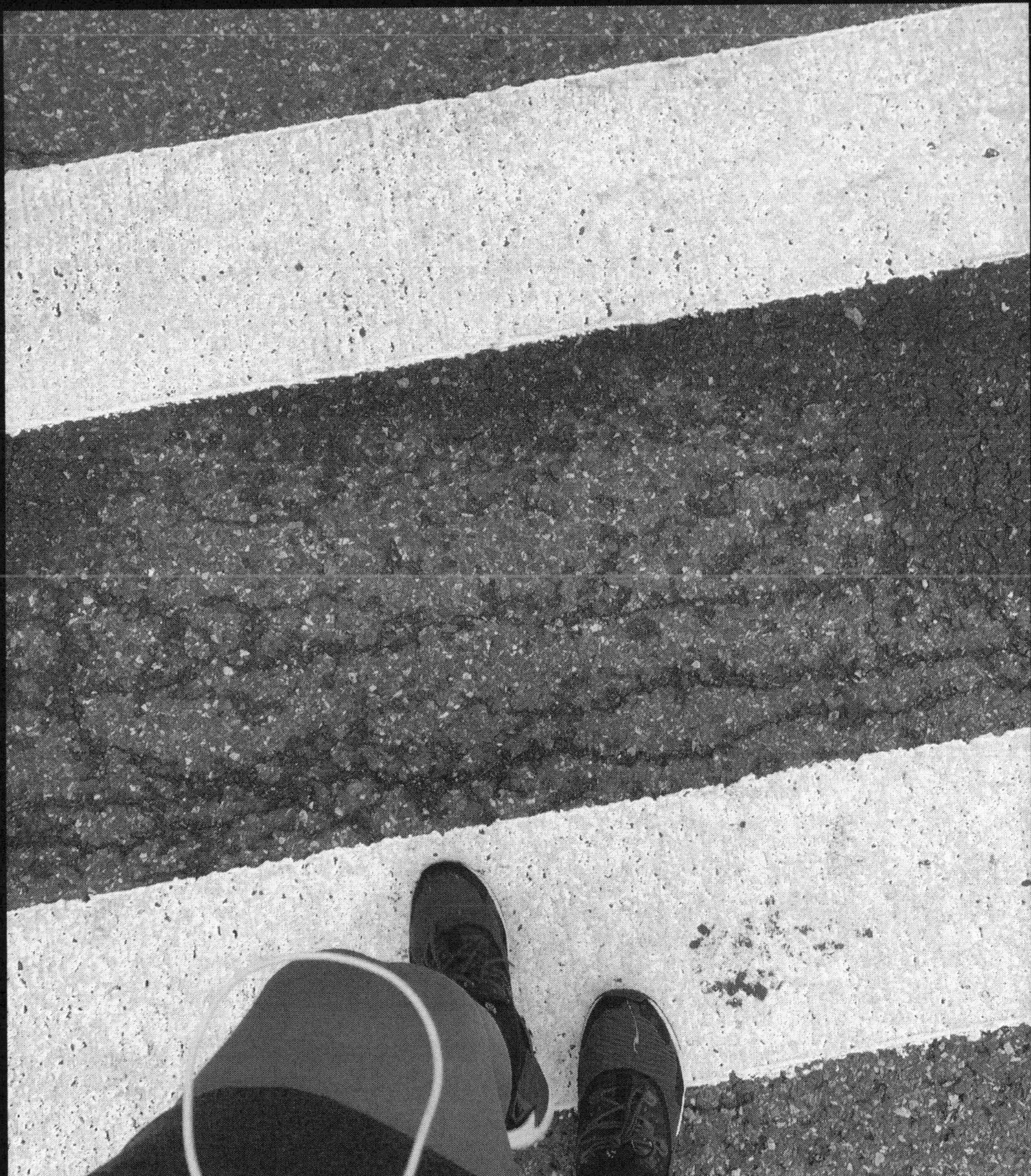

eric bunnag booth

is a collector and marketing expert living and working in Singapore. He is the cofounder of MAIIAM, a contemporary art museum in the northern kingdom of Chiang Mai, Thailand.

Forwarded message
From: Chomwan Weeraworawit
Date: 31 May at 15:41
Subject: Philip Huang for MAIIAM t-shirts
To: Eric Booth
Cc: Philip Huang

Dearest Eric,

Hope all is amazing. Finalising t-shirt details so we get them ready for the opening!

What we can do is 80 t-shirts—hope this is ok!

Size 0 (xs) = 10

Size 1 (s) = 20

Size 2 (m) = 20

Size 3 (l) = 20

Size 4 (xl) = 10

Total = 80

If they go quickly we can order more! They were only able to send over a roll of the organic cotton that we use this month and have ordered more already so can put in a second order if this sells out! I'm getting them valued right now and will let you know what the wholesale total for the shirts are ka.

Here is a draft of the design. 2 options:

1) All black on white.

Our crew neck is a bit wider than in this picture. I've also done a colour option here.

2) Grey and orange (with MAIIAM slightly bigger in front)

Let me know what you prefer. We can also do half/half. For the screen print I think water—

based with some texture unless you prefer it to be rubber? In a next email sending hang tag mock ups.

Thanks!

xxx

C

ps. we can also do some limited edition ones in indigo! I think we are going up middle of June so can do a very small run. I know Philip wanted to experiment!

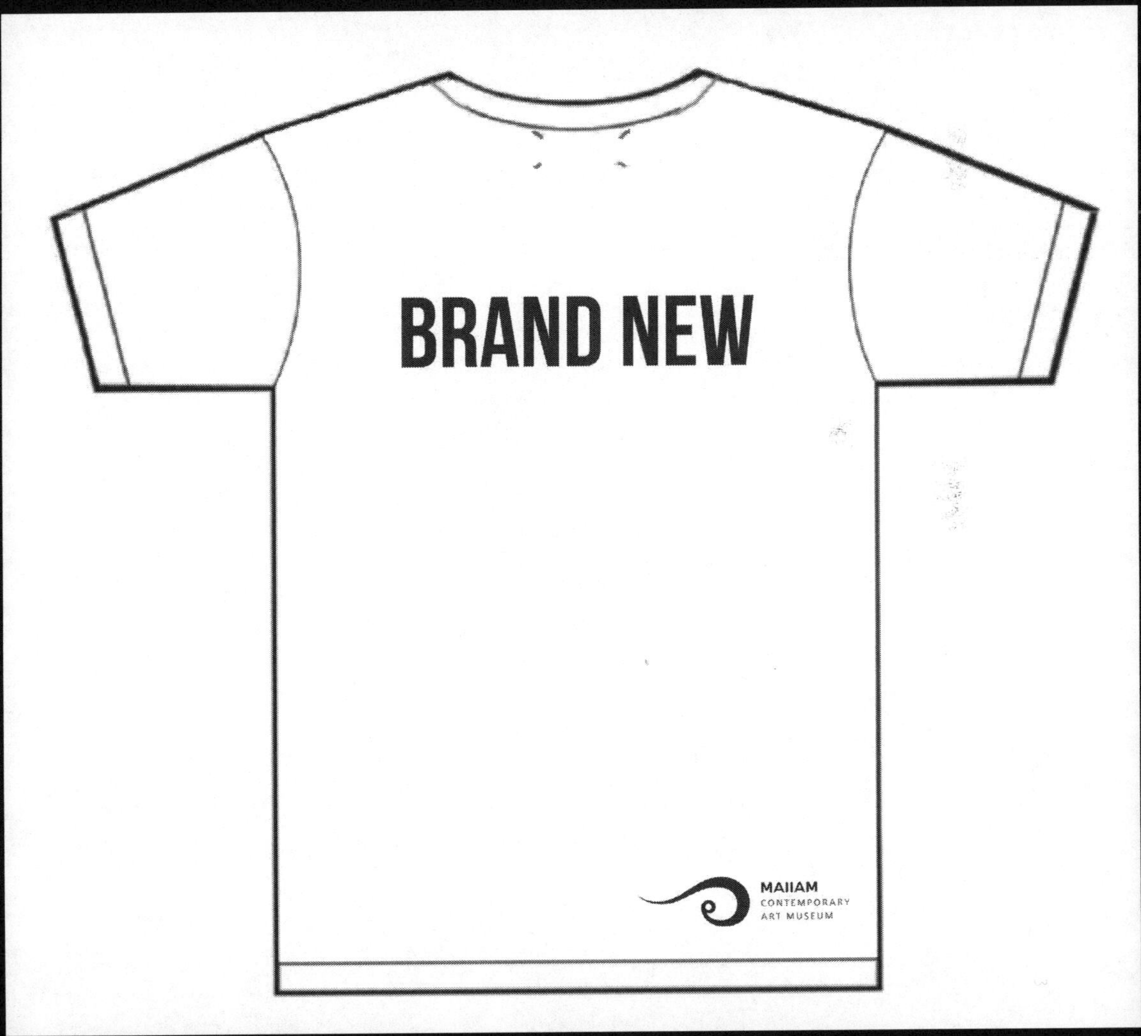

Forwarded message
From: Rachaporn Choochuey
Date: 31 May 2016 at 15:51
Subject: MAIIAM - photo round #1
To: Eric Booth, Gridthiya Gaveewong, Jean-Michel Beurdeley
Cc: Asrin Sanguawongwarn

Dear JM, Eric and P'Jeab,

I am sending the photos we shot last week. I chose 12 out of about 200. Let us know what you think.

If you are fine, we will upload the hi-res version in the dropbox for the press release. We can make digital and print versions.

Best,
Racha

From: Eric Booth
Date: May 22, 2016 at 10:47:55 AM EDT
To: Holly Crawford
Subject: Re: how is your week coming along

Dear Holly,

1000 apologies!

It's been impossible for me to take time off from my work and museum in progress. We have 40 days until the opening. All is on schedule but the preparations are overwhelming.

If you have a few minutes...pls see

https://www.facebook.com/MICAMchiangmai/

I'm sorry to let you down, but hope you will understand.

Best regards,
Eric

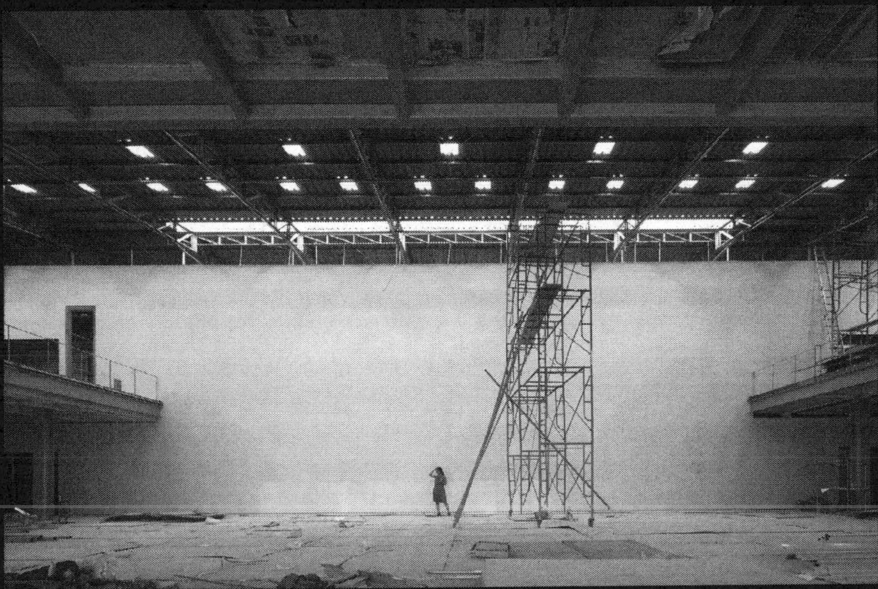

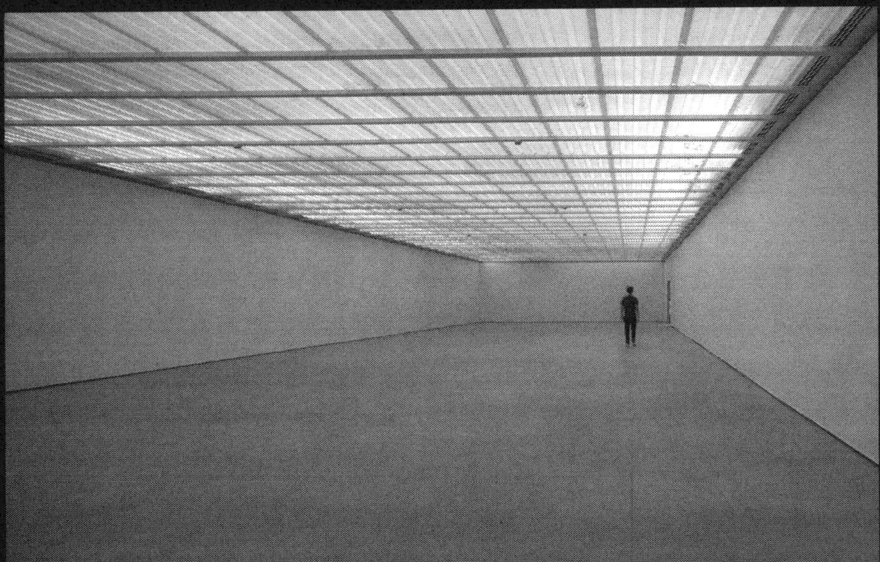

alymamah rashed

is a Kuwaiti visual artist who investigates the discourse of her own body as a Muslima Cyborg, fluctuating between the east and the west. The Muslima Cyborg rests in a liminal spectacle that compartmentalizes the collective tangibility of the mind, the body, and the ornament.

مع [في] ومع [خارج] الحدود:

With(In) And With(out) Borders: The Typology of Metamorphic Spirituality

تصنيف الروحانية المتحولة

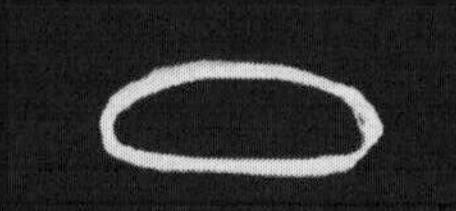

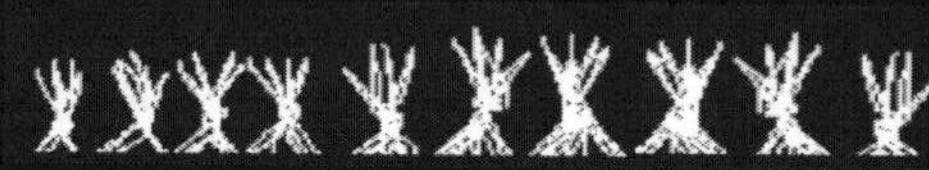

When my body stands within a rect-
angle, the sensation and the sensed
are in convergence with one anothe
-r. When my body
stands w- ithin a r-
ectangle, I embed
my gravity to birth a
leakage of self illum-
ination. When my
body stands within a r-
ectangle, I am facing
the center of the earth
and circulating with it's
motion to arrive
into a higher sky.
When my body
stands within a rectangle,
I lay in between
my veiled gardens
and my mass-pro-
duced ornament.
When my body stands with-
in a rectangle,
I am rooted to the surface of my prayer
rug. I have found my afterimage birthed
from the veiled sky. My palms touch the

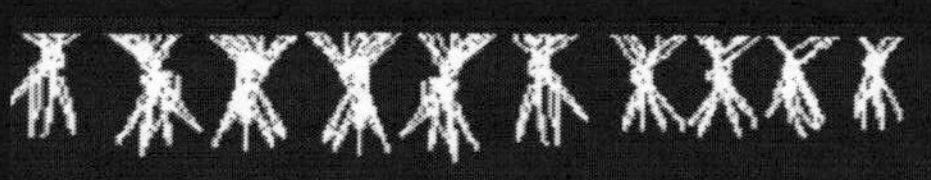

أرض
ground

Before the prayer rug was a woven carpet, the prayer rug was originally a **Khumrah/خُمرة/palm frond** that the prophet prayed on. The prayer rug is an object of the organic. The prayer rug was green. During early Islamic history, the prayer rug transformed into a carrier of images. The early prayer rug birthed the **mihrab/محراب/niche** and a simple design of the doorway to heaven. It is fascinating to see the prayer rug's origin as an assemblage of palm fronds transforming into an object of religious imagery. The image eases one's transcendence to the otherworldly. The image becomes literal in comparison to the organic plant. The organic plant is an object of life. The image is an imprint of sensation. The object's materiality is able to dictate the sensuality and spirituality of prayer. However, the materiality of the prayer rug has been eradicated due to the birth of the image. Furthermore, differentiating between the mass produced versus the handmade prayer rug is not a commentary on materiality since both formations are contained within a similar form and shape. It is a conversation of craftsmanship in relation to capitalism's mode of producing commodities. The collection of images on the prayer rug became the material for the contemporary prayer rug. The contemporary prayer rug is a rectangle with edges and borders in which a practicing Muslim would place themselves within to pray and converse with Allah. However, this act of webbed seclusion seems to be mechanical rather than fleshed.

When your flesh, bones, and spirit enter within this rectangle, are you aware that you have entered a phenomenological space of unity? What do your spiritual senses replicate within your mind? Does it depart from the concrete? Or does it caress your abstract surroundings? These are all questions that withhold the presence of awareness beyond instinct and temperament. The borders of the rectangle are not constraints that hold you to a ritual that is automatized. Rather, the borders of the rectangle represent a self generated mapping that sets your seclusion within your own relationship and shaping of Islamic faith. In other words, the space that one would bound themselves within would offer the possibility of a preexisting spiritual typology. Finding one's own spiritual typology within the prayer rug shall lead them to find their subjectivity outside of earth.

(It has always been within you and I)

Yet, within this fluctuant desire lays the yearning of grounding one's self to a unified understanding of time in relation faith. "Conceiving of space as a static slice through time, as representation, as a closed system and so forth are all ways of taming it. They enable us to ignore its real import: the coeval multiplicity of other trajectories and the necessary outward-lookingness of a spatialized subjectivity."[1]

Another crucial point that determines the act of personalizing one's borders is the imagery, colors, symbols, and shapes that are weaved within the prayer rug itself, whether the rug was handmade or mass produced. Most Islamic scholars and sheikhs would agree on the fact that the prayer rug's decorativeness should not distract you from the act of praying. However, this regulation seems to have a crucial point that does not recognize its capacity and validity. Spiritual mapping begins during the act of selecting purchasing your prayer rug.

---

1 Massey, Doreen, ed. "The Life in Space." In For Space, 59. London: Sage Publications, 2005.

I choose the prayer rug that resides within my own collective image of my personal faith.
I choose a prayer rug that aligns with my illumination rather than someone else's.
I choose an image that illustrates the intangible sensation of my Islamic spirituality.

When one reframes their approach, they are able to have a higher sense communication between themselves and Allah during the act of prayer. However, I must insist that this is something that should not be based on one's sense of materialism that is strictly built on the outer image of one praying within the borders of prayer. Rather, the act of being conscious about your own prayer rug may carry the potential of drawing the illiteracy of divine sensation. It should be a step that frees you from the tangible eventually. The contemporary ideals of a prayer rug are listed under the objecthood of commodification, which converges religious practices with capitalism. However, this convergence offers a sense of ownership. When you consciously chose your prayer rug, your prayer beads, or thob you automatically form an intimate relationship towards your object. This at least occurs in the early stages of lookingness. This sense of lookingness then departs the object and becomes sensational and internal. According to Mino Moallem, a Professor of Gender & Women's Studies at the University of California Berkeley, Moallem explains this continuity of religious practices through commodification seems to offer an extension of faith that converges two realities. The prayer rug territorializes prayer by creating a material boundary between the sacred and the profane, or that with the potential to corrupt. "One could argue that, while prayer carpets and prayer rugs alike depict recurring imaginary spatial motifs such as the tree of life and the Garden of Eden, prayer rugs incorporate spatiality into everyday modes of being in the world. They channel individual moments in time and space towards the universalist impulses of Islamic practices.2" Furthermore, Moallem raises a crucial point that views the prayer rug as a portal between two existences: earth and the unknown. "They also mediate between the material and the spiritual, linking the embodied presence in the "here" and now to the virtual and heterotopia of "there" through the spatial purification of space and perpetuity of time3." Therefore, the variation of imagery, symbols, and colors of prayer rugs available in contemporary times, is in fact resulted by commodification, capitalism, and tourism. However, these forces can be seen as modes that personalizes and strengthens one's faith. Humans need an external visual extension that can embody their conceptual and internal thread eventually. (knowledge as faith)

As a result, the imprint of your prayer rug, an earthly object, shall reside within you to lead you to a metamorphic space. You transform and fly to higher grounds every time you pray. You will pray on different prayer rugs and grounds. It will not matter because you have already surpassed the stage of earthly personalization and have entered into the space of love, light, faith, and divinity that lays between **you** (earth) and **Allah** (infinity).

My **body** / **جسم** /**jism** is not from
the same
womb
as yours.
caresses a higher ground.
caresses a higher ground.
caresses a higher ground.
My **body** / **جسم** /**jism 's** imprint
caresses a higher ground.

Underneath the leakage of the
crescent.
My **body** / **جسم** /**jism**
intertwines
with its limbs.
Our oasis lays
within
the
same **sky/**
سماء/ sama'
Our multisensible
bodies/ /أجسام
ajsam return
to a different

2 Moallem, Minoo. "Praying through the Senses: The Prayer Rug/Carpet and the Converging Territories of the Material and the Spiritual." Conversations: An Online Journal of the Center for the Study of Material and Visual Cultures of Religion, 2014. Accessed June/July, 2019. doi:10.22332/con.ess.2015.1.

3 Moallem, Minoo. "Praying through the Senses: The Prayer Rug/Carpet and the Converging Territories of the Material and the Spiritual." Conversations: An Online Journal of the Center for the Study of Material and Visual Cultures of Religion, 2014. Accessed June/July, 2019. doi:10.22332/con.ess.2015.1.

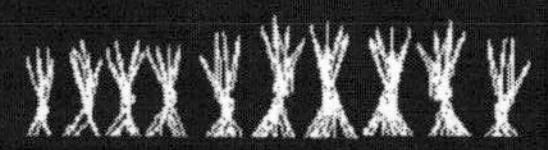

ground. ground. ground.
ground. ground. ground.
ground. ground. ground.
ground. ground. ground.
ground. ground. ground.
ground. ground. ground.
ground. ground. ground.
ground. ground. ground.
ground. ground. ground.
ground. ground. ground.
ground. ground. ground.
ground. ground. ground.

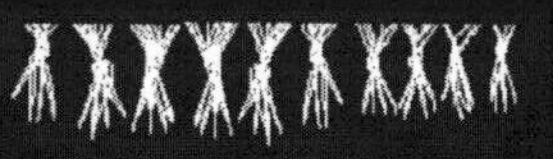

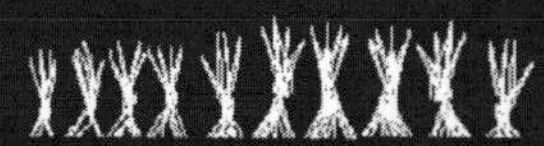

ground. ground. ground.
ground. ground. ground.
ground. ground. ground.
ground. ground. ground.
ground. ground. ground.
ground. ground. ground.
ground. ground. ground.
ground. ground. ground.
ground. ground. ground.
ground. ground. ground.
ground. ground. ground.
ground. ground. ground.

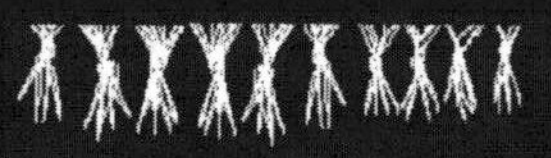

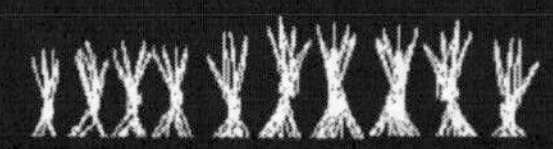

ground. ground. ground.
ground. ground. ground.
ground. ground. ground.
ground. ground. ground.
ground. ground. ground.
ground. ground. ground.
ground. ground. ground.
ground. ground. ground.
ground. ground. ground.
ground. ground. ground.
ground. ground. ground.
ground. ground. ground.

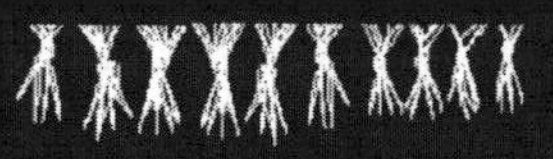

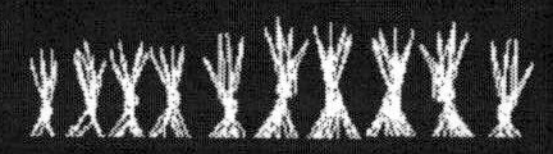

ground. ground. ground.
ground. ground. ground.
ground. ground. ground.
ground. ground. ground.
ground. ground. ground.
ground. ground. ground.
ground. ground. ground.
ground. ground. ground.
ground. ground. ground.
ground. ground. ground.
ground. ground. ground.
ground. ground. ground.

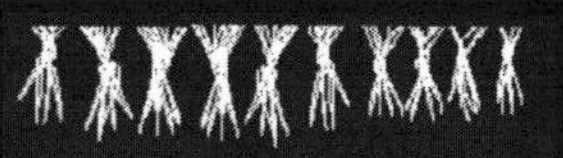

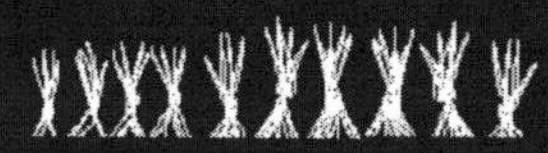

ground. ground. ground.
ground. ground. ground.
ground. ground. ground.
ground. ground. ground.
ground. ground. ground.
ground. ground. ground.
ground. ground. ground.
ground. ground. ground.
ground. ground. ground.
ground. ground. ground.
ground. ground. ground.
ground. ground. ground.

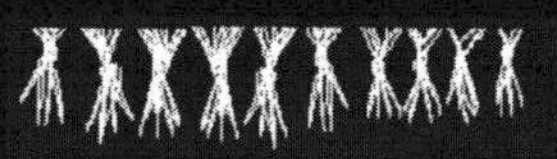

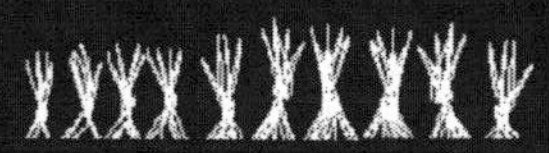

ground. ground. ground.
ground. ground. ground.
ground. ground. ground.
ground. ground. ground.
ground. ground. ground.
ground. ground. ground.
ground. ground. ground.
ground. ground. ground.
ground. ground. ground.
ground. ground. ground.
ground. ground. ground.
ground. ground. ground.

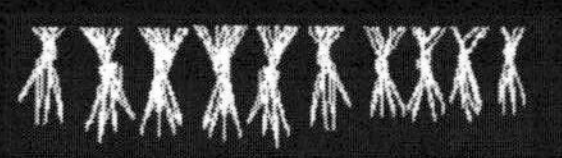

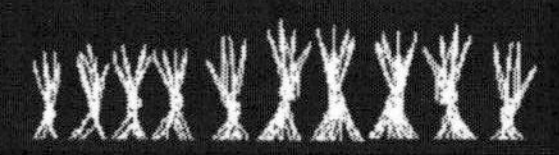

ground. ground. ground.
ground. ground. ground.
ground. ground. ground.
ground. ground. ground.
ground. ground. ground.
ground. ground. ground.
ground. ground. ground.
ground. ground. ground.
ground. ground. ground.
ground. ground. ground.
ground. ground. ground.
ground. ground. ground.

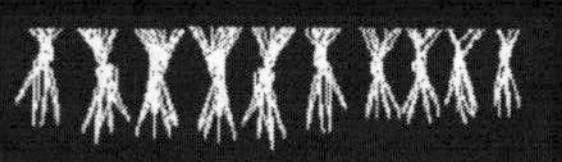

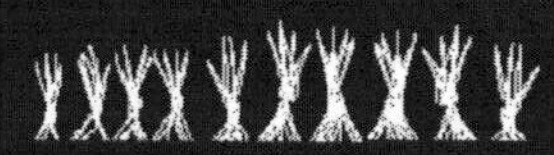

ground. ground. ground.
ground. ground. ground.
ground. ground. ground.
ground. ground. ground.
ground. ground. ground.
ground. ground. ground.
ground. ground. ground.
ground. ground. ground.
ground. ground. ground.
ground. ground. ground.
ground. ground. ground.
ground. ground. ground.

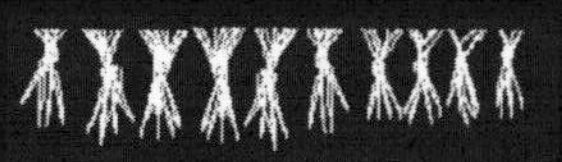

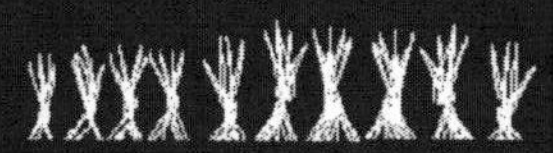

ground. ground. ground.
ground. ground. ground.
ground. ground. ground.
ground. ground. ground.
ground. ground. ground.
ground. ground. ground.
ground. ground. ground.
ground. ground. ground.
ground. ground. ground.
ground. ground. ground.
ground. ground. ground.
ground. ground. ground.

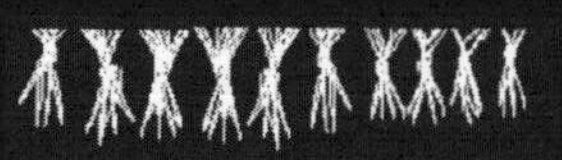

Through this metamorphic fluctuation, it is important to acknowledge the following condition:

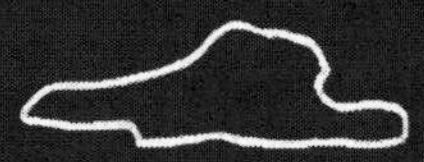

The **body /جسم /jism** (you) is separate from the object (prayer rug).

The prayer rug is an object created by the **body /جسم /jism**.
However, the mind **soul/روح/ruh** converges
the **body /جسم /jism** and the prayer rug together to birth
abstraction.

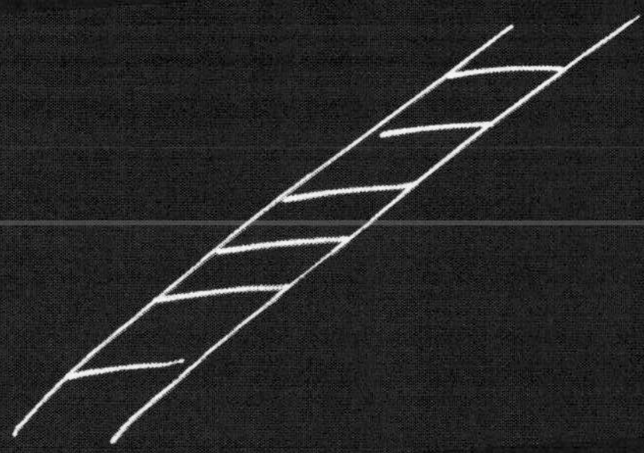

In "Francis Bacon: The Logic of Sensation" by Gilles Deleuze, Delueze presents the reader with the following question: "Why still paint today?" The answer seems to birth abstraction as a mode of spiritual freedom and expansion. This same answer is applicable to the question of prayer, In other words, "Why do I still pray today?", and the prayer rug itself, "what is the role of my prayer rug?" These are questions that must be asked to raise your spiritual relationship to a higher degree.

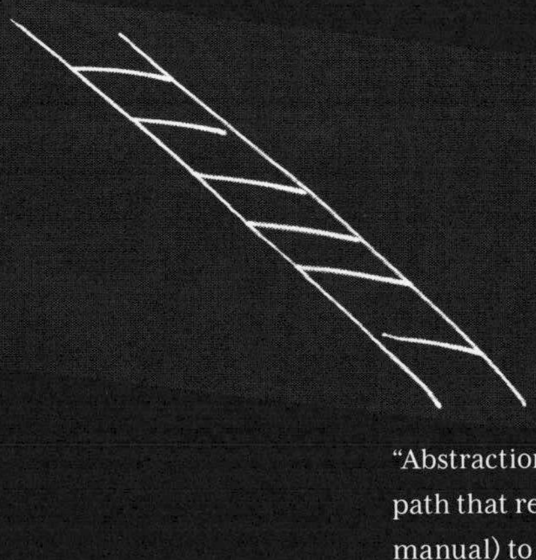

"Abstraction would be one of these paths, but it is a path that reduces the abyss or chaos (as well as the manual) to a minimum: it offers us an asceticism, a spiritual salvation. Through an intense spiritual effort, it raises itself above the figurative givens, but it also turns chaos into a simple stream we must cross in order to discover the abstract and signifying Forms."[4] Humans are constantly searching for salvation, freedom, and security.

Therefore, we must challenge our own automaticness.

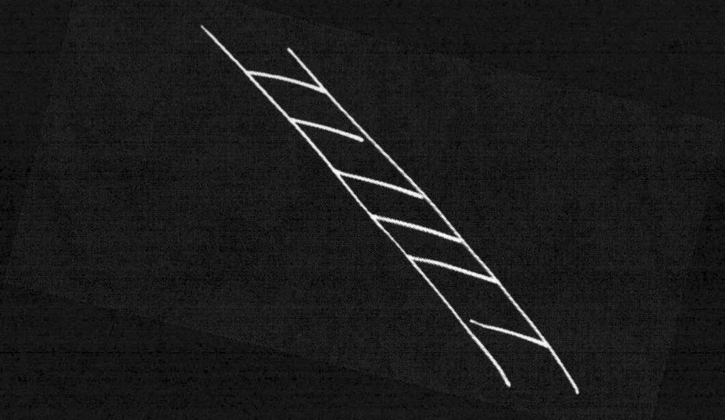

Prayer is a conscious action of faith.

It should not be something that is
performed without the presence
of your

—

soul

JJ99SS /

/ ruh

4 Deleuze, Gilles. "The Diagram." Translated by Daniel W. Smith. In Francis Bacon: The Logic of Sensation, 103. London: Continuum, 2003.

When I converse with Allah,
I am present.
I am here (earth)
and
I am there (belief).

I will continue to
challenge
my habits (settlement)
to raise my being

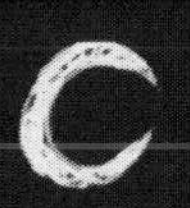

into light.

(afterimage)
(afterimage)
(afterimage)
(afterimage)
(afterimage)
into light. (afterimage)
(afterimage)
(afterimage)
(afterimage)
(afterimage)
(afterimage)
(afterimage)
(afterimage)
(afterimage)
(afterimage)
(afterimage)
(afterimage)
(afterimage)
(afterimage)
(afterimage)

ةىولت ةروص

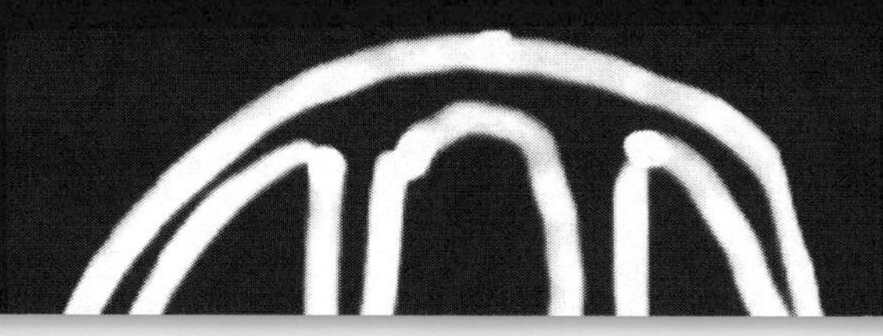

edward winkleman

is an independent curator, author co-owner of Winkleman Gallery. Winkleman also ran the wildly successful blog, operating under his namesake, that became a repository for artists seeking insight into the art world.

We're far enough away from it now that I can share this story (and laugh about it). During the well-attended Opening Reception of the latest Moving Image [an art fair in New York that Murat Orozobekov and I organize] a bit over a week ago, a fashionable friend of ours commented on how my choice of a light brown suit with a pink shirt was boldly diving into Spring. Normally I would have obsessed over whether she was really suggesting it was too soon to abandon the ubiquitous black, particularly in the art world, but at that moment the season appropriateness of my wardrobe choice was the very least of my worries. But let me back up.

Earlier that day, shortly before we opened to the public, we were putting the final touches on the fair. Everyone else on the team was out on the fair floor turning on monitors and such, but I just couldn't accept a series of scuff marks on our Office/Gallerist Lounge walls left by the previous event organizers who had rented the tunnel. So, I grabbed a paint roller and set about making it perfect.

Now I know it's idiotic to paint in a suit, but I was extremely careful (and didn't have a change of clothes anyway), and in fact was quite pleased when I finished and washed my hands to see that I hadn't got a drop on me. Not on the front anyway. Murat comes back into the office and asks, in typical Muratese, "What's on your ass?"

Yup, you guessed it, two huge circles of white paint, one for each cheek that must have brushed up against the wall at some point in my haste.

Mind you, the fair is opening in minutes, I have no other clothes, and our home is an hour at least back and forth plus changing, so my only option is to try to clean my pants. Fortunately it was water-based paint, so I grab some wet paper towels, twist my torso as far as I can, and try rubbing it off. That wasn't going too quickly though so Murat locked the office door and I dropped my trousers half way to get at the back better.

That too proved inefficient though; they needed to be cleaned on a flat horizontal surface. Murat volunteered to take them to the restroom while I waited in the office.

"I am NOT sitting here in my underwear while you go out for who knows how long!" I protested.

"Well, here, try my sweatpants," he tried helpfully.

Of course the only thing more absurd and obscene than me in my tighty whities, dress socks, and snow white legs would have been me bursting out of Murat's tiny sweatpants. No, that wasn't going to happen.

"Well, here," said an increasingly exasperated Murat, throwing me a black tablecloth, "Wrap that around you."

I looked like I was going to a surreal South Pacific funeral with my suit top and black sarong bottom. But at least my legs were no longer freezing.

Eventually Murat came back from apparently deciding the best way to wash my pants was to hurl them straight into the Hudson. They were positively soaked.

"Well...I had to clean them," he declared.

"Arghhh!" I believe was the extent of my appreciation at that point. I grabbed a few rolls of paper towels and tried soaking up as much as I could, but it was becoming increasingly obvious I would be opening the fair with a very soggy bottom and looking like I pissed myself if we couldn't figure something out.

"There's a heater in the hallway," Murat said, grabbing the trousers and heading out again.

"Lock the door!" I hollered after him.

Normally the office of any fair is like Grand Central right before it opens, with deliveries, dealers checking in, fire department officials, etc, all needing to enter. So it felt like an eternity as I waited in my skirt, and sure enough before Murat returned someone was pounding on the door. Hard.

Hoping it was Murat I ventured, "Who is it?"

"Building maintenance" came a deep gruff voice. "I need the cart you have in there."

"Just a minute," I insisted, hoping Murat would notice the epic humiliation about to descend on me and come running back.

One minute. Two minutes. Three minutes. The pounding resumed, the doorknob jiggled. "What if he gets the keys?" I suddenly thought.

"Murat. Murat!" I pleaded into the walkie talkie. "Please come back. Now!"

"Don't go in there!" I heard Murat instruct, perhaps a touch too strongly. The building guy protested that he didn't like people ordering him about in his own building. A pissing match ensued, which of course Murat won, but now he was upset with me.

Finally, though, I got my pants back, still damp, with a much lighter stain of white paint, but I had no choice; I had to wear them.

Whether it was too early in the season was my last concern about my clothing as the fair opened. Fortunately no one who attended seemed to notice I kept twitching my butt.

martha wilson

is a pioneering feminist artist and gallery director, who over the past four decades created innovative photographic and video works that explore her female subjectivity through role-playing, costume transformations, and "invasions" of other people's personae. She began making these videos and photo/text works in the early 1970s while in Halifax in Nova Scotia, and further developed her performative and video-based practice after moving in 1974 to New York City, embarking on a long career that would see her gain attention across the U.S. for her provocative appearances and works. In 1976 she also founded and continues to direct Franklin Furnace, an artist-run space.

Dear Holly,

Thanks for this invite! Please let me think about it. More soon!

XOXO Martha

Dear Holly,

Wednesday I will interview Martha Rosler at Pratt, Thursday I fly to Zurich to perform for the 100th birthday of Cabaret Voltaire. It's a pretty busy time! I do not think I will be submitting anything to your book project after all.

Sorry for finking out!

All best wishes,
Martha

Dear Holly,

What's hanging me up is the non-linear art-life part. Lists are linear, aren't they? I never write stuff like "check email" on my To Do list; that's a given. I write the tasks— which I'm not going to reveal in print! And the non-linear art stuff I write in my journals—I'm not going to reveal that either, because it is in process and not a work yet. So I don't think I can come up with anything I would like to represent me. Sorry!

I am in Taipei until Thursday. Feel free to argue some more, but I think this is not going to happen.

Thanks for asking me,
Martha

doug harvey

graduating with an MFA in painting from UCLA in 1994, Harvey has written extensively about the Los Angeles and international art scenes and other aspects of popular culture, primarily as the art critic for *LA WEEKLY* and *Art Issues*. His writing has also appeared in *Art in America*, *The New York Times*, *Modern Painters*, *ArtReview*, and numerous other publications.

Hey Mikey,

It looks like a great show as usual but I would have to a] visit it, b] be writing art reviews these days, and c] be willing to do so for no money for Artillery. I loved the video of you being buried alive in your little sculptures though. Artillery should just put that up!

The collaboration is alive. I will shortly have your painted elements completely excised and ready to be assembled and fixed in the Final Configuration. Finland Ho!

D. Harvey

"The caricature or stereotype of The Eskimo has a life of its own, with interesting similarities and differences in relation to stereotypes imposed by Europeans on other Native Americans. Certainly these cartoonish generalizations were a form of semiotic imperialism, but in the case of Eskimos, there weren't as many natural resources to get all Manifest Destiny about, so they were given more credit for their ingenuity and resourcefulness, and allowed to retain—in simulacral form anyway—humor, mystery, nobility and cultural autonomy that were eradicated from the profiles of more real-estate savvy aboriginals."

Greetings Mannlicherista

MC will be appearing on the LA experimental radio program "Glossolalia" on KXLU FM (& kxlu.com) on Monday between 6-8PM. If anyone wants to SKYPE in and be a part of the mix, let us know. We're planning a loosely chronological retrospective, but we'll probably be layering stuff, so there's wiggle room for improvisation.

R. Happening

"Last Chance to Gaze Upon My Giant Golden Testicles! Viewers who encounter my piece "Stranger Fruit (for Nazario Conchuza Gonzalez) AKA Gilded Disc®otu m'" (1997/2016, Enamel on mirror tile fabric, polyester fiber fill stuffing, defunct bumble balls) at Nick Brown's "Werewolf" show at Charlie James Gallery are unlikely to remember it from my 1997 solo debut at POST, where it was one component of an "experimental narrative circuit" entitled "St Sebastian Tom Sawyer Cathy Mishima Expo 67," so here's a link to my admittedly skimpy documentation:

HTTP://DOUGHARVEY.LA/DOUG_HARVEY.PHP?ID=59

Later, in an essay for JOAAP's "Failure" book I described the work thusly:

Descending in tandem from the rafters was the gender-corrected biorchid soft kinetic sculpture Disc®otu m', a sack of mirror-encrusted fabric containing two motorized vibrating wads of material. I've always been puzzled by Duchamp scholars insistence that the title of his last painting Tu m' was an abbreviation of the French expression "Tu m'emmerdes" or "you're shitting on (bugging) me." As far as I can tell, it's just a guess—it could be completed with any French verb starting with a vowel. Why not "Tu m'blank" as in "You blank me," which, rather than sealing the tomb on painting because of some specific affect (irritation, beshitment, boredom), emphasizes (and probably expresses doubt in the validity of) thevery hierarchical subject/object binary model of communication (and by extension reality itself) by which it achieves its agency. Disc®otum' in addition to presenting a disembodied teabag of Damocles that visually mimics the geometry-bound domes, was intended to expand Duchamp's contraction, doubling it with mirrors and subjecting it to seizure. Lazarus,

Come forth!'"

Hey everybody—

I've organized a field trip to the Getty to hear Anselm Kiefer speak next Weds evening—but I could only book 8 tickets. They're free but they'll go fast— if you could all book your own, we'd be in good shape. I've also posted links to a couple of documentaries about Kiefer as well as Thomas McEvilley explaining his "Shape of Ancient Thought" on the blog.

Prof. Doug H

Hi John
Still looking for a place to live! I guess I could have kept doing my KCHUNG show. Oh well, I'm keeping busy anyway.

For the Eternal Telethon, maybe we could do the regular Mannlicher Carcano Radio Hour slot on the Saturday from 11:30-1:30—if there's enough bandwidth to accommodate skyping the other participants together for the actual radio broadcast. I'll have to check who's on board that weekend, though.

Who's coordinating performances at Human Resources now? F is looking to do a launch party for our forthcoming ltd ed cassette (ONLY 50 copies—one is earmarked for KCHUNG though) in July.

Doug H

I'll tell you one story—when I was in undergrad I had a summer job at the art school summer camp for kids, as a sort of shepherd—I didn't have to teach, just shuffle the kiddies from one place to another. As a surprise for the painting instructor (my friend Richard, who was sort of in the middle of an identity crisis) I got the kids to surround him and chant this [Children of the Italia Conte School intoning "Keeep calm... keeep calm... WATCH YOUR STEP!!!"] He giggled nervously and rolled his eyes for the duration. It seemed like a good idea at the time. Later I think he was arrested for stalking Leonard Cohen.

Hi Wendy,
I am just following up regarding your request for individual bios for the members of F. They are attached below.

Marnie Weber's multidisciplinary practice encompasses performance, film, video, sculpture, collage, music and costuming. Weber's early years were grounded in performance art, before moving into filmmaking and later large-scale installations, all the while continuing a practice of collage, creating limited edition records as an art form, and performing and recording music. www.marnieweber.com

Doug Harvey is an artist, writer and critic, independent curator, experimental musician, and educator who lives and works in Los Angeles. His activities may be monitored online at www.dougharvey.blogspot.com and www.dougharvey.la.

Daniel Hawkins is a Los Angeles based multi-media artist and experimental musician.

For more information visit:

www.danielhawkins.info and www.desertlighthouse.org

F for Freak

F is a Los Angeles art-rock supergroup whose motto is "Simplicity Through Noise" and who have developed a practice rooted in improvisational ensemble playing using electric guitars (played with rubber mallets and other extended as well as traditional techniques) and vintage synthesizers, in various combinations of three. Their debut album Fauxmishwas released Sept 2, 2011 and later this year they will be releasing a limited edition cassette titled FF. The members are established in their own right and include Daniel Hawkins, Marnie Weber, and Doug Harvey.

"Lipman appears to have developed his obsession just in time, as several of the participants—particularly Beckett's go-to actress Billie Whitelaw and Grove Press publisher and "Film" producer Barney Rosset (both creative titans in their own departments) are themselves teetering on the brink of the Void in their interview segments. Rossett, whose flickering memories of a missing prologue to the Beckett short sparked Lipman's passion, was the source of the missing footage as well as surreptitious audio recordings of the pre-production meetings. These are pretty great, but there isn't enough to them to justify a feature length deconstruction."

Bolton, here's the short essays on Lllyn Foulkes and Carol Caroompas—I'm finishing them up in reverse. They're both a little long. Should get the Margaret Nielson, Mel Henderson, and Martin Kersels to you in the next couple of days. Let me know if you need them as docs—my Mac upgrade has forced me to use Pages, but I can manage something...

BTW, the Foulkes piece wasn't actually in the Hammer show, but it's reproduced on the catalog's back cover in the 1963 Artforum piece by John Coplans!

And yes, I can do a Jean Lowe as well—I love her work. Is it a bookcase?

"At the same time, he put the built-in nostalgia and social critique of assemblage on the back burner. Instead, his new paintings seemed to demand a place at the forefront of contemporaneous avant-garde painting—compositions based on postcards and other printed matter mined the quotidian quotations of the emerging Pop generation; his rag-smear textures began to look more like Art Informel than Max Ernst; and his sections of precise geometric stripes picked up the Minimalist gauntlet hurled by Frank Stella and his followers."

good evening professor,

I'm sorry i missed the assailments. I was wondering if you could open it for me for a day or 2 because I was away for my aunt's funeral in canada and left my laptop and kind of was out of focus mentally to do work. I would ge=reatly appreciate it. Also this will not happen again. I do apologize and I hope you understand. Thank you

Eleanor X

OK, I've given you a 5-day extension on the first week's assignments, and opened the modules for everyone forever.

Prof DougH

Ive tried opening them but they were locked. I'm have difficulty. looking a father is probably the worst feeling and Its hard to cope is there anyway you can unlock them cause i can't get in. i didn't se when u wrote me back I'm sorry for the excuses cause ethic sins me.

Eleanor X

Greetings Mannlicherista

MC will be accompanying John "Let's Paint TV" Kilduff during a live performance at an LA club called Pehrspace Saturday Night. Mr Kilduff will probably be delivering one of his motivational painting demo lectures while walking on a treadmill and possibly juicing a variety of vegetables or somesuch (if you're unfamiliar, just look on youtube). Let us know if anyone wants to skype in and we'll patch a laptop through the PA.

R. Happening

"My last seizure was in my first year at art school, in the library, looking at a thumbnail magazine reproduction of one of Richard Prince's appropriated cigarette cowboys, thinking I wanted to rephotograph the tiny B&W image, blow it up and present it as my own work. A trapdoor of infinite regression opened in my brain, and I fell through—past uncountable reappropriations of Marlboro men, into darkness. It would make an excellent Jim Shaw piece!"

Thanks to everyone for participating in "practice, Practice, practice: Abstract Spirituality in Los Angeles Painting, Sculpture and Performance" and the "pPperformance Night"—both were powerful in the depth of their psychological and spiritual resonance, their formal and sensual strength, and their idiosyncratic synergy from seemingly diverse, even contradictory traditions. The "catablog" is intended to be an ongoing thing, so I'll be adding material in the future. I hope to curate, publish, and organize workshops and other public events on this theme in the next year or two, so please keep in touch!

Did I forget to mention that attending the Kiefer lecture counts for 30% of your final grade?

Prof. Doug H

Hey

I'll leave the two bootleg covers for SASSAS on the porch. Mine—The Shaggs BUDOKAN! is an actual bootleg cover from the parallel dimension where I am King. Unfortunately, the vinyl itself didn't make it through the wormhole. MA's is "Overcoming Excellence...with Ron Beegle!"—from a projected series of unsanctioned recordings of motivational business speeches, named after her show from 2008.

D

Hi WW

I'll see if I can pull something together—maybe just a collage of stuff I'm currently working on....

Is it OK to announce AC is publishing 'patacritical Vol2? I want to generate more of a buzz this time, and solicit specific contributors...

ischa tallieu

lives and works in Brussels, Belgium, and holds a Master in Art History and a Post-Graduate Specialisation in Theatre Studies. From 1997 until 2014 she was director of Galerie Fortlaan 17 and since 2014 she runs Tallieu Art Office.

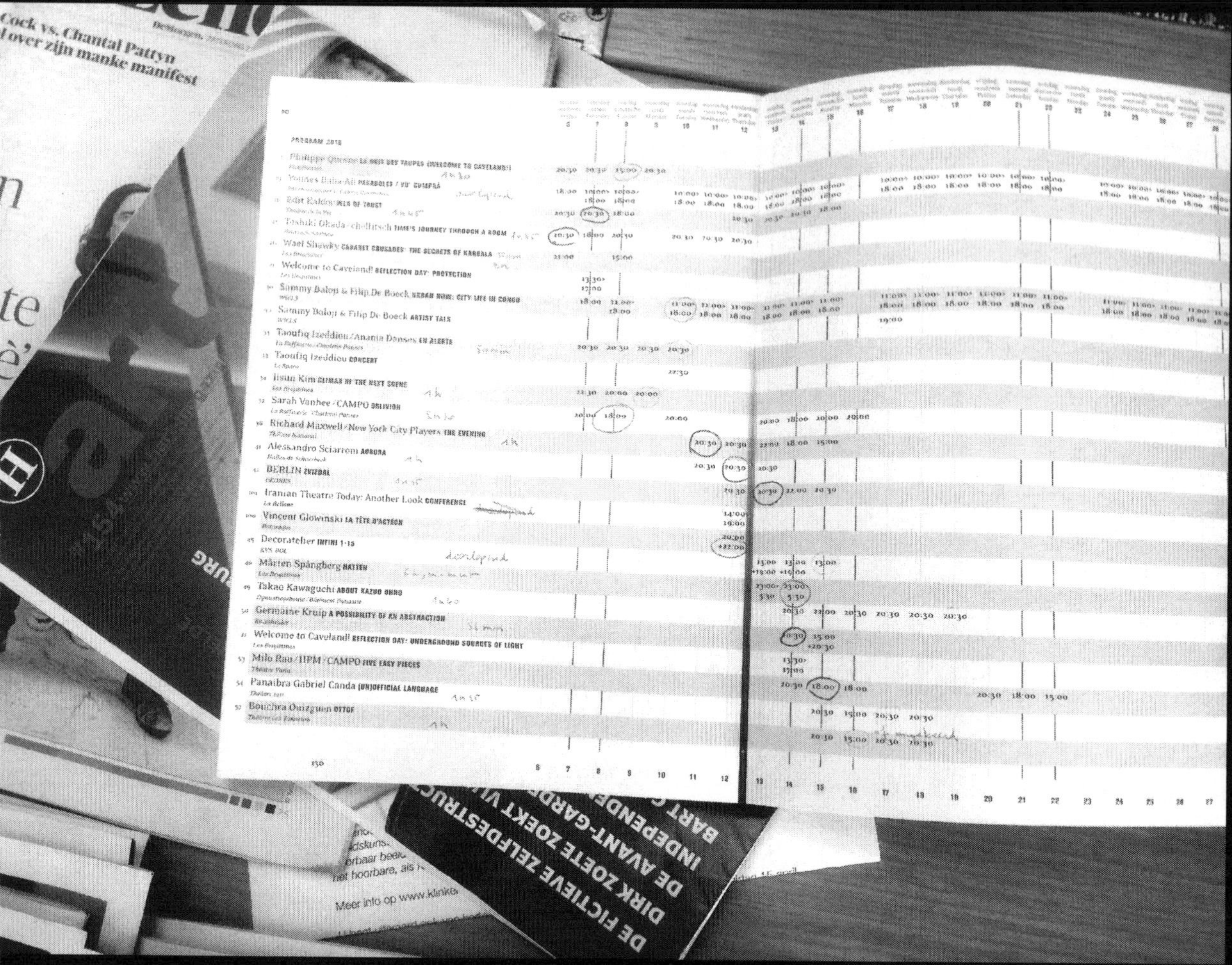

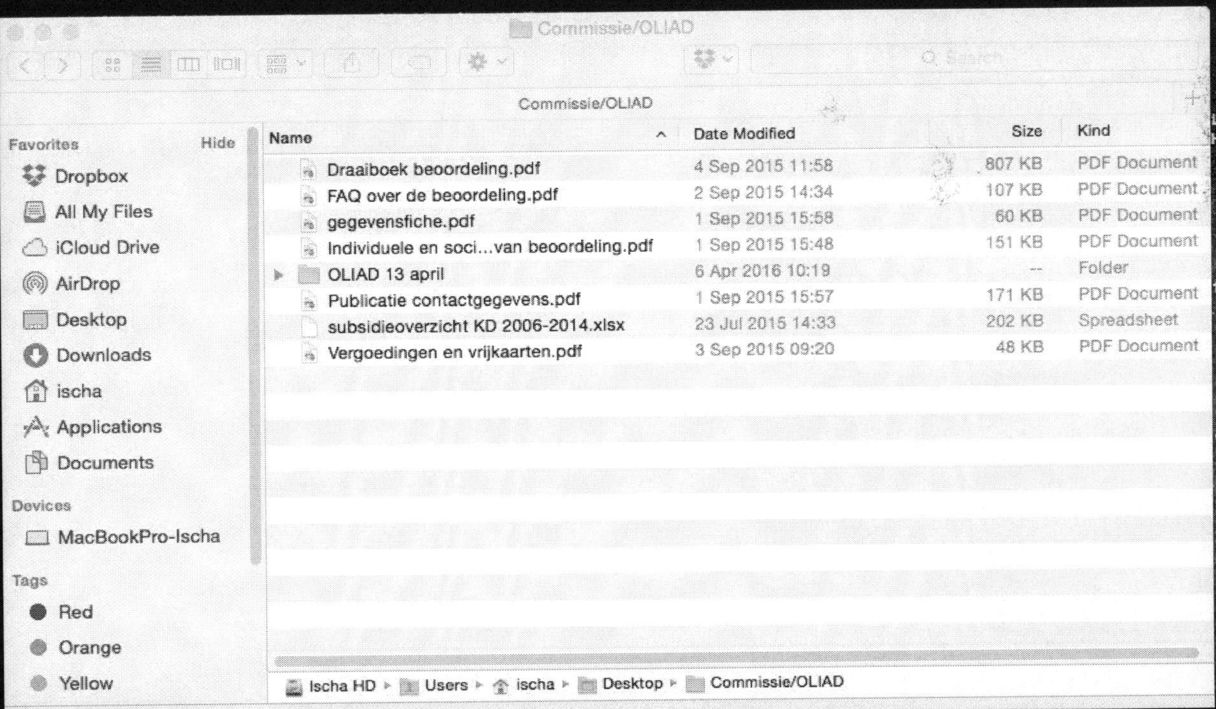
Commissie/OLIAD
Favorites
Hide
Dropbox
All My Files
iCloud Drive
AirDrop
Desktop
Downloads
ischa
Applications
Documents
Devices
MacBookPro-Ischa
Tags
Red
Orange
Yellow
Name
Date Modified
Size
Kind
Draaiboek beoordeling.pdf 4 Sep 2015 11:58 807 KB PDF Document
FAQ over de beoordeling.pdf 2 Sep 2015 14:34 107 KB PDF Document
gegevensfiche.pdf 1 Sep 2015 15:58 60 KB PDF Document
Individuele en soci...van beoordeling.pdf 1 Sep 2015 15:48 151 KB PDF Document
OLIAD 13 april 6 Apr 2016 10:19 -- Folder
Publicatie contactgegevens.pdf 1 Sep 2015 15:57 171 KB PDF Document
subsidieoverzicht KD 2006-2014.xlsx 23 Jul 2015 14:33 202 KB Spreadsheet
Vergoedingen en vrijkaarten.pdf 3 Sep 2015 09:20 48 KB PDF Document
Ischa HD ▸ Users ▸ ischa ▸ Desktop ▸ Commissie/OLIAD

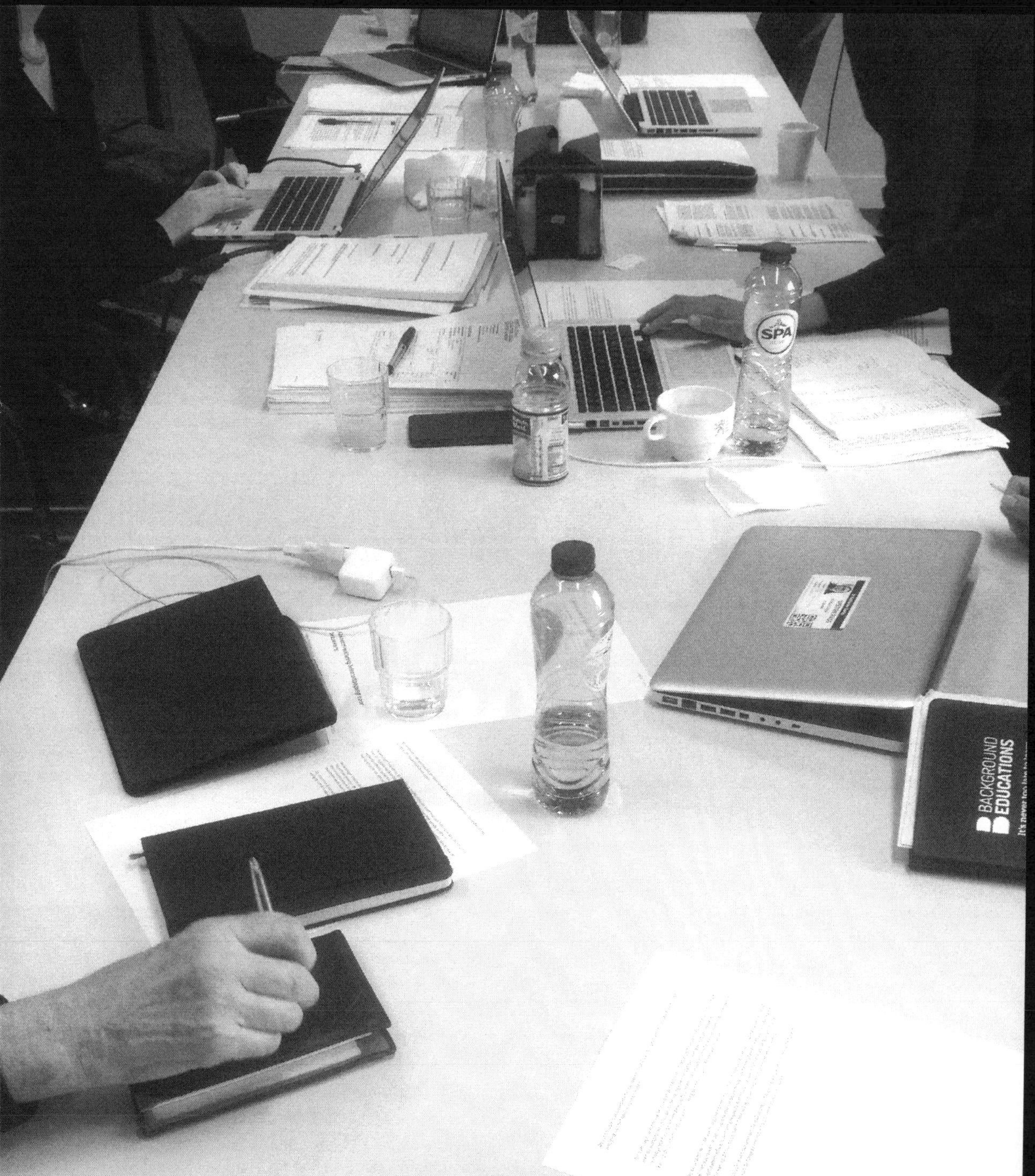
SPA
BACKGROUND
EDUCATIONS

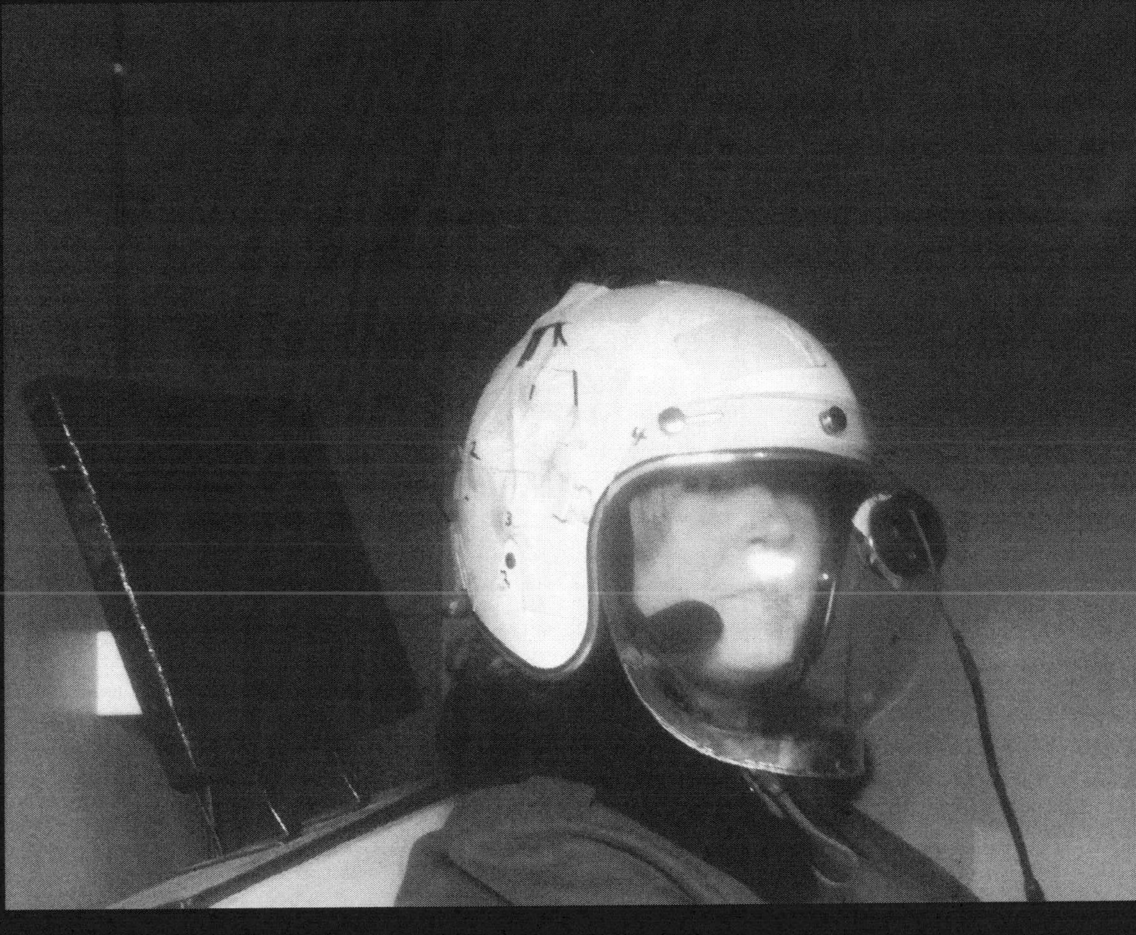

Ischa Tallieu <ischa@artoffice.be> Today 16:26
To: Ischa Tallieu <ischa@artoffice.be>
Txt

IT

Essence is therefore not in things, nor even in the link between them, but in the space that this link crosses. And reveals, each time.
The important thing is to understand that space is not static, but that it only exists because we move through it.
It is also our source of happiness and life, while at the same time being dependent on us.

Grégoire Polet (in catalogue CONNECTED)

Sent from my iPhone

27 April

Week 17 of 2016

Kalender

April 2016						
M	T	W	T	F	S	S
				1	2	3
4	5	6	7	8	9	10
11	12	13	14	15	16	17
18	19	20	21	22	23	24
25	26	27	28	29	30	

May 2016						
M	T	W	T	F	S	S
						1
2	3	4	5	6	7	8
9	10	11	12	13	14	15
16	17	18	19	20	21	22
23	24	25	26	27	28	29
30	31					

Varscenefest + Scenetekstivalen

08

09

10

11 — 11:00 Tale Naes - 1:100 Presentation Stipendium Project - Scene-text
Tromsø Bibliotek

Noon

12:30 The Unsaid - The Unheard
Halogaland Teater, Tromso

13

14

15

16

17 — 17:00 Mental - the vacuum cleaner (UK)
Small Projects, Tromso

18

19

20 — 20:00 I went mental and all I got was this lousy T-shirt - The Vacu-umcleaner
Rådstua Teaterhus, Tromsø

21

• All-Day Events

27/4 Varscenefest + Scenetekstivalen
Location: Tromso (NO)

• Timed Events

11:00 to 12:00 Tale Naes - 1:100 Presentation Stipendium Project - Scenetext
Location: Tromsø Bibliotek

12:30 to 13:30 The Unsaid - The Unheard
Location: Halogaland Teater, Tromso

17:00 to 18:00 Mental - the vacuum cleaner (UK)
Location: Small Projects, Tromso

20:00 to 21:00 I went mental and all I got was this lousy T-shirt - The Vacuumcleaner
Location: Rådstua Teaterhus, Tromsø

Page 1/1

Resent-From: Ischa Tallieu <ischa@artoffice.be>
"der barna sover"

Dear Ischa Tallieu

Thank You for participating in the presentation of my Artistic Research project and the reading of "Where the children sleep". It was so interested in hearing you comments - and since this is research - I would so much have apreaciated if you could write me a couple of lines about your experience in the eventyr-room on the 27th of april.
It will be usefull to me in many ways.
As an artist, as a person - and too my research.

I hope you find the time.

Yours sincerely Tale Næss

elizabeth gower

has been exhibiting innovative work, including collages and wall hangings, since 1976. Her interest lies in the human desire to create order from the chaotic. Exploiting the associations evoked by such banal material, her work has often been connected with a feminist sensibility; however this framing should be countered with recognition of the strong aesthetic concerns at play.

Portrait of the Artist as a Young Woman is an extensive archive of photographs spanning over four decades from 1974 to the present. Each image documents my various studios, work processes and exhibitions as well as the witnesses who took the photographs.

Over that time the form of my work has changed but the consistent process has involved collecting and collating data and materials including retrieved printed papers, product packaging and mass- produced imagery that are cut and rearranged into geometric systems; repeated texts and lists that form extensive chronologies and multiple location photographs configured into linear timeline installations.

I have selected 7 days from Portrait of the Artist as a Young Woman that record the transition of anemerging artist through mid-career to the present.

In my final year at Art School I moved into a series of grand disused Victorian rooms above a suburban arcade with, my artist partner (a fellow student). This space radically influenced the scale and scope of my work over the next seven years.

The photograph records large paper works in progress for my third one-person exhibition in Melbourne. The semi-transparent paper sheets hanging from the ceiling were later re-worked and extended into a nine-panel installation that was included in the 1979 Sydney Biennale, Art Gallery of New South Wales.

At the time, I was a high school Art teacher three days a week and a waitress at a local French restaurant two nights a week. I was involved with the burgeoning Women's Art Movement and a member of the LIP, feminist Art journal collective. In 1977, I left for a five-month study tour to Europe, a London, New York and a studio residency in Paris. This was my first overseas trip, I took $1000 in traveller's cheques and the book 'Europe on $10 a Day'.

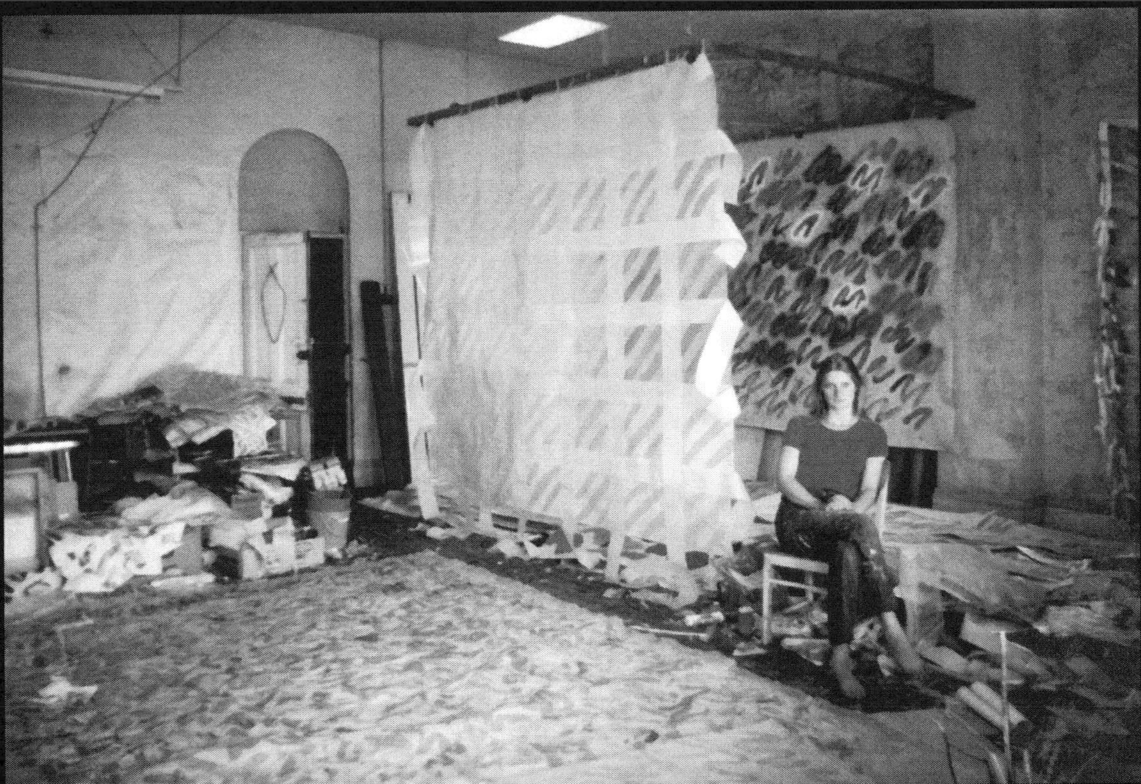

Chapel Street studio, Prahran, 1976 (photographer: Howard Arkley)

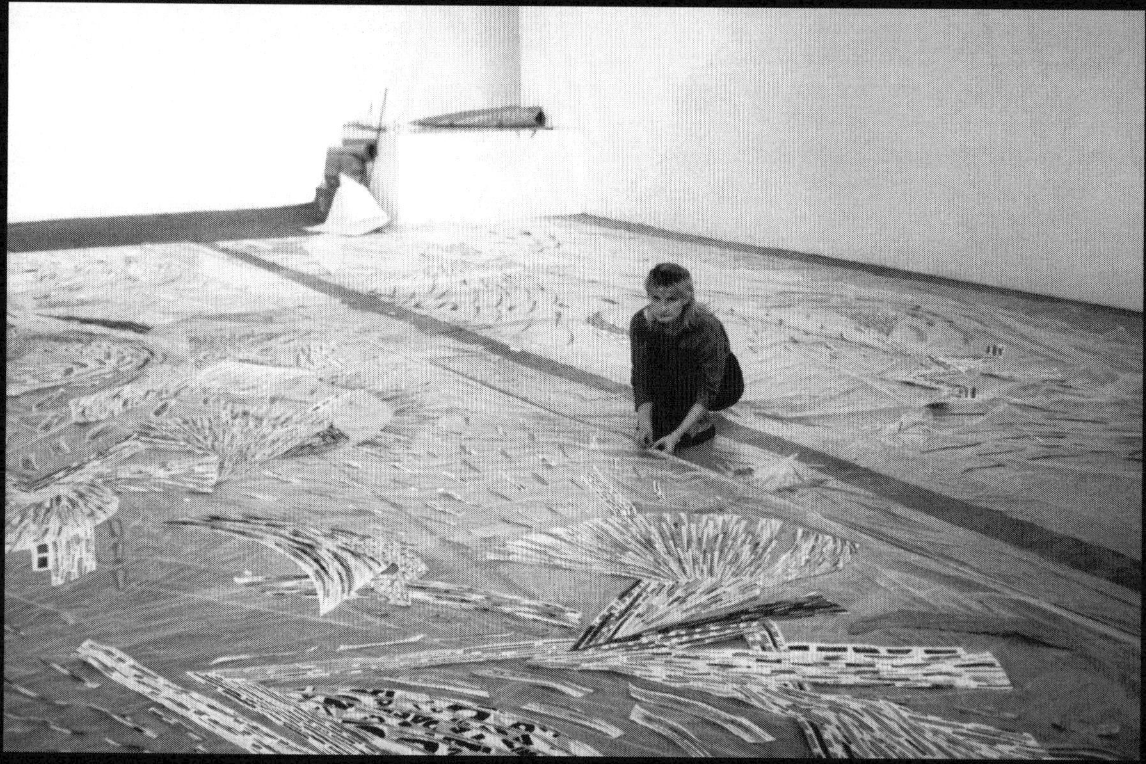

Installing 'All Life Long' Christine Abrahams Gallery, Richmond, 1984 (photographer: Louise Neri)

In this photograph, I am threading a rod through the top of the front layer of an eight-metre-long (26 feet) installation before it is hoisted up and hung floor to ceiling from the beams. This was the day before my wedding and I was hoping to be out of the gallery before nightfall.

The work was first developed in the studio as a shaped wall-work made from shredded billboards and posters. It was then expanded into a free-hanging installation during a residency at the Tasmanian School of Art, Hobart, later included (with the addition of text) in Australian Perspecta at the Art Gallery of New

South Wales. And then, with the addition of another layer, at the Art Gallery of Western Australia. Most of my installations are temporary and often modified and adapted years as a direct response to subsequent sites.

My studio at this time was a large warehouse in the heart of Melbourne. Artists had begun to move into abandoned buildings in the laneways of the city and I worked and lived there 'illegally' for two years. I subsidised my practice as a part-time Tutor (initially the only female staff member in the Painting Department) then contracted Lecturer, at the Victorian College of the Arts (VCA).

I am holding my son Ivan in front of a large painting, Visual Overload, in a small studio in my house. I had just picked him up from crèche after a busy day teaching at the VCA where I was now the first female Head of the Painting Department. This position was full-time with one research day, and I worked in the studio at night and on the weekends whenever possible. I knew only one other woman who was a mother, an artist and a teacher, so there were no role models.

When this photograph was taken I was also pregnant with my second child, Hannah, and six- months later my mother died. Eventually juggling three careers was unworkable, I knew one had to go and it could only be teaching. So, I resigned and reconciled myself that I had achieved some milestones for other women artists to build upon.

I was fairly confident that my art career would be fairly viable, as I had been awarded a couple of commissions and a few works were selling. In addition, my partner who was also an artist, had a parttime Lecturing position at a University, so there was some regular cash-flow that we optimistically thought could support two art careers and a family.

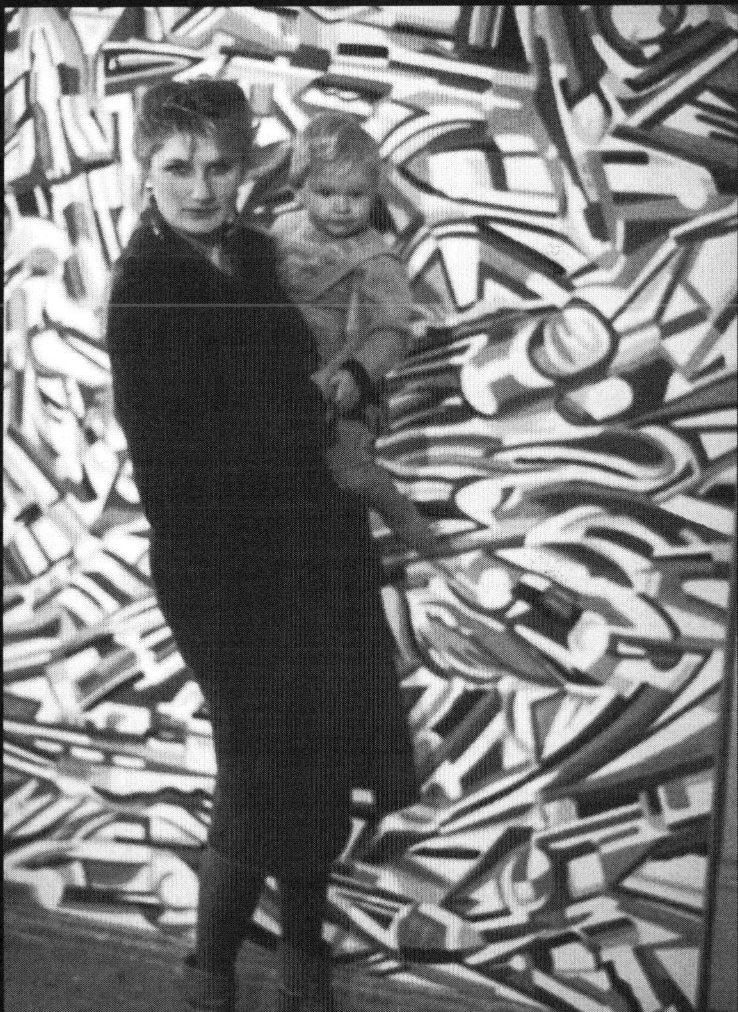

Beach Ave studio, Elwood, 1987 (photographer: John R. Neeson)

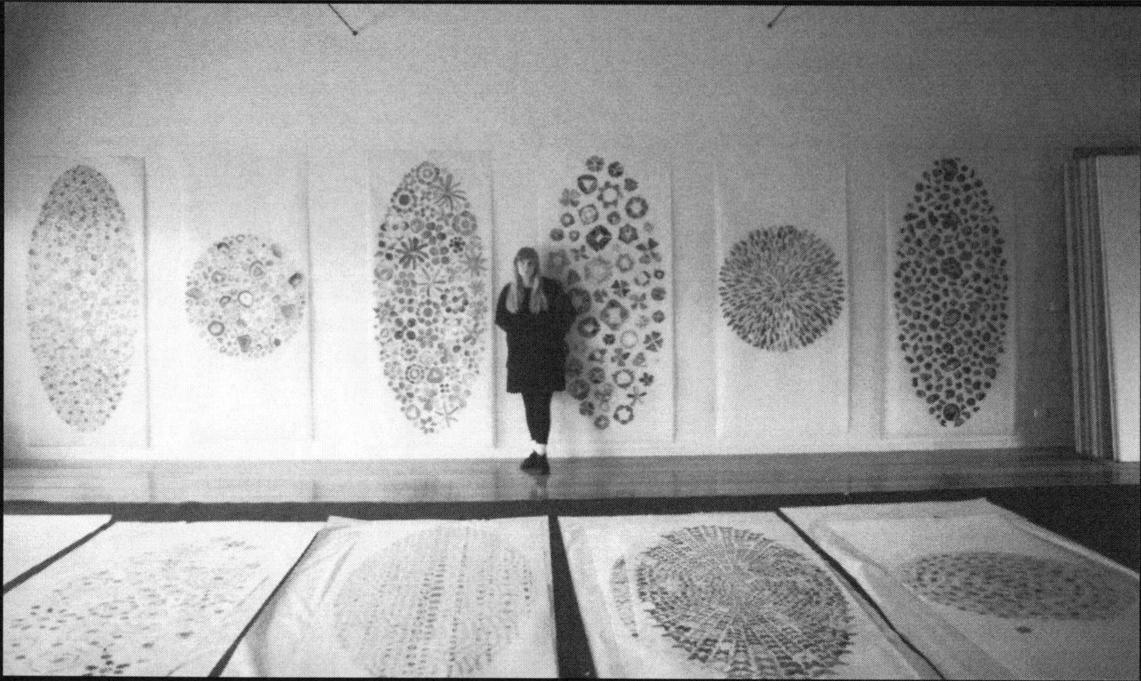

Beach House Hall studio, Elwood, 1996 (photographer: John R. Neeson)

Although I had a small studio at home, when I was awarded a large commission to do twelve mural-sized paintings for an apartment block, it was necessary to rent a large hall at the end of my street. I would work on these (stacked to the right in the photograph) while the children were at school and at night when they were asleep, if I could get away.

In this studio, I also completed a series of twenty-two drafting film sheets collaged with thousands of cutout images of the natural world. These were begun three years earlier and along with a 10,000-word essay, were submitted for my MA at RMIT University. This body of work collectively titled Chance or Design (seen on the wall and floor) were a counterpoint to another recent series made from cut-out images of manufactured products and objects. They were exhibited at Ian Potter Museum, Melbourne with a substantial catalogue and toured to five regional Galleries the following year. I travelled to each venue to supervise the installation, but this was only possible because my partner and I shared parenting responsibilities, and on two occasions I managed to orchestrate these journeys as school holiday destinations.

This is a press photograph from the Sydney Morning Herald newspaper, showing the terrazzo floor Idesigned for the foyer of the Sydney Olympic Superdome. I was awarded this commission and in the same year a residency at the Australia Council Barcelona studio, soon after being invited to return to theVCA as a Senior Lecturer, which meant juggling three jobs again and a very hectic life. However,opportunities such a major commission and a highly competitive residency do not come along that often,so I took up the challenge.

For an artist who had always worked independently and within my own timeframe, the Olympic projectwas a huge learning curve that included flying back and forth to Sydney for meetings with projectmanagers, architects and site supervisors; physically drawing the imagery onto the 500 square metre(5382 sq.ft) floor within a building site; supervising teams of labourers cutting-in the design and pouring terrazzo; overseeing quality control; and dealing with a constant series of deadlines and schedules.

The situation was made somewhat easier because the children were older and more independent andmy partner who was now doing PhD research was not locked into a fixed employment schedule.

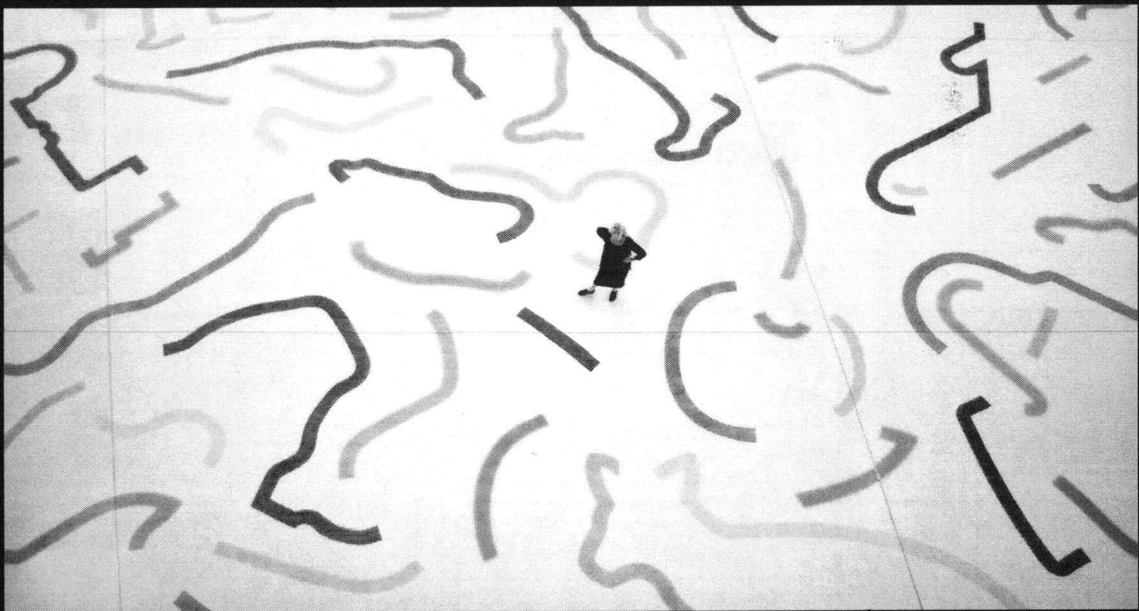

Sydney Olympics Superdome foyer, 2000 (photographer Brendan Esposito)

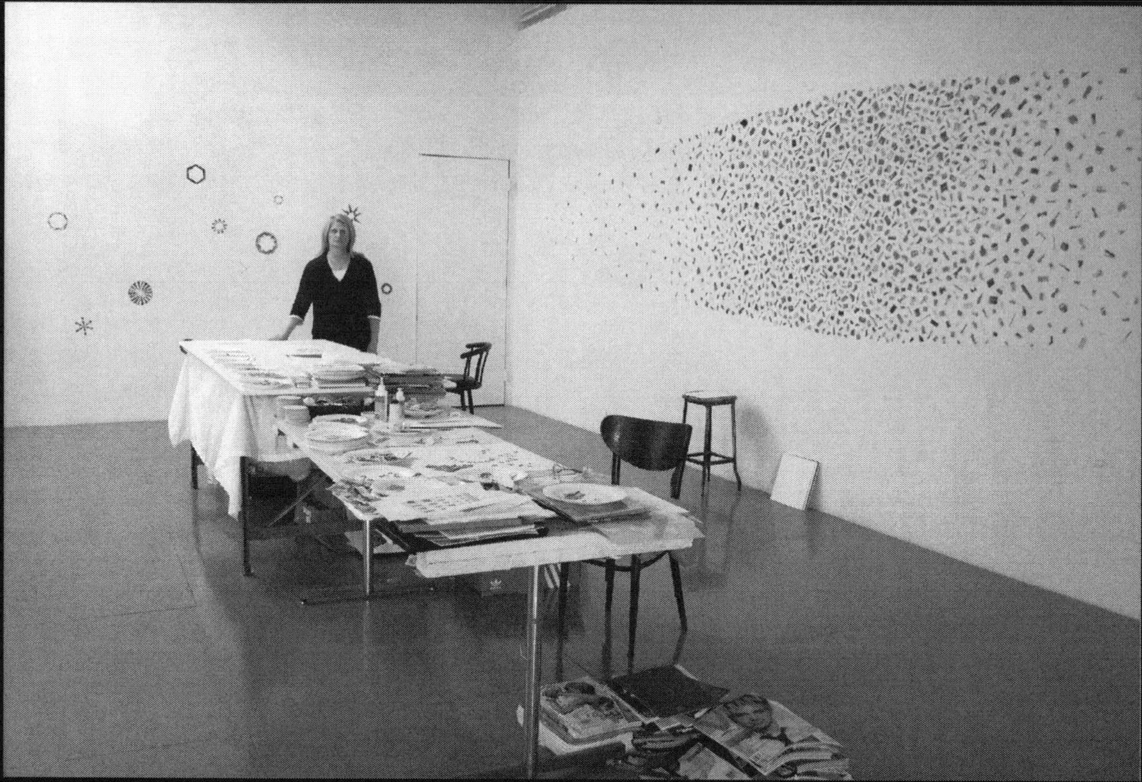

Greene Street studio, New York, 2008 (photographer Kathy Morano)

This photograph records the Australia Council's Greene St studio in SoHo, a highly competitive residency that includes a stipend. I had actually stayed at the studio in 1977 with my then partner who was the recipient and I had always wanted to return. But children under 14 were not permitted so I bided my time, then applied a few of times until the application was successful. By 2008 they were both at University and old enough to stay in Australia on their own for the duration of the residency and were able visit briefly for Christmas.

I took sabbatical from my Lecturer position at VCA but continued my PhD research (VCA now affiliated with the University of Melbourne required staff to have a doctorate). During the residency, I worked on various exhibition projects at AC Institute in NYC; Longwood University Virginia (seen in progress on the wall), and group shows at UICA, Michigan and Brevard Art Museum, Florida.

Studio residencies are generally coveted by artists as they provide 'time out' from jobs and commitments and allow for full time practice without monetary distractions. This is a very rare experience as most artists have to subsidise their practice with a 'day job'. In retrospect, the New York residency (and previous ones in Barcelona and Paris) marked turning points in my work and still inform my current practice.

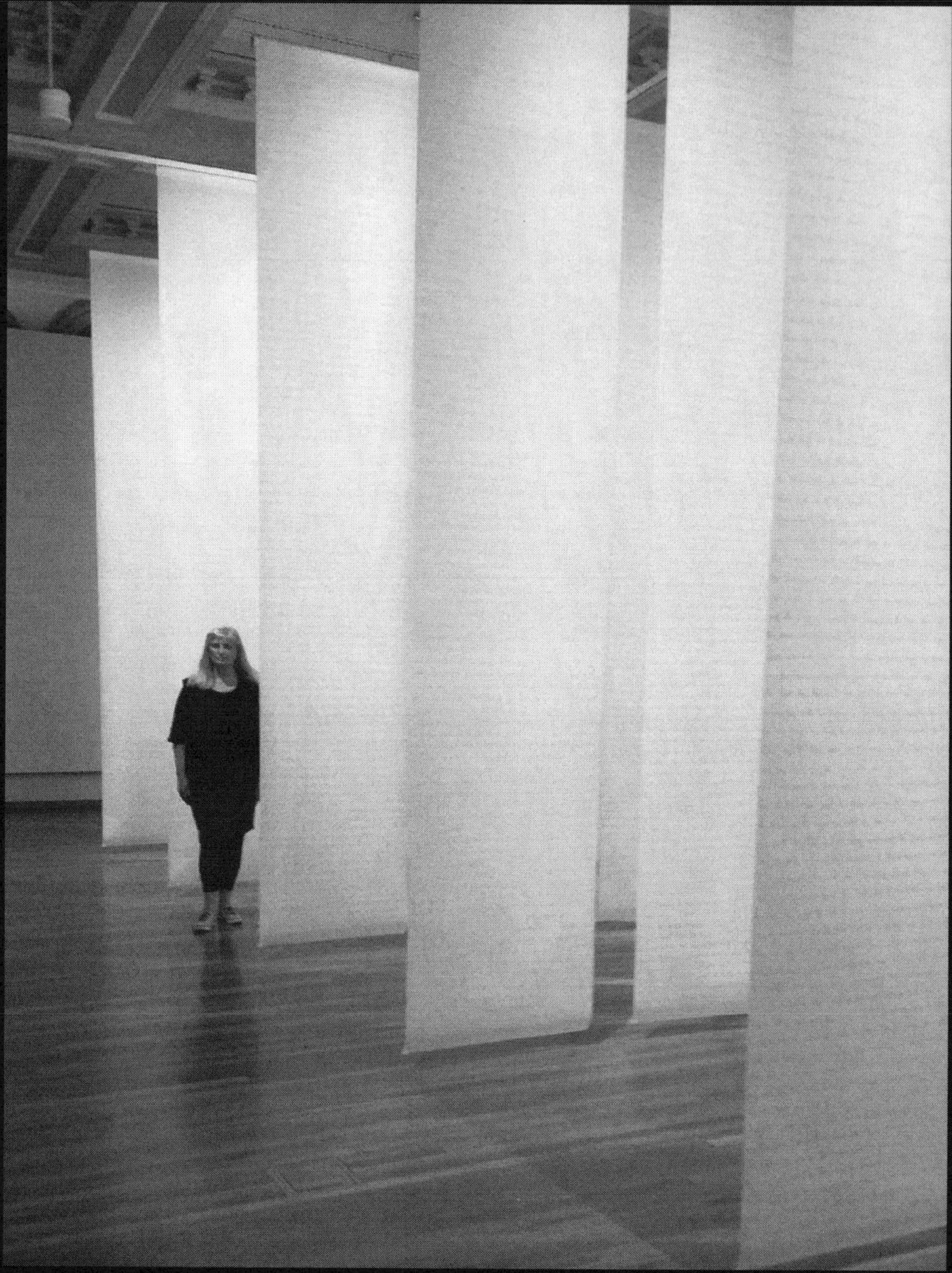

She loves me he loves me not' RMIT University Gallery, 2016 (photographer Suzanne Davies)

The installation he loves me, he loves me not, documented in the photograph, consisted of twenty rolls of drafting film each with phrase handwritten 21,915 times (the number of days I had lived until the date of the show and asked the question). The phrase is written on behalf of women across cultures, who are conditioned to seek approval, permission and sanction from the generic 'he' (i.e. father, brother, boyfriend, husband, male deity, and more generally the boss, colleague, critic or audience). This was the fourth manifestation of the project.

The first, completed in 2007 during a residency at Cité International des Arts Paris, was a wall installation on seven rolls of baking paper, which was posted back to Australia for an exhibition This Crazy Love. In 2009, the phrase was repeatedly written in white chalk directly onto black walls, and then as a performance in the Live on the Limo project at The Armory, in which the passengers pulled petals from a daisy while reciting the phrase. Both of these projects were auspiced by AC Institute, NYC.

As I was working on the 2016 installation, I was diagnosed with breast cancer. However, as the work was almost complete and I had funding for a catalogue, I finished it before the operation. The photograph was taken as I was about to start a month-long course of radiotherapy – as they say the show must go on! I taught for one more year after this show. I am now a full-time artist for the first time in my life, and currently have a major survey of recent works at the Geelong Art Gallery.

brian curtin

is an Irish-born art writer, lecturer, and curator of contemporary art. He holds a Ph.D. in studio art from the University of Bristol and has been based in Bangkok since 2000. He writes and curates on dialogues between contemporary art, Queer theories and studies in visual and material cultures. His commentary, essays, interviews and reviews have been published in *Art Journal*, *Flash Art*, *Artforum*, *Art Asia Pacific*, *Circa*, *Frieze*, *Journal of Curatorial Studies*, *Parachute and Craft Research*, amongst others.

SATURDAY, FEBRUARY 13

I am remembering the last time I was happy. It was for a few months before this month. But now the cumulative impact of a boring trip to Japan, a visit to my insane father at the family home and my distracted boyfriend has caught me in a wave that won't recede or crash. I feel held in a bobbing soup of boredom and soft trauma.

I've begun using sleeping pills, or, more exactly, fragments of pills because I hate the morning grogginess that sleeping on artificial aids give me. But these little things allow me to impose order on my day, once I wake early. A long essay I am struggling to finish reflects everything else: disassociation and inarticulateness to be occasionally challenged by sharp insights that are only ever left hanging. I have no conclusion in mind.

SUNDAY, FEBRUARY 14

Today I attended a series of public talks about historical aspects of literary and urban cultures in the city I live. These talks are praised locally for merely existing. To try and ascertain intellectual value would be offensive to the efforts of those who make these efforts. I listened to tales of colonial histories turned into soap operas that were so un-ironic as to be queer. These are fairy tales written by stupid people but the lack of moral lessons is enticing. If I could ascertain value the cultural scenes I am part of wouldn't care anyway. I decided that I exist within a set of relations that are equal in pressure and unequal in value. But deciding which to sever is currently impossible.

MONDAY, FEBRUARY 15

My boyfriend has begun smiling again. A handsome doctor offers me a menu of tranquilizers, some of which are illegal. He tells me not to use the pills too regularly because they are "highly addictive". I begin writing through a backlog of promised essays and other types of texts for artists.

The absolute freedom I have to write what I write is perverse.

Artists never ask for re-writes. They trust that all I write is important. It isn't, and I encode slurs and sleazy thoughts within self-serving commentary and lite opinions on politics.

TUESDAY, FEBRUARY 16

Attended a seminar led by a conventional documentary photographer. The world is in a perpetual state of conflict, so we should not fear conflict. I am happy that this insight reflects much of my current reading on photography. The camera obscura should have taught us that photography receives the world and is unpredictable in its results. The many images we consume daily cannot define the world for us but are testament to that impossibility. They tell us much about a lot – time, the photographer, the fact of history – but little about the world itself.

Spent the afternoon at an archive, thumbing through old photographs. These photographs are almost comical in their "naïve" colors and their compositions speak to an older world or a sensibility that appears so sincere in its lack of trappings, or affects. I resolve to seek out a quote I remember from Kant about how aesthetics saves us from captivation by the world.

WEDNESDAY, FEBRUARY 17

Tranquilizers dull my senses in a very irritable way.
I am a fraction less alive than I want to be and my sense of vulnerability segues into defensiveness. I cannot maintain civilized or even the most throwaway conversations with my colleagues.

THURSDAY, FEBRUARY 18

The buzz about a new gallery, and an exhibition by an artist I've worked with often, carries me to the opening party. The crowd is cool, a likely in-group, so I don't experience the anxious boredom that typically grips my stomach when speaking to the figures of indifference that typically float through these artificial events. The paintings are bruised Impressionism. They could mean so much here and are never likely to mean much anywhere else. I drink a lot and become happily drunk.

FRIDAY, FEBRUARY 19

I go to meet a man I've never met before, he is from another country and staying in a hotel. We have exchanged pornographic images via phones and computers for a number of months now. I suspect he is in love with me because he becomes impatient if I do not immediately respond to his demands for digital intimacy. Also, he is a native of a country that is famously repressive. I meet him with no sense of hesitation, no trace of fear, and kiss him confidently, then strip him and myself and fuck him with every conceivable position. Intimacy no longer has anything to do with sex for me. A guy I see occasionally performs sex with my body so mechanically that there could be no possible reflection of the subtly wonderful times we spend together in public.

My hotel lover doesn't contact me within hours of leaving his hotel. I expected him to.

anne mckeown

is a multimedia artist combining rational and conceptual processes with intuitive inquiry. With concept in hand she calls on chance, accident and random samplings to form the basis of her work.

A PARTICULAR MEMORY

It was the feel of the air in that moment, the darkening evening, allowing merely a blur of detail, an opening of time.

In an old familiar neighborhood; but not MY neighborhood; I was remembering mine, matching my historical perception of place and time. I wondered if I were to take the turn here could I re-enter, to be again inthat time with that love, warmth, ease...return is not possible, of course.

Memory, the delicious sensation of re-experiencing a past state, in a moment, it is possible to go beyond surface memory to feel deeply a full sensation of being in one's past. The fullness of the sensation evokes a further sensation of wonder. Yes, it is possible to be in that past.

The experience of wonder can be retold. We want to learn how to communicate, how to tell our experience in our own way. When we tell our story we wait for applause, a smile, the agreement of others. For a moment we know they have seen us.

We want to learn how to travel through this place we find ourselves in, to find solutions, to create what makes us feel most ourselves. We want to be seen. We want to be aware, to be here, to feel the richness of being human.

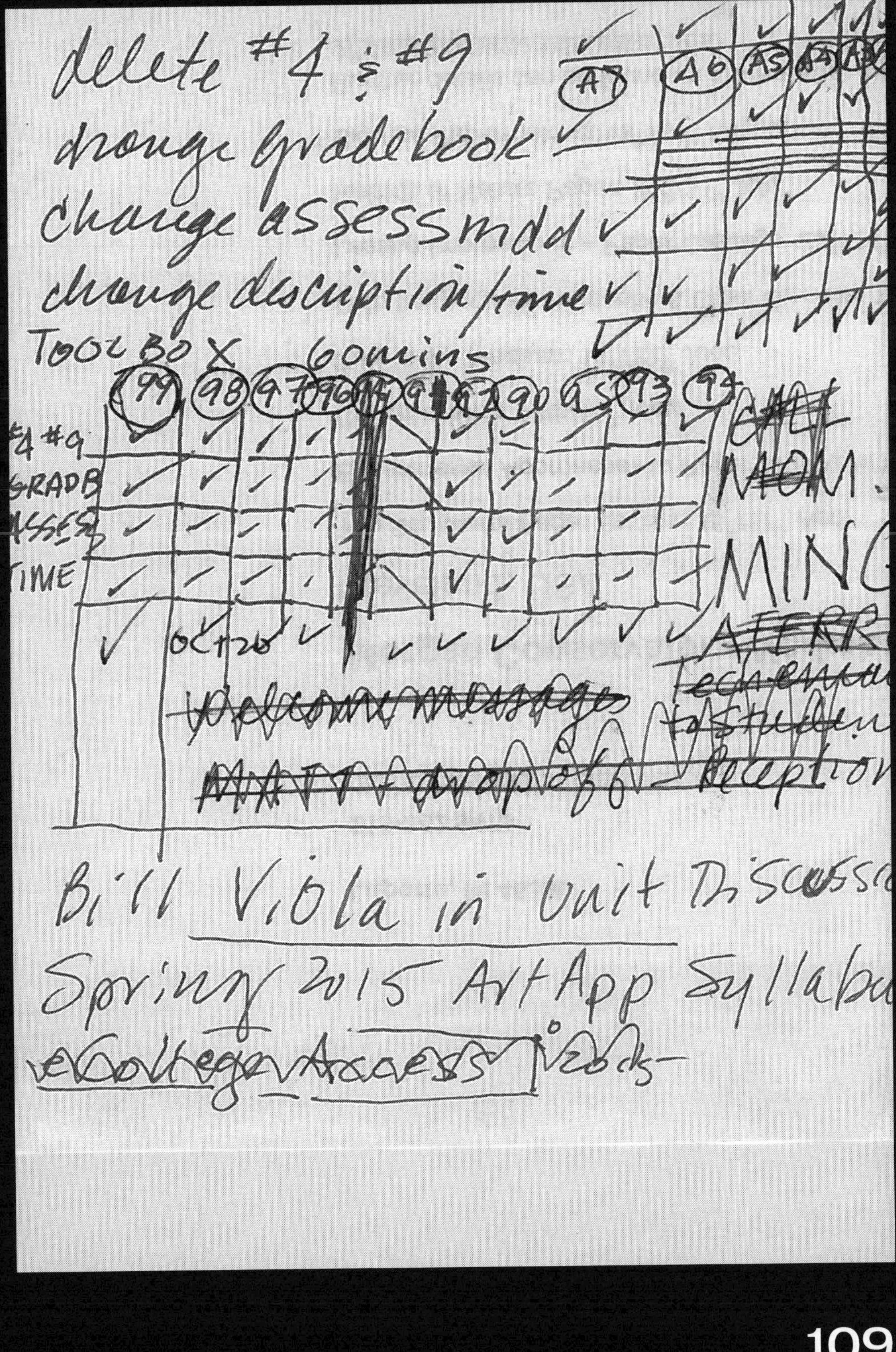
delete #4 & #9
change gradebook
change assessmt
change description/time
TOOLBOX
60mins
#4 #9
GRADB
ASSES
TIME
OCT 20
MOM
MIN
Bill Viola in Unit Discuss
Spring 2015 Art App Syllabu

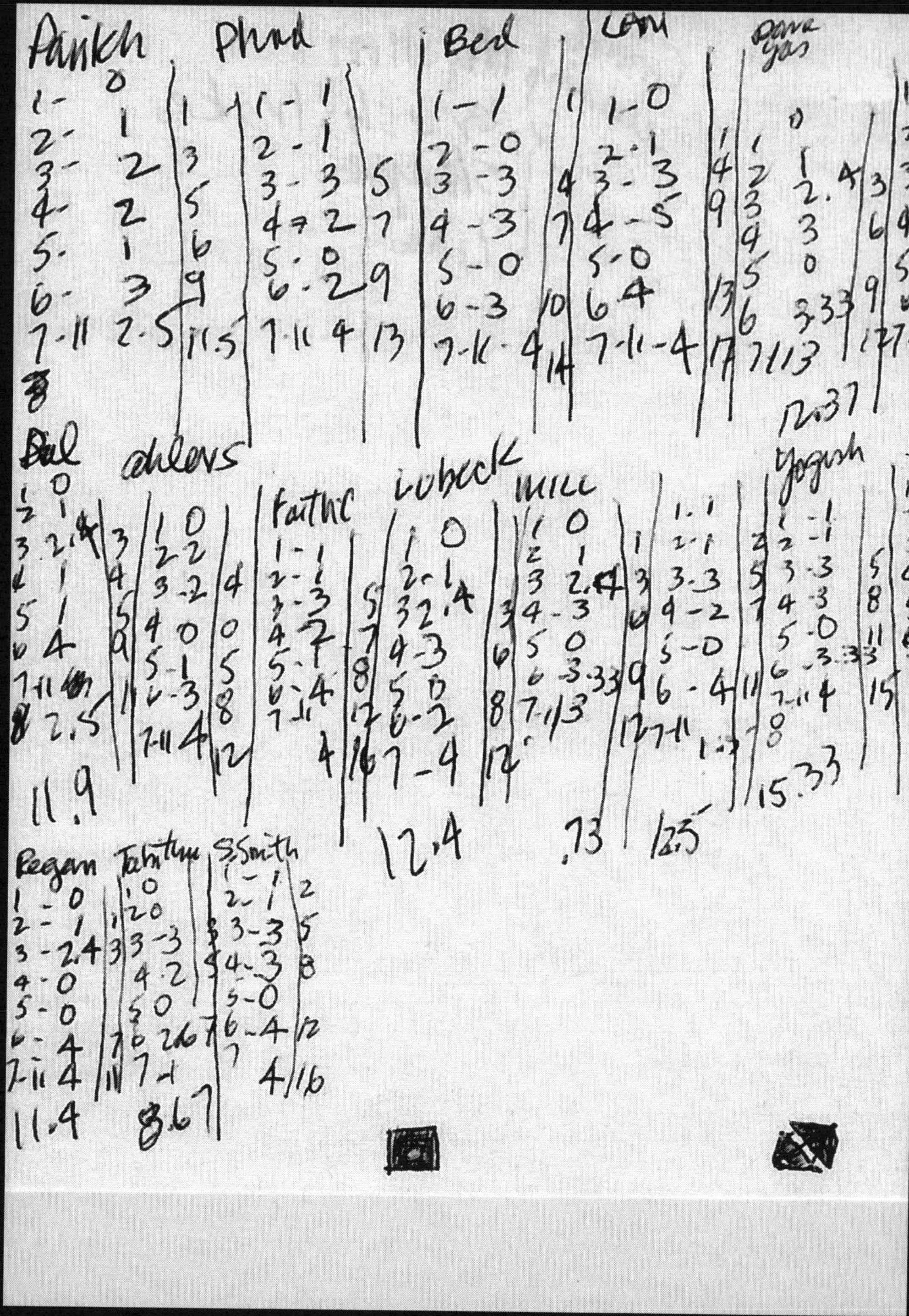
Regan
S.Smith

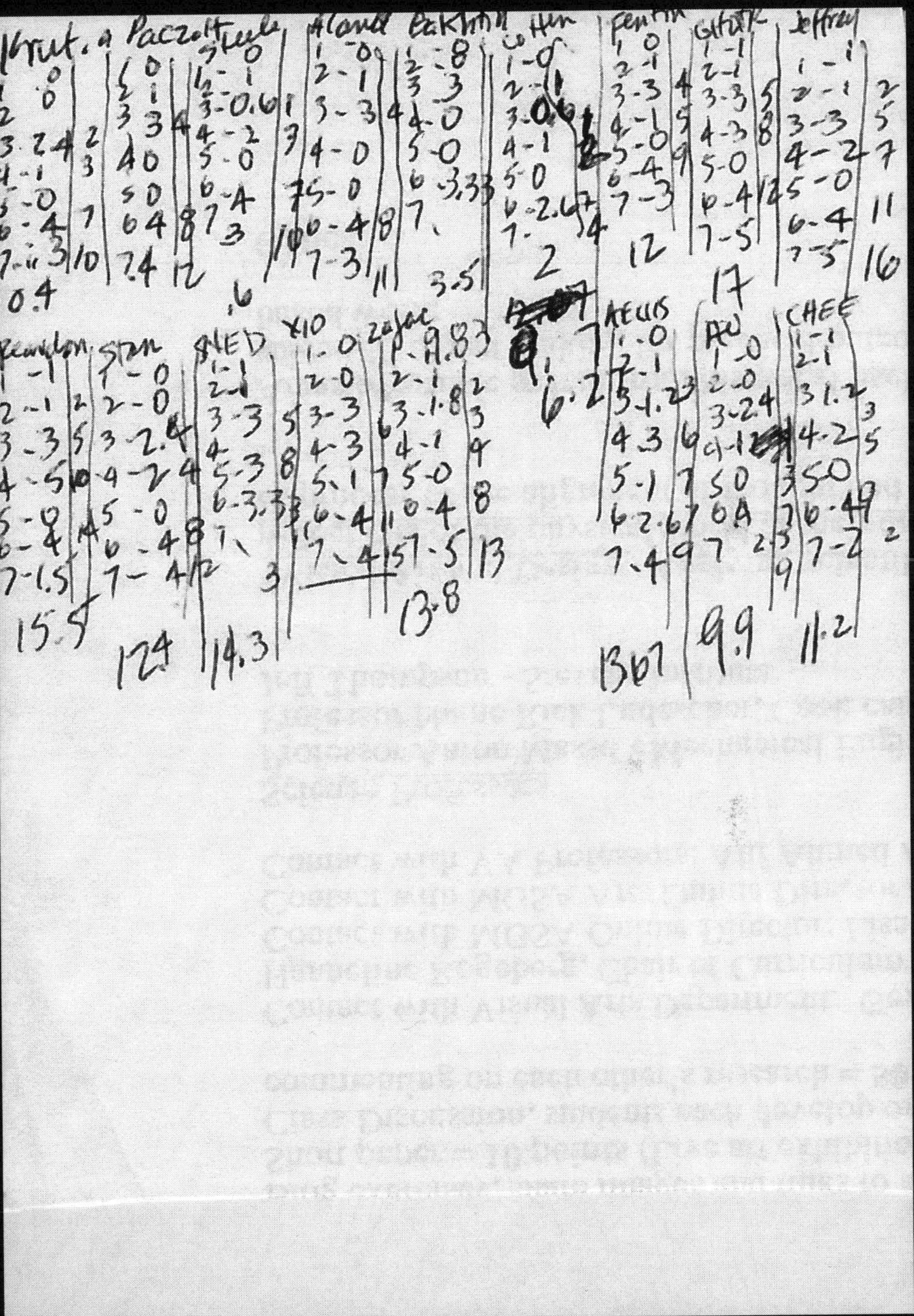

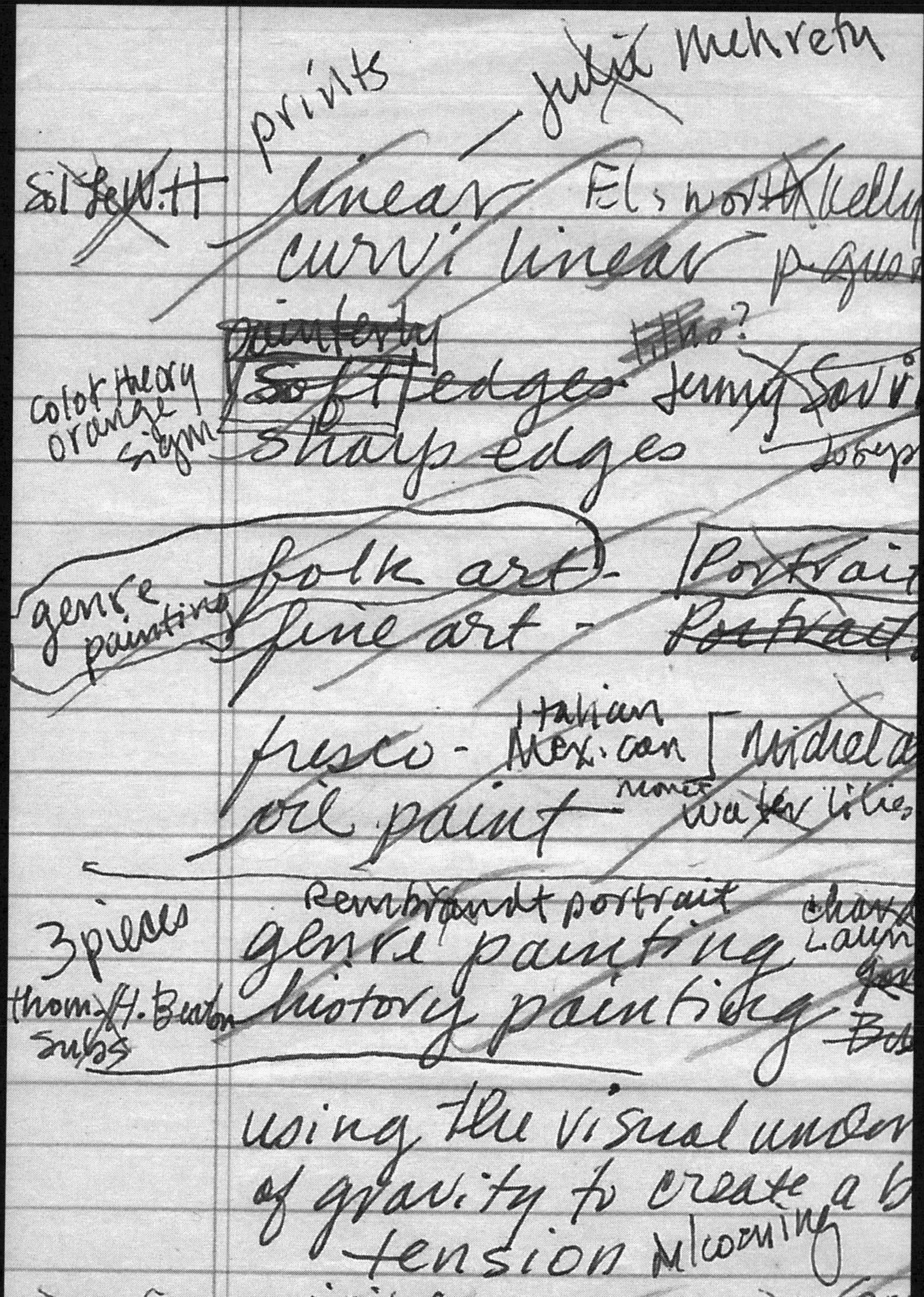

prints — ~~Julia~~ Mehretu

Sol LeWitt — linear — Elsworth Kelly

curvi linear

~~painterly~~ litho?

color theory orange sign — ~~Soft~~ edges — Jenny Savi

sharp edges — Josep

genre painting — folk art — Portrait

fine art — ~~Portrait~~

Italian Mexican

fresco — Michela

Monet

oil paint — water lilies

Rembrandt portrait

3 pieces — genre painting — char Laun

thom H. Benton subs — history painting — Bo

using the visual under

of gravity to create a b

tension incoming

more visible

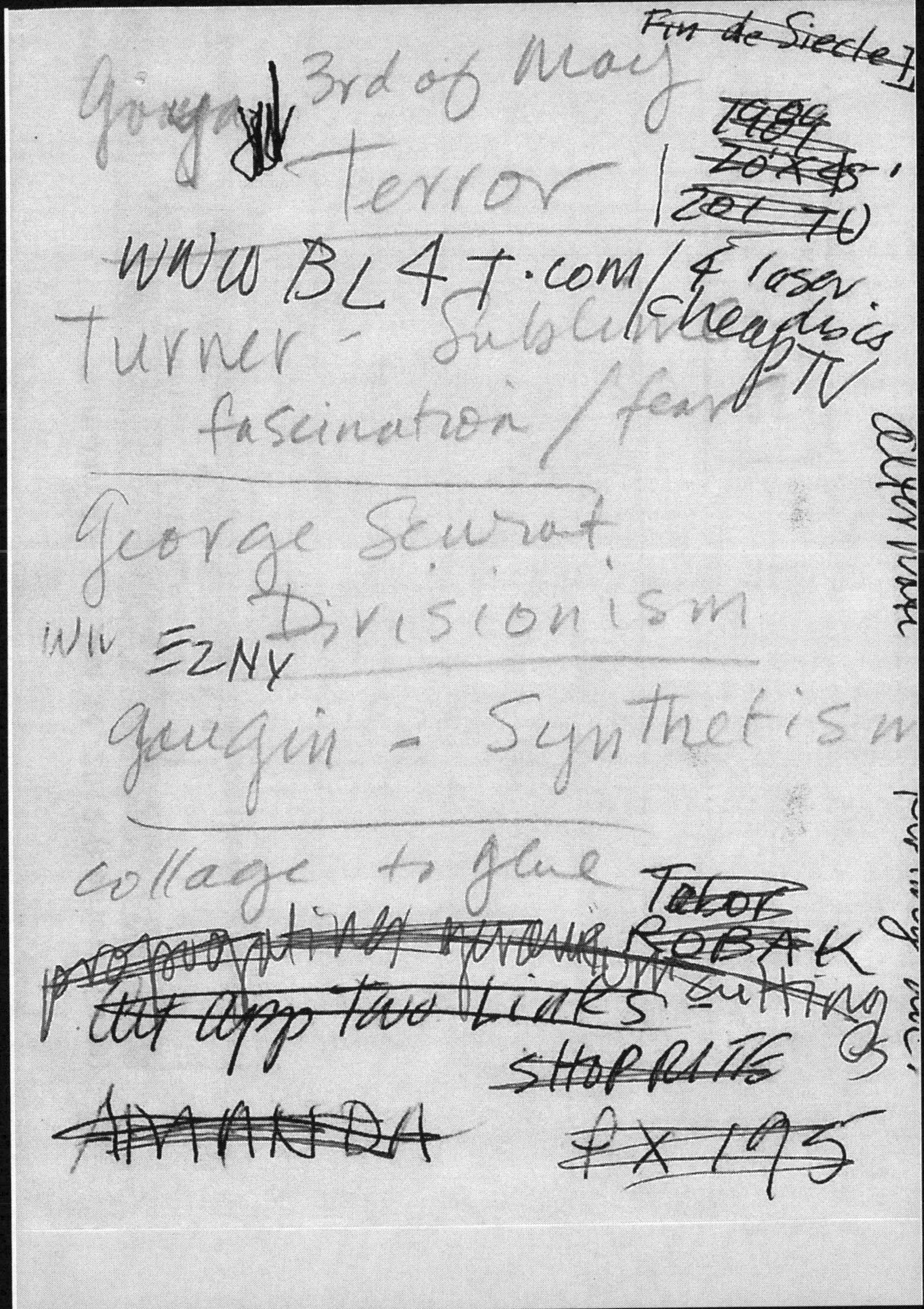
Goya 3rd of May
Terror
WWW BL4T.com/
Turner - Sublime
fascination / fear
George Seurat
Divisionism
Gaugin - Synthetism
collage to glue

tracy snelling

works in sculpture, photography, video and installation, She give her impression of a place its people and locale. Her work derives from socioology, voyeurism, and geographical and architectural location.

ONE

Arrive to Berlin, February 10.

My good friend and collector Marcus is a film distributor and he generously gets me into events and soirees. A film hero of mine is charming me over dinner.

I wonder where I am and if it's all real or some kind of fantasy my mind thought up to distract me from the move.

Berlin is cold.

TWO

I need to get to work,to make a sculpture for a meeting in Frankfurt about my commission.

Train to the hardware store for wood and supplies.
English is rare in these stores.
Scowls and frowns.
People don't seem happy the further out you go.

But maybe the smiles in California are at times masks for something darker.

After I return from my German hardware store experience, I get a durum doner near the corner S-bahn. The young Turkish man smiles as he hands me my food, tries to ask where I'm from.

THREE

Meeting in Frankfurt for a commission;
Myself and some other artists, exhibition architects, museum people.
Third meeting. Some have become friends. Nice times. Drinks, conversation.
And then it's over, you're back in Berlin.

FOUR

Meeting a friend of a friend. Museum opening, lots of people. Not quite connecting, but up for the challenge.

Look at the show.

Comment.

Listen.

Respond.

Someone is blowing bubbles in the project space of the man's friend.

He melts down. Anger. Grabs the guy, pulls him out, threatens to throw him down the stairs. I am horrified. Fascinated.

I stand far enough back so that people do not know that I am with him.

I cover my mouth with my scarf as I laugh (nervously or incredulously?) at the insanity of the situation. He does not throw him down the stairs.We leave and he says he might have overreacted.

He's not proud.

What a strange night of art viewing.
Is this Berlin?

FIVE

I'm in a small town called Kortrijk in Belgium to install one of my Clusterfuck installations - - the biggest one yet. The local audio/video technicians scratch their heads and frown as I tell them I need someone to install the four projectors, media players, and speakers. They didn't know, they said.

My large sculpture that I built in China isn't working. We test it with another transformer the other assistants have (which ends up being broken, in hindsight), and I rewire the whole sculpture, testing as I go. It finally works and then I do a few more things and nothing works.

Fuck.

Turn it on its side and start testing once again. I wired one thing backwards. Fix it and it all works.

Move it into the installation, plug it in, go to screw in a light bulb to the fixture I bought in China, and poof. The bulb pops and smokes.

Shit.

Turn it off, replace the cheap Chinese fixtures. Finally, it all works. The technicians are nice, just understaffed and overwhelmed.

The last installer finishes my last projector the next day, a few hours before the opening. I photograph everything, change in the bathroom at the art space, like so often is the case.

Nice opening, drive back to Brussels, big, late dinner with Jerome and a welcome sleep at the nearby hotel.

I fly back, a week or so before the bombs go off at the airport and train station.

SIX

Fly to Milan for the opening of "2050: A Brief History of the Future," based on economist Jacques Attali's book.

The next day I turn the TV on in the morning after my run. I see a bomb in an airport but everything is in Italian. Where is it? I soon find out it's in Brussels. So sad that this has happened there. Assholes killing people in the name of religion? Change? It never works.

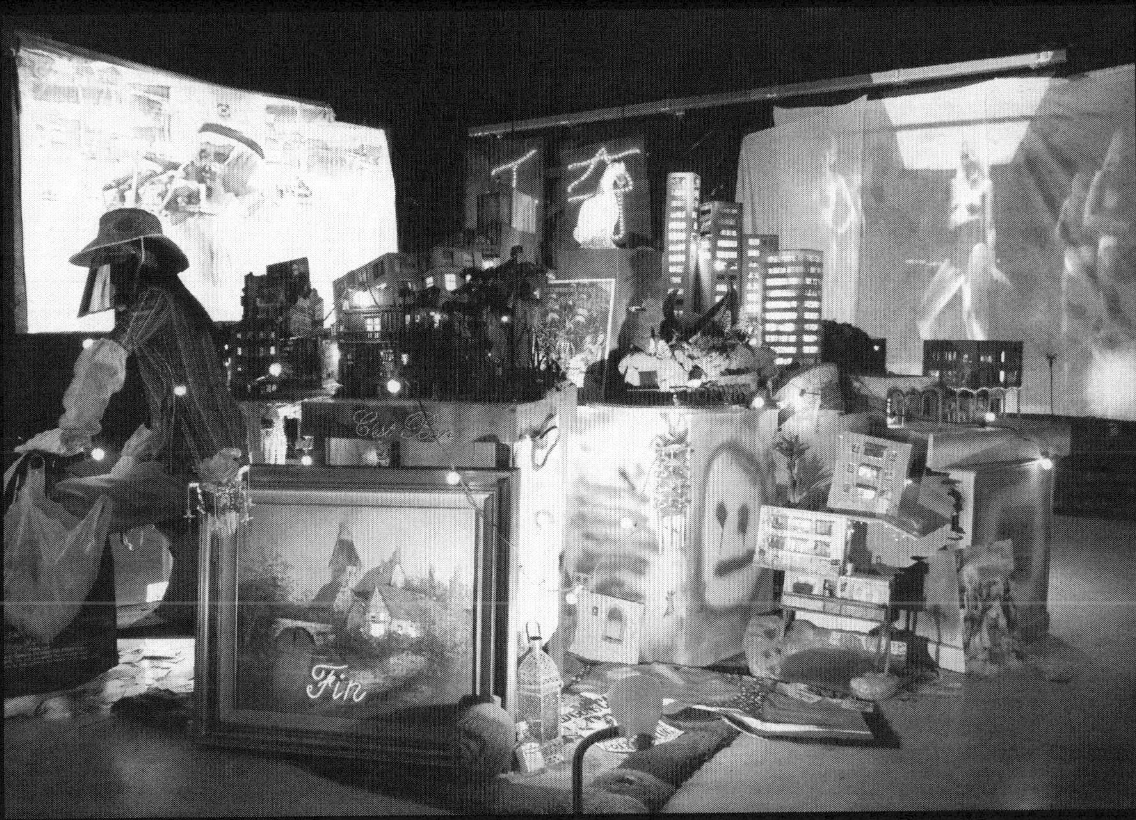

I go down to the Palazzo Reale to check my sculpture and make a few fixes. There is a press conference. I cannot tell what they are saying, but apparently Attali speaks of what happened in Brussels and of the importance of artists–not taking a positive or negative stance, but rather the act of artists observing and reporting what they see. One of the curators doesn't fly in from Brussels because he is in shock from the bombing.

Later, the opening is happening. Our exhibition is quite amazing--artists I have admired for many years, installed next to my work. Louise Bourgeois, Francis Alys, Philip-Lorca diCorcia, Edward Ruscha, and it goes on. I meet John Isaacs, another artist in the show that also shows with my gallery in Brussels. He's like a movie star¬–handsome and charismatic. And very nice. As no dinner is arranged by the museum, he invites me along with his art writer friend and wife, and another collector couple. We eat, talk, laugh, and drink. They recommend the Milanese risotto, which is twice cooked and flat like a pancake, instead of creamy and rich. He says it's the food of peasants, but I imagine if you eat it enough you develop a taste for it... The cocoon of the art world sometimes makes for quick, close ties, and fast friendships.

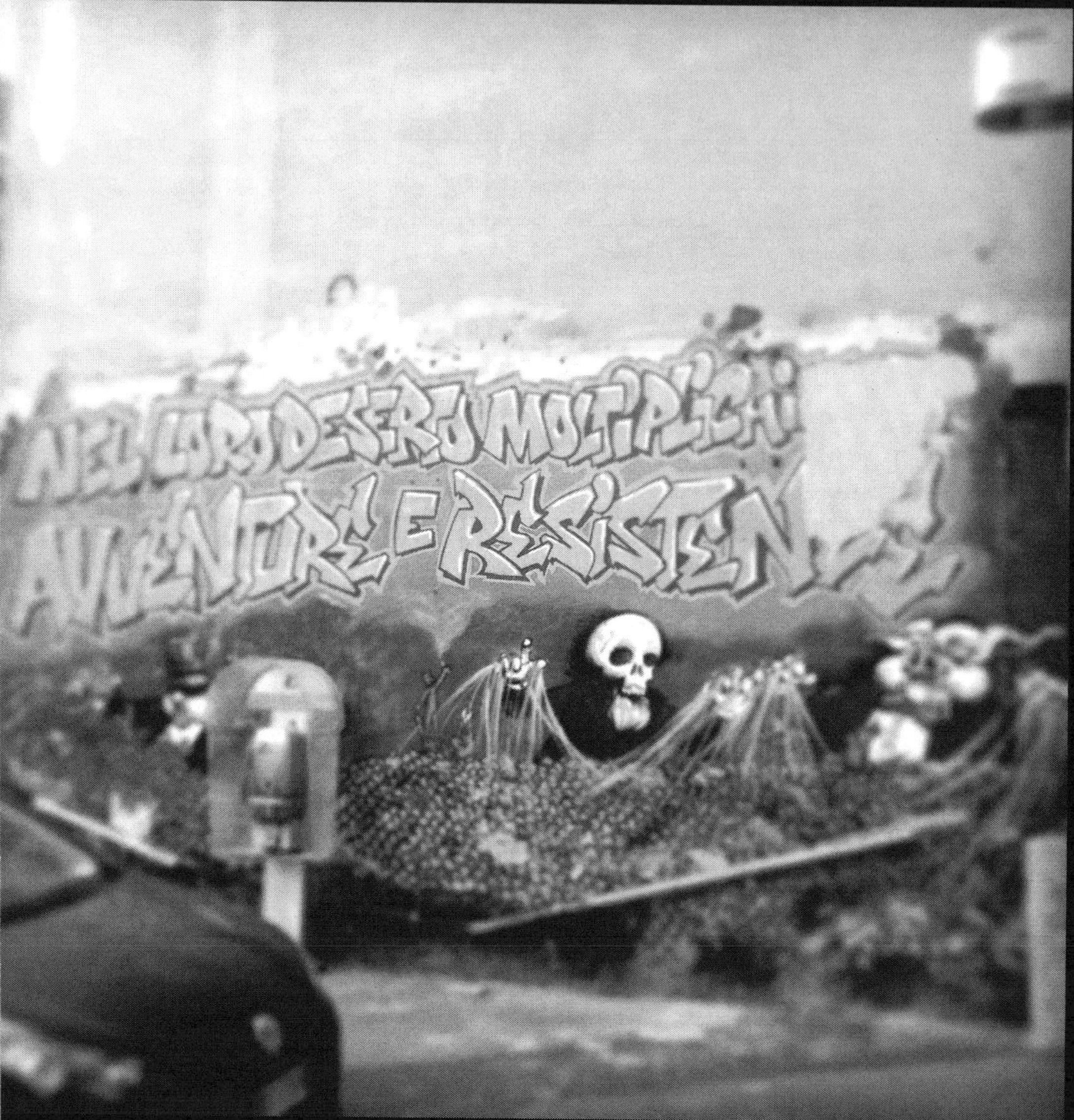
NEL LORO DESERTO MOLTIPLICHI
AVVENTURE E RESISTEN

The next day, the flight is in the evening and John and I share a taxi to the airport and talk about Abu Dhabi, Berlin, art, inspiration, Stanley Kubrick, making a living as an artist and his family while we wait for our delayed flight. The pilot doesn't tell us the reason for the flight delay until we are up in the air. He said a woman on the incoming flight had a panic attack because she saw an Arab on the flight and thought he was a terrorist.

SEVEN

Working in Berlin. I've been here for a month and a half. It's starting to feel more natural and like home, but I miss having my close neighbors who are also close friends. Here in Wedding, in the huge building with studios and businesses, few people live here and you barely see them, which leads me out of the studio for interaction, thereby making me more distracted and work less...

So today, I went out for an early lunch, came back, and somewhat worked. And I distracted myself with the computer. Then worked more. It's like walking in molasses. Watching paint dry. So slow.

While starting to work again, I have an idea. For weeks I've been thinking I need to find a company to cut out all these windows for my plywood building facades. And right there, the idea comes. It's brilliant. I can get it all done so quickly, without spending a ton of money or hiring a company or assistants, at least for that aspect. I start to work, using a t-shirt as a mask/bandanna, and my sunglasses as protective eye gear. I don't want to wait until tomorrow to start. So I figure out how to do it tonight.

I wonder if the procrastination, computer distraction, wandering aimlessly in the grocery store, is all necessary for this to come. I've just figured how to save weeks of time, so a day of fucking around seems like nothing. Maybe it was the visit to a small bondage/rope tying bar the night before, purely for sociological and artistic research, mind you... Whatever the reason, something clicked and a brilliant idea came.

I think I should embrace the fucking around more.

It's all about balance.

The solution is wonderful and the project is good–a 4 or 5m high x 3m wide wall of dense low-income apartment buildings, like one would find in China, for instance, but filled with people from all over the world, about overpopulation and the human condition on a grand scale. A similar piece to my One Thousand Shacks installation, which is a large wall of small scale shacks referencing extreme global poverty.
But in the wake of the Brussels and Pakistan terrorist attacks, not to mention the mass destruction of Syria, should I focus on that? So much is happening that can't be ignored. I question everything once again, and decide to just procrastinate, writing these words instead.

alana austin

is a sculptor and knicknack creator from New York. Her artistic drives are centered around process and construction rather than a “finished” product.

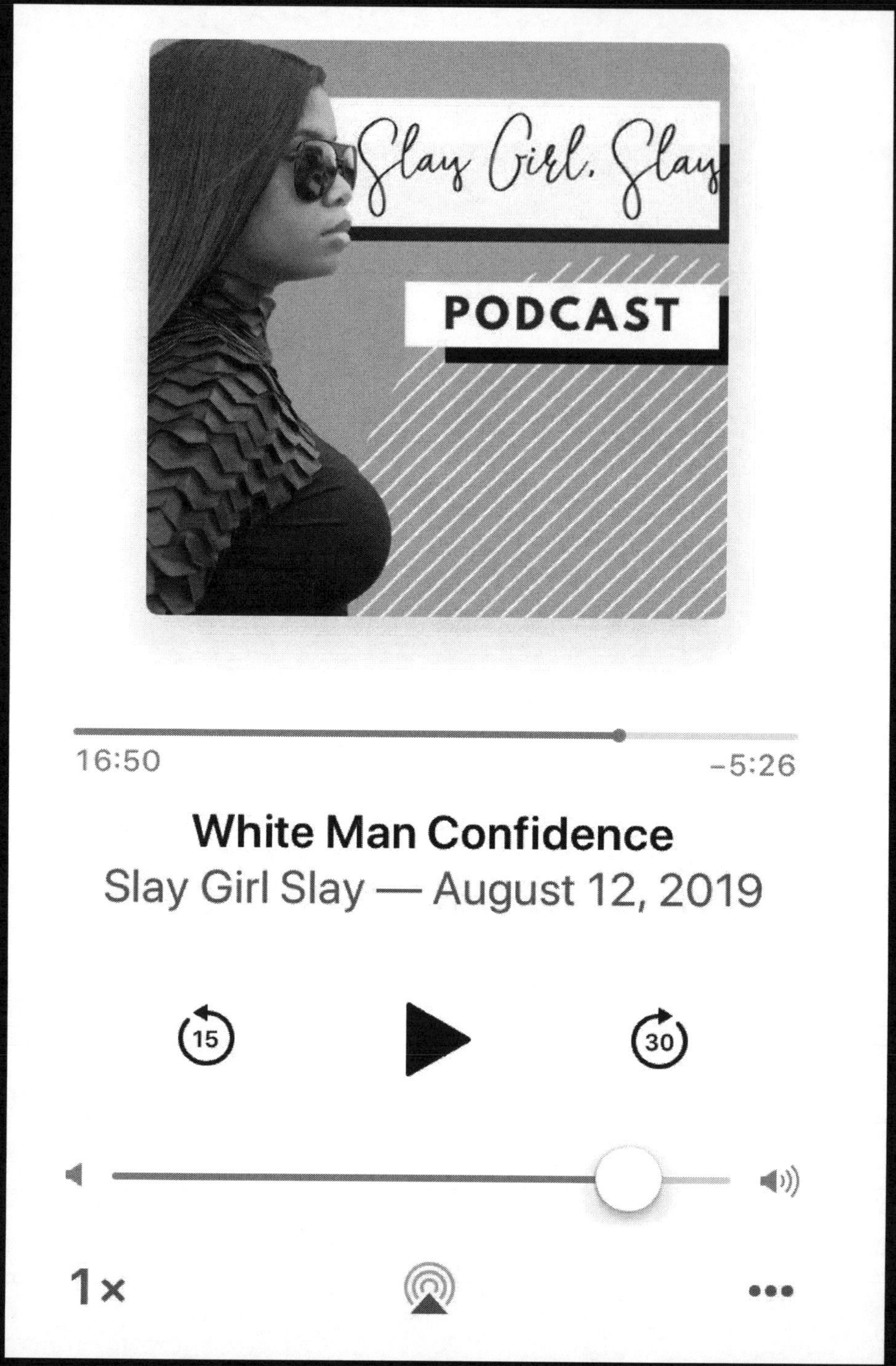
Slay Girl, Slay
PODCAST
16:50
−5:26
White Man Confidence
Slay Girl Slay — August 12, 2019
15
30
1×

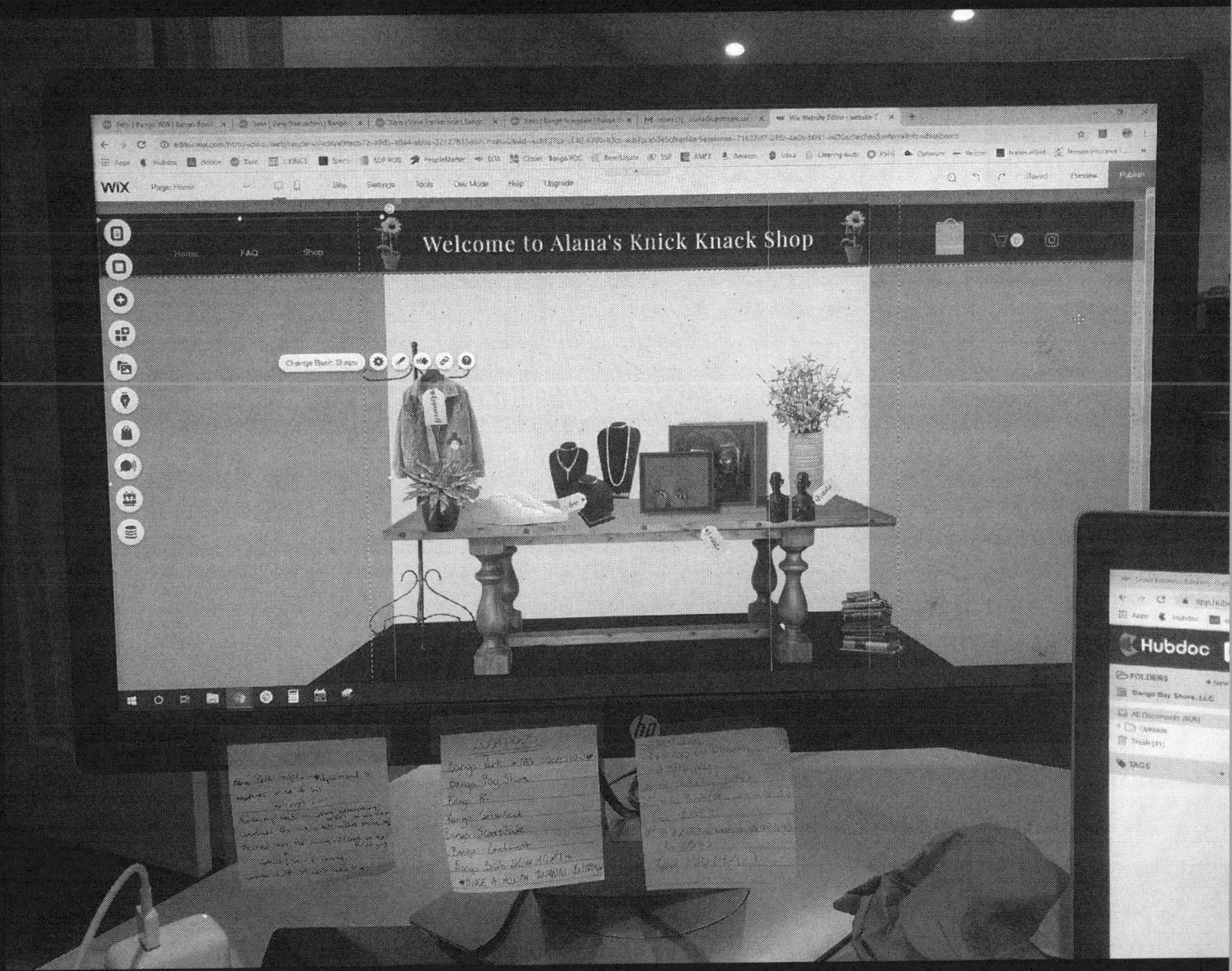
WIX
Welcome to Alana's Knick Knack Shop
Hubdoc

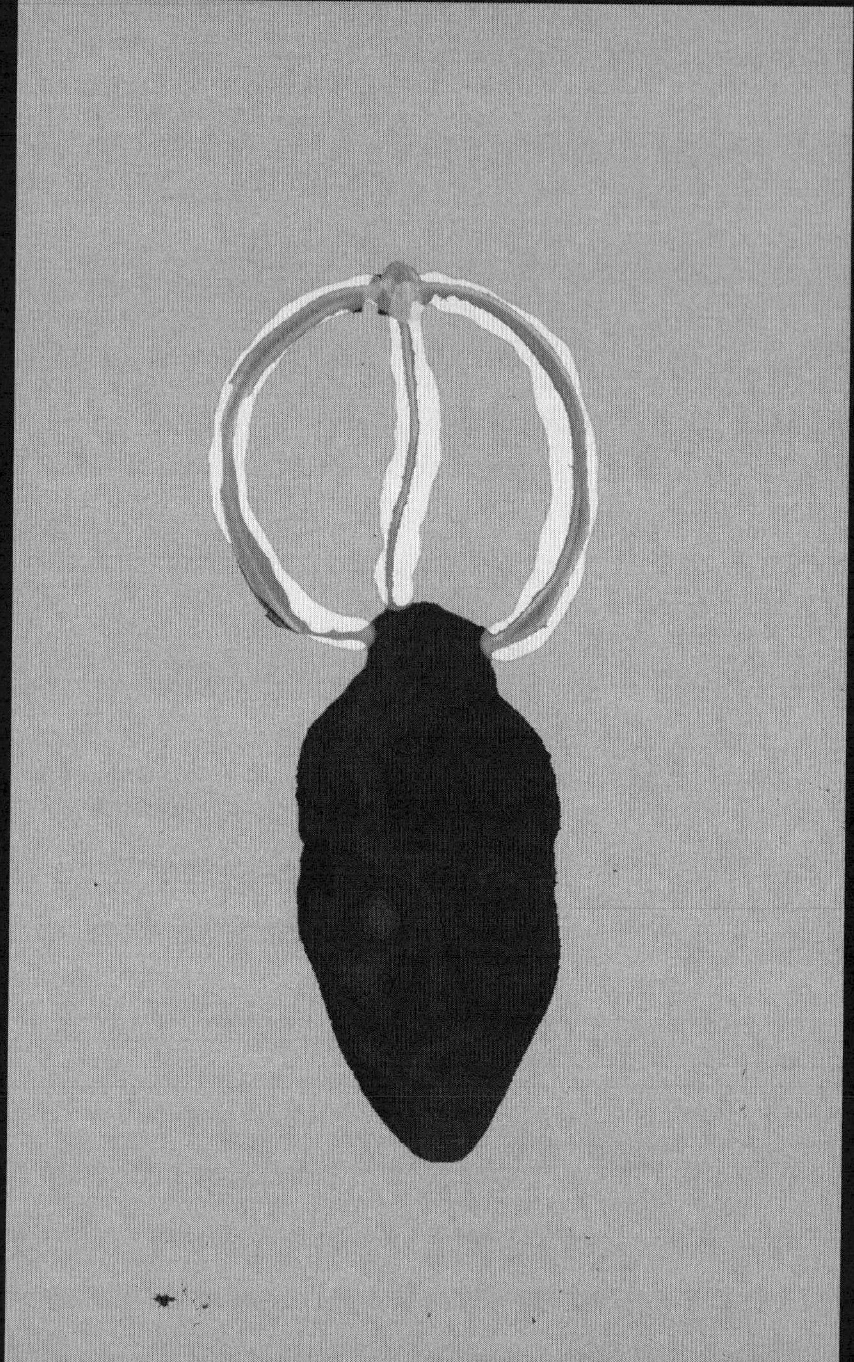

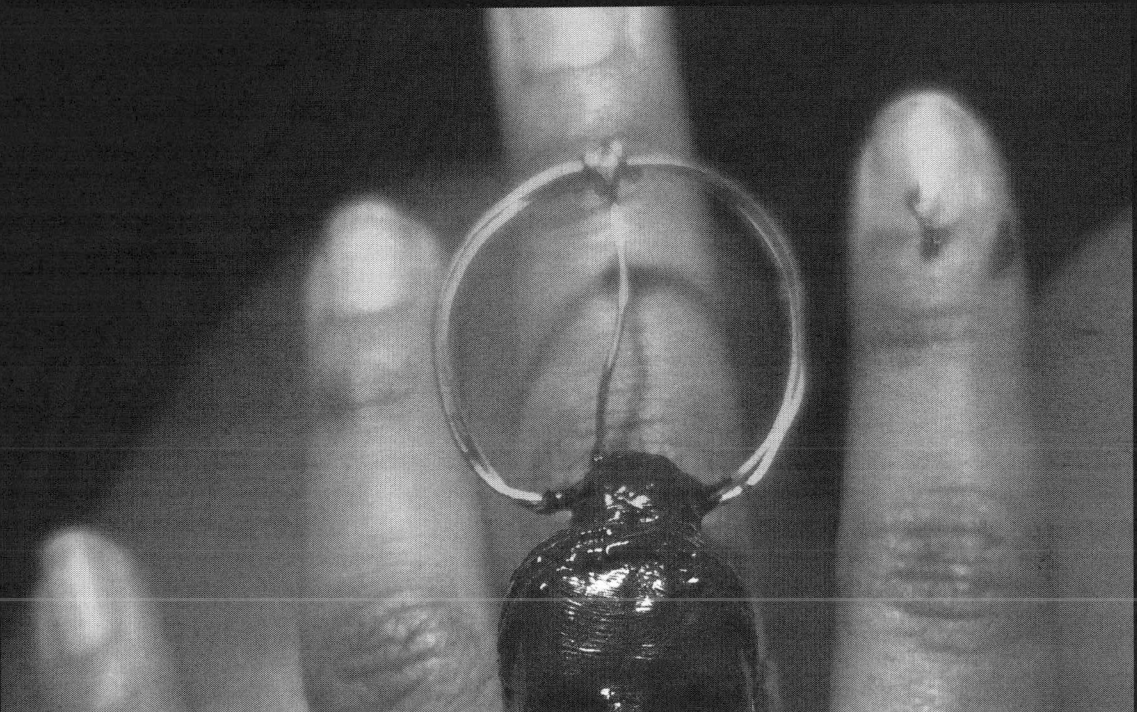

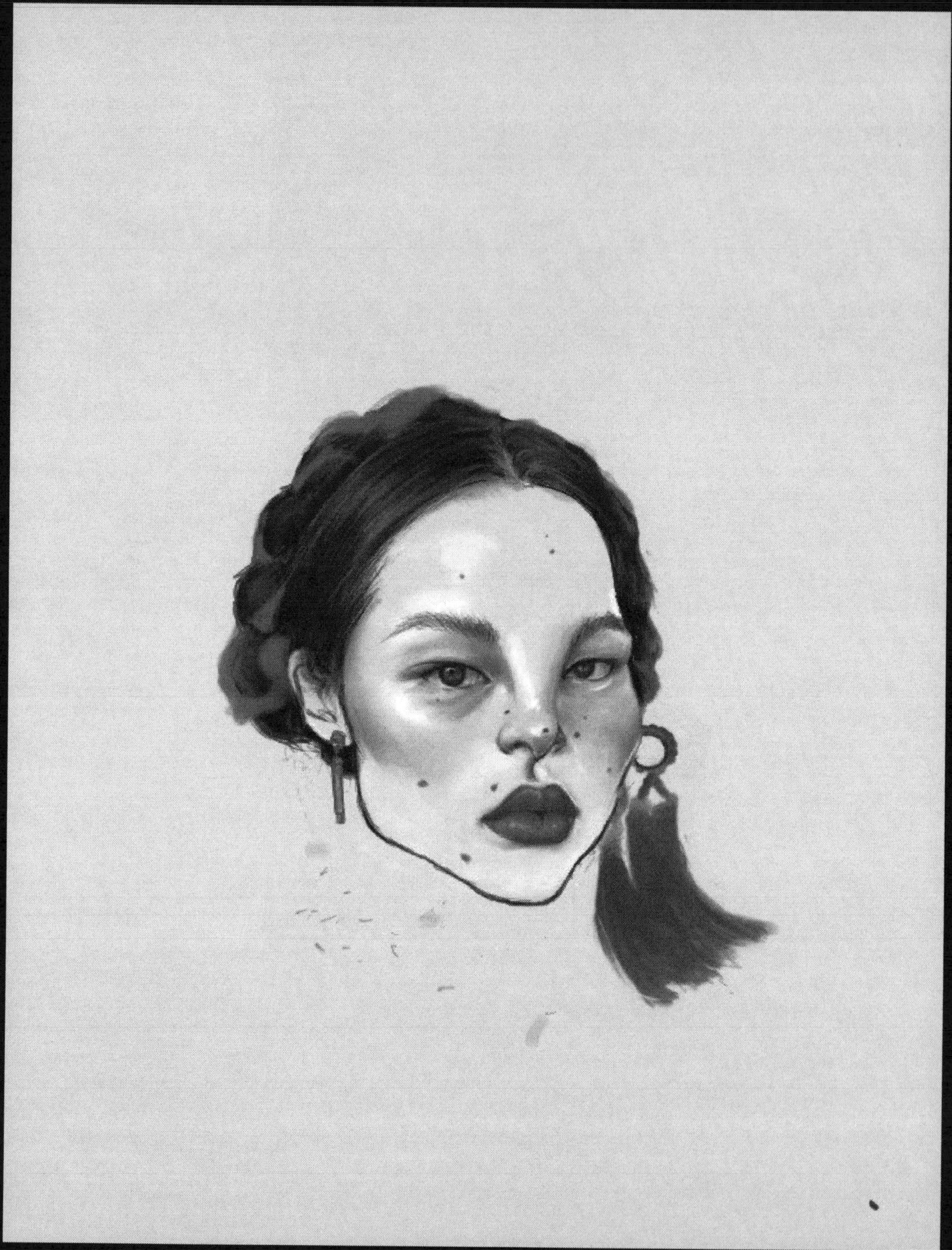

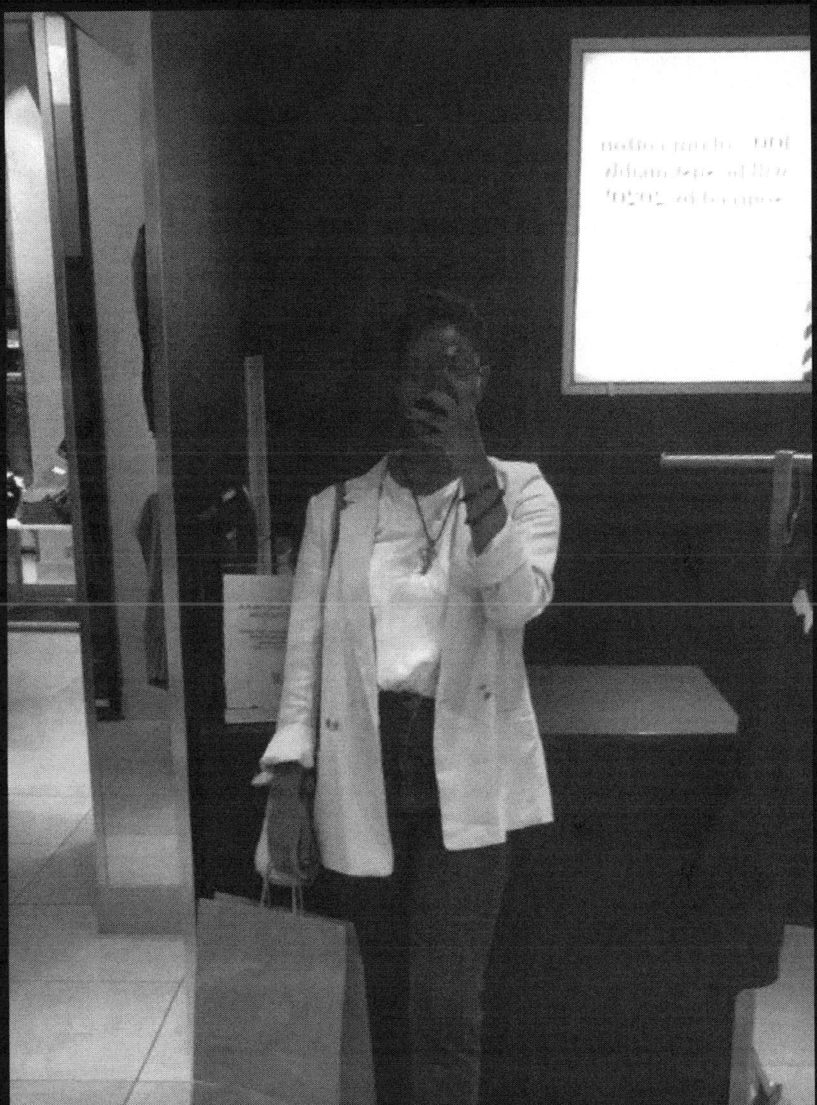

cristin mcknight sethi

is a historian and curator with a specialization in textiles and folk art. Her research and teaching interests include textiles and folk art, the intersection of gender and practices of making, networks of circulation and exchange, the anthropology of art, and postcolonial theory. She has published on contemporary craft in India, the history of natural dyes in Asia, and the production and circulation of folk embroidery during the late nineteenth century.

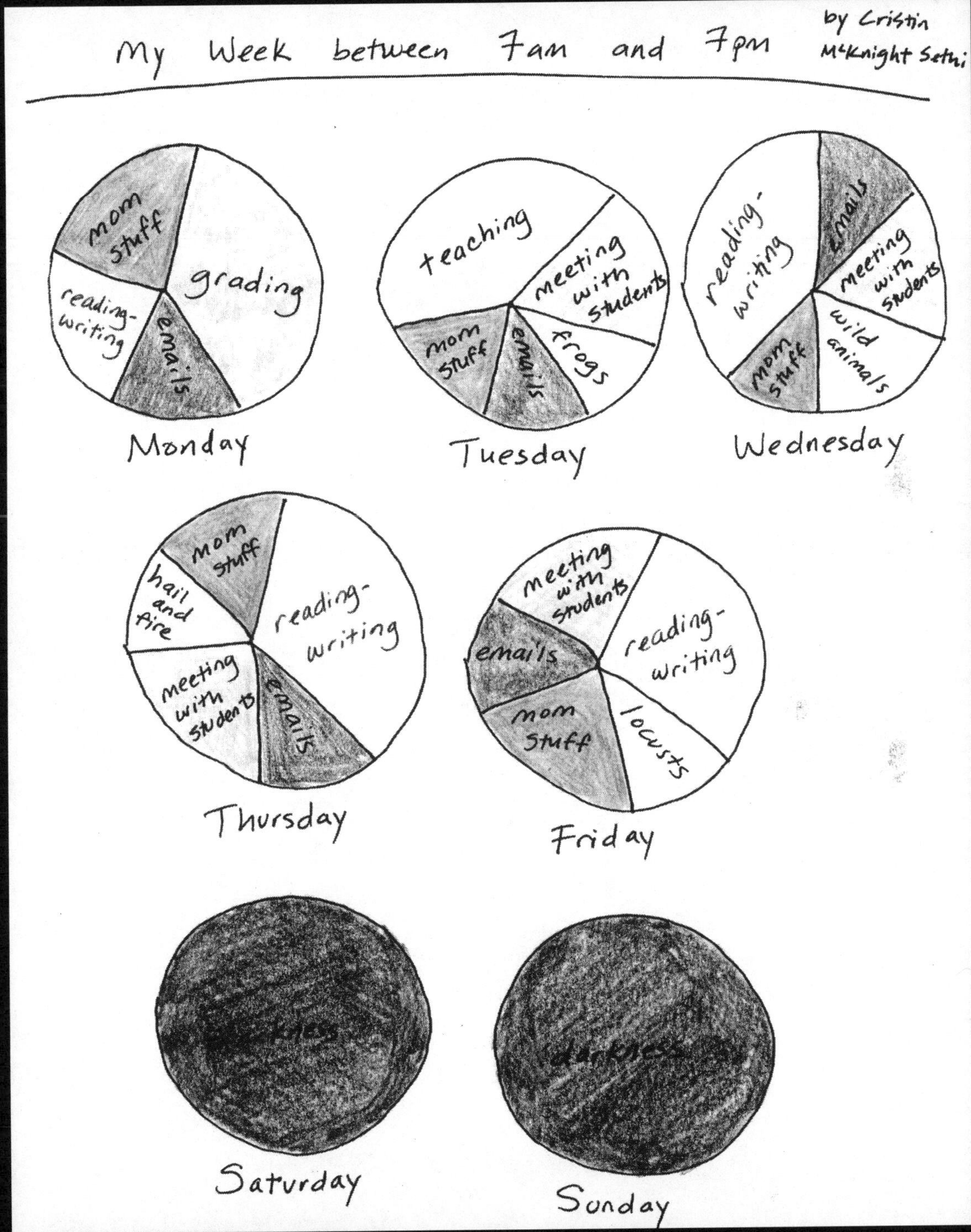
My Week between 7am and 7pm
by Cristin McKnight Sethi
mom stuff
grading
reading-writing
emails
Monday
teaching
meeting with students
mom stuff
emails
frogs
Tuesday
reading-writing
emails
meeting with students
wild animals
mom stuff
Wednesday
mom stuff
hail and fire
reading-writing
meeting with students
emails
Thursday
meeting with students
emails
reading-writing
mom stuff
locusts
Friday
Saturday
darkness
Sunday

orlan

is a world renowned French artist. She creates sculptures, photographs, performances, videos, and videogames to augment reality, using scientific and medical techniques like surgery and biogenetics. ORLAN makes her own body the medium, the raw material, and the visual support of her work. She has won the E-reputation Award, designating the most observed and followed artist on the Web.

DAY 1

Jubilanty
As a un cyclop
I swallow
Electric cables
The trip between the earth and sky
My eye, uneasily
Creature

Among the creatures
Probabilty calculation
My skull as
A suspended lid
I paint a pear
Uninhabitable orbit
No pussy
stretching

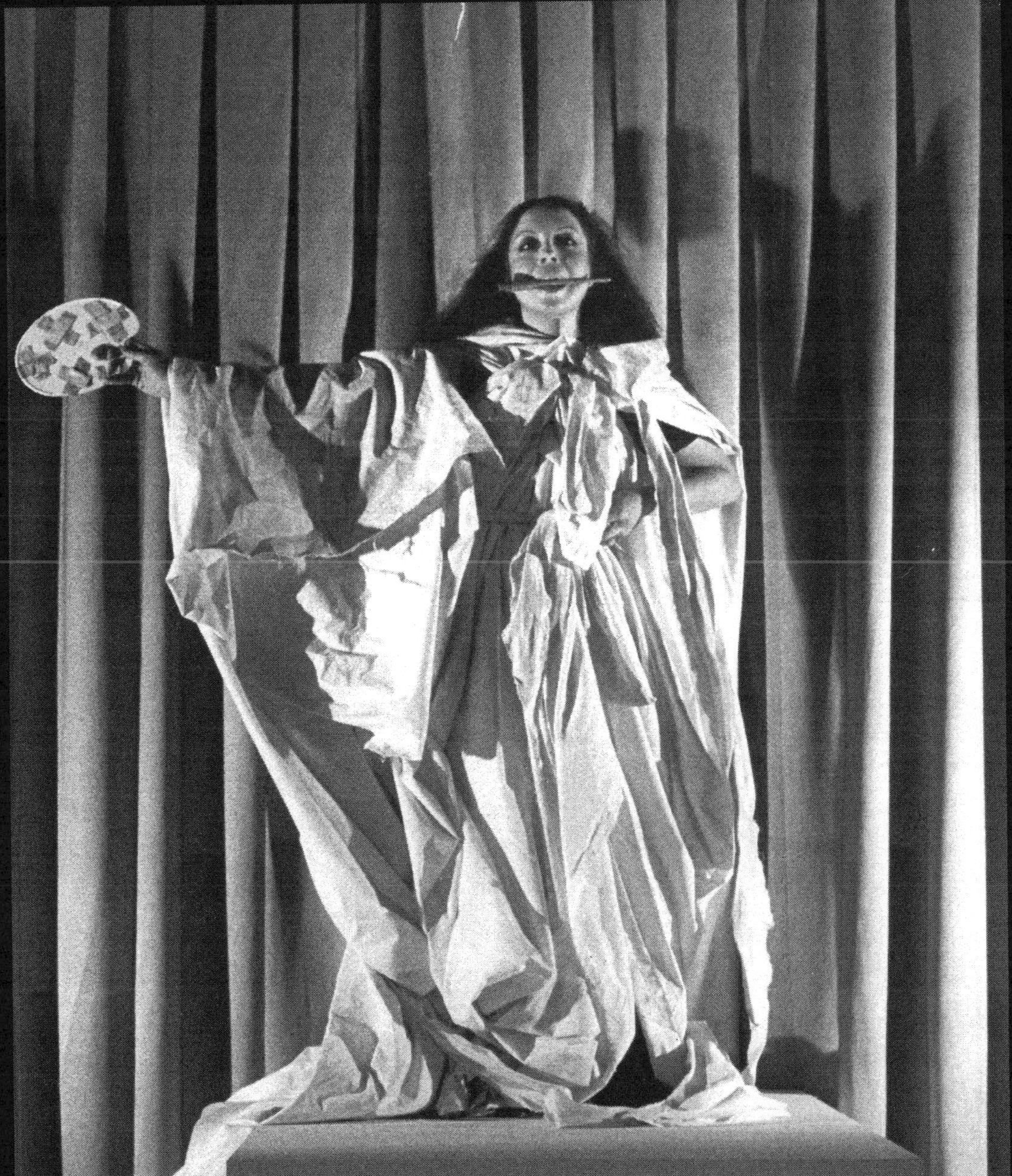

DAY 2

About
Here we are
Accustomed
Approximately is cheerful
Propensity lazy
Looking falls

The snow
Necessary link
Break judgment

At rebous (doesn't exist in english) I rub on a tree a trunk
Languid

Sick if me
Orphan disease
About

Experience the doubt
State Loan eve

Again

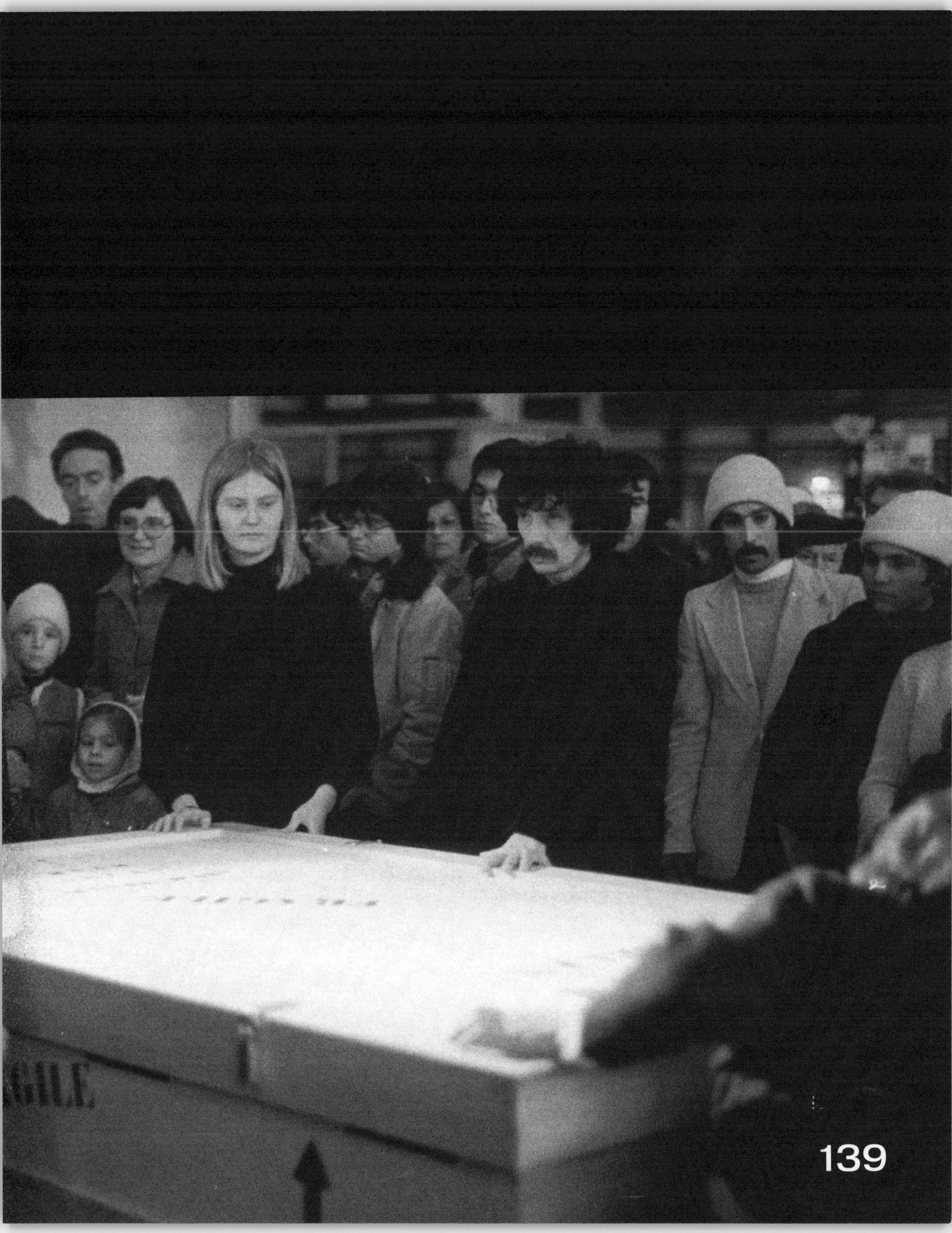

DAY 3

Assembly
Construction
But now
Number of words
Gusts reduction
Bring thinking
Reflection
Disturbance

Anatomic

Mirage

Of your sexual body
The difference
borderless
surroundings
Halos sperm

Friction

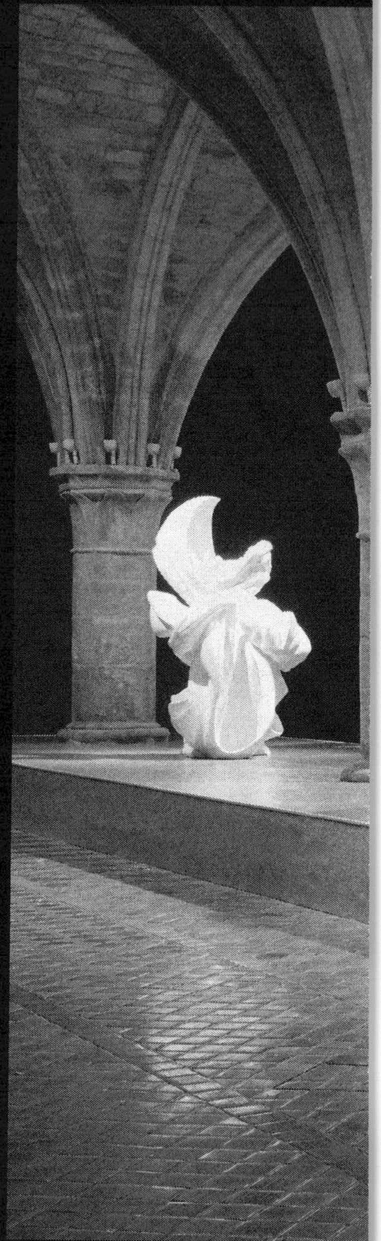

DAY 4

The limit
« Weighs nerves »
superimposed holes
time to time
climb to the top
a membrane
sickens me
the organs are there
will delight countless…
lexicon
sensation
efforts of imagination
obstruction

state of

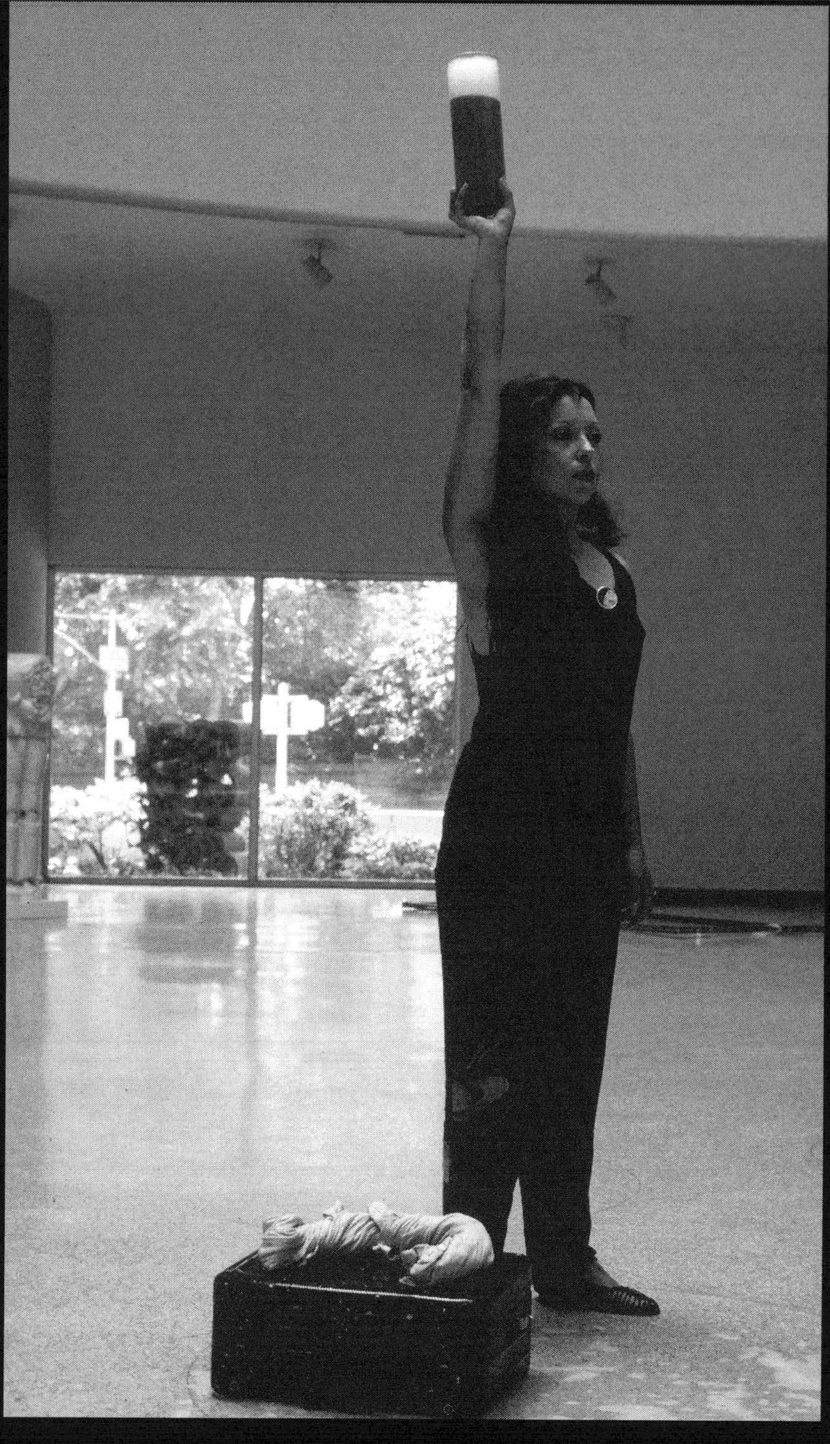

DAY 5

Day with fruits
The sea to watched
Obligation
The « He »
Have a rock and palm trees phallus

unavoidable
Watchable, remarkable

Water hot prowl
With coconut balls
Are laughing
Monkeys jumps
Cliché side by side...

Fins are without engine
Beautiful fan
Without power

holidays

vacant emptiness without takeoff

the falls

are (not) at the end of the world
old sweat dreams...
whatever we do, we say

it sticks
with or without noise

there is « chut »...

DAY 6

Cold warm
Is not like
Warm cold
Choice of vocabulary
Word order
From the particular
To the general
All
The plan
The plan set
Not bad is not

Diet

Is not warm
Always

Confident

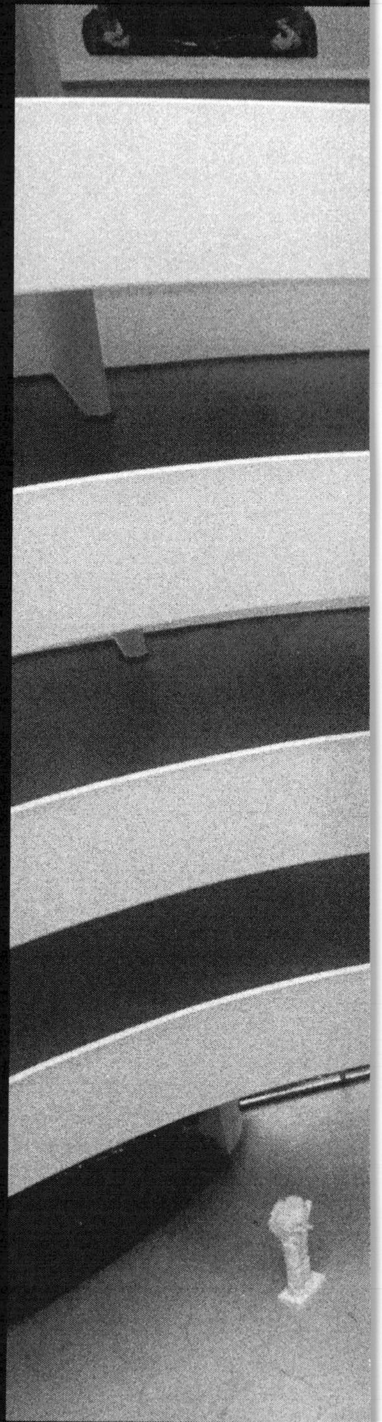

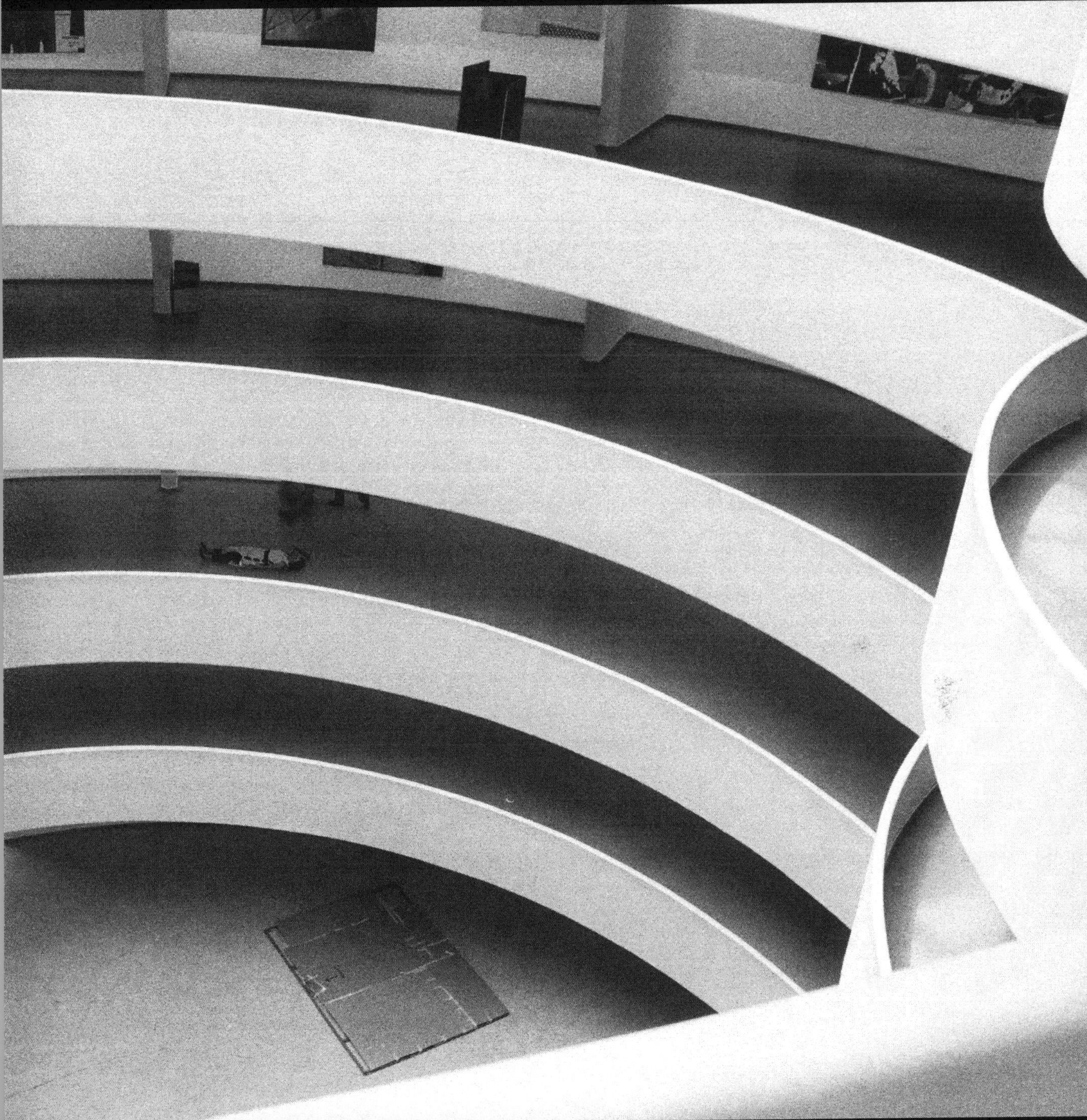

DAY 7

Breakdown
Reconstitution
No oppression
Contractures
Departures of
Internal enemies
I spread
It rustles
Furtively
Camera of my
Mouvements
Full Battery
Odorous
Seminar worlds
In epilepsy
Furiously
Echos
Of my torn voice
Serious forgetful
Schizophrenic duo
Cling on my shoulders
Incriminate to the time
SS service

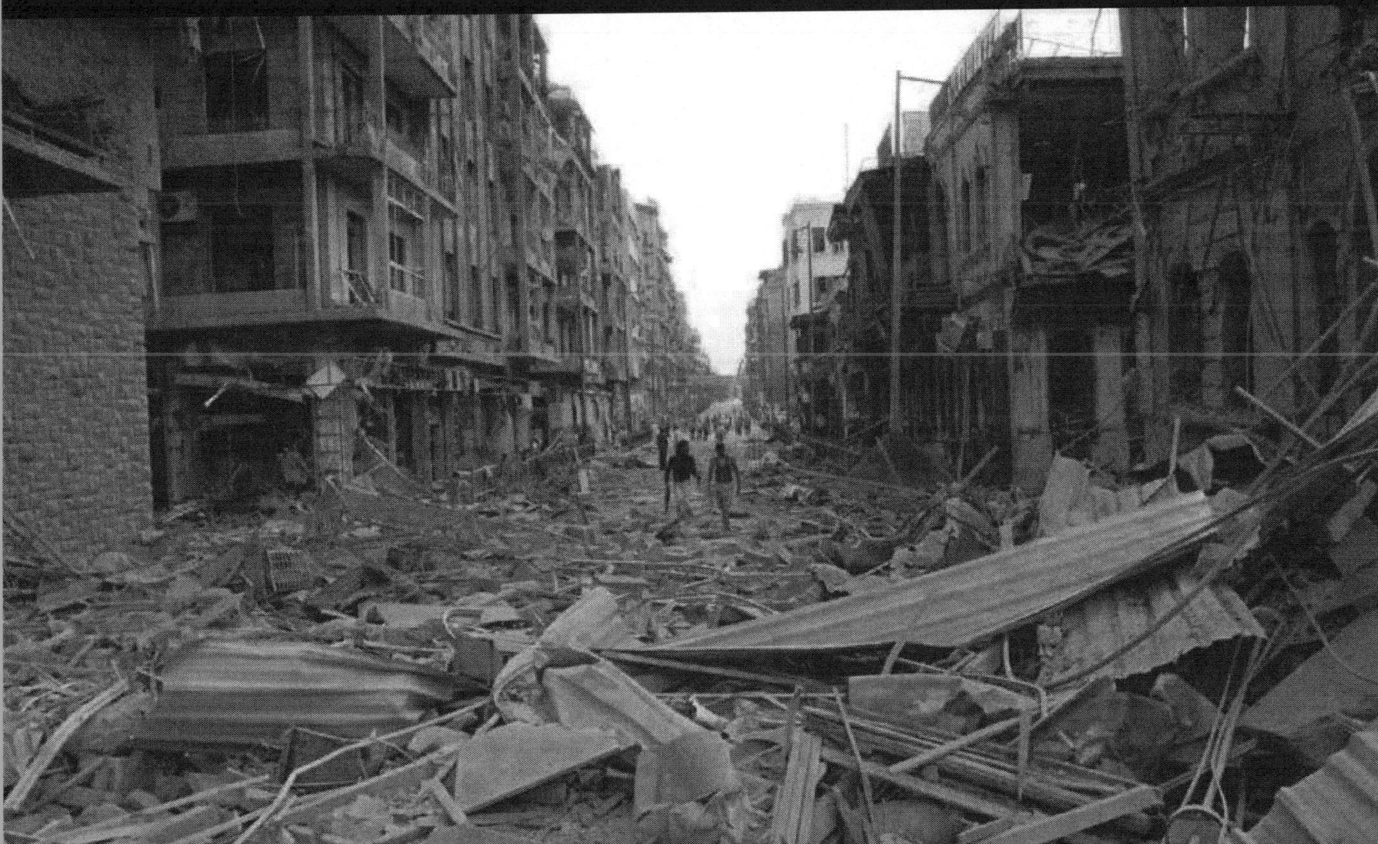

john murchie

was the former Associate Curator at the Art Gallery of Nova Scotia. He has worked as a baker, cook, curator, farmer, writer and researcher.

A WEEK IN & OUT OF THE STUDIO: MONDAY TO SUNDAY FEBRUARY 15 – 21, 2016

As a person of habit, I try to keep a schedule: breakfast, gym, office work, studio work, lunch, studio work, make dinner, tv. These days I also spend time trying to finish the renovations on the studio - always slow work for some reason.

Started in November what may turn out to be a series of small paintings that move in a somewhat different direction although still of the same cloth as those of the past many years. So working on two of those.

Given the repetitive nature of my practice, I have before me any number of works at one time: a couple of crossword paintings including a "large" (for me) triptych; a re-enactment/re-creation of Canadian Art Stands on Its Own, a painting I made about 20 years ago but which now sadly needs rehabilitation; two paintings from the Alphabet Series; several research drawings as well as the two previously mentioned paintings. Now and again, but not this week, I also work on some long term paint projects, some of which have been on-going for many, many years such as Canadian Loonie (1 of 1,000,000).

Reading can, and does usually, come throughout the day. As an aside, I was flipping through Artforum International (February 2016) sometime during the week in question and realized how very tired I am of art as the gesture.

dee hibbert-jones

is an Academy Award nominated, Emmy® award winning filmmaker, internationally recognized artist, and Associate Professor of Art at UCSC. Her work incorporates animation, installation, public art and documentary film examining power and politics: how people manage and who gets heard. She explores diverse subjects from land use and wasted resources, to criminal justice and indigent rights: examining what is considered valuable and who is dismissed as valueless.

OSCAR PLANS: FEBRUARY 23-29

Avalon Hotel 9400 W Olympic Blvd, Beverly Hills, CA 90212
Oscar tickets should arrive at our hotel if not 8949 Dee & Nomi Arrive

TUESDAY FEBRUARY 23

8:00am Flight DELTA 2755 8:00am-9:25am. Arrive.

12:30pm Lunch with Jamie wolf (Dee & Nomi only)

6pm-7pm Rose and Lucy arrive with dress consult Dee

7:00pm Shorts program (Dee & Nomi + guest)

WEDNESDAY, FEBRUARY 24

9am shorts tv
1pm-3pm Diane von Furstenberg lunch w/ Dee & Nomi
4.00pm Meeting with Ondi
5:45pm Academy's Samuel Goldwyn Theater. Gala event:
Samuel Goldwyn Theater in Beverly. Reception is at 6:30pm
The event starts at 7:30pm with the documentary feature
and shorts nominees. The event should be roughly 2-2.5 hours.

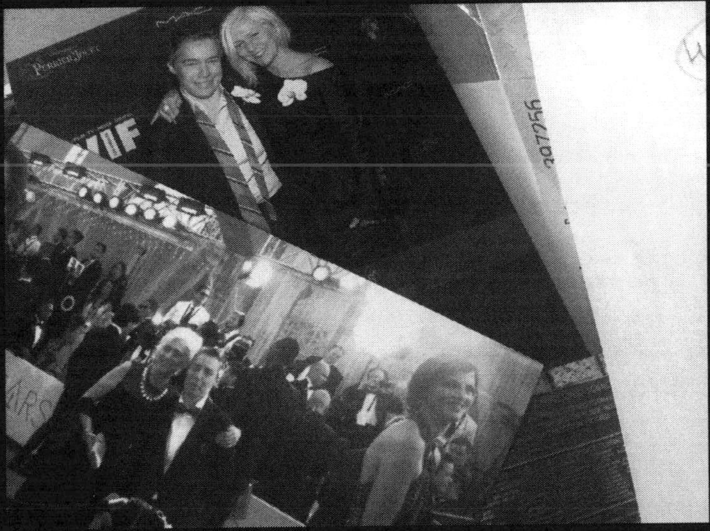

THURSDAY, FEBRUARY 25

10am WRadio.com.co | Astrid will be handling interview

11:30am Hair Marc Bedford Drive Beverly Hills

6:30pm Nominees dinner invite (Nominees ONLY)

a.o.c. Restaurant 8700 W. 3rd Street

FRIDAY, FEBRUARY 26

Call mum

Daphna, Miriam, Moishe, Max flight DELTA 2757.
9:00am. arrival 10:25am

Babysitter: Lauren Friday from around 4:30 onwards

5pm-8pm Great British Film Awards Fig & Olive West Hollywood Women In Film 9th Annual Pre-Oscar Party at 8117 Sunset Boulevard Hyde Sunset Kitchen + Cocktails. 9th Annual Celebration of the 2016 Female Oscar Nominees.

8:30pm Austin Law Group is hosting a celebration all invited.

SATURDAY, FEBRUARY 27

8:30am-11pm	IDA's program Writers Guild Theater 135 S. Doheny Dr, Beverly Hills, CA 90211
6:35pm	Screen Chau, Beyond the Lines (34 min)
7:00pm	Screen Last Day of Freedom (32 min) Photo opp and meet and greet with moderator
7:30pm	Moderated Q&A with all filmmakers
8:00pm	Shorts Awards (us and a guest) Paley Center for Media 465 North

SUNDAY, FEBRUARY 28

10:30am	Press agent meeting
10:45am	Set up in your room.
1:45pm	Leave for Oscars 5.30 pm Dolby Theater Hollywood and Highland Center 6801, Governors Ball Hollywood Boulevard #170, CA 90028, LA

raquel hazell

is an artist and publisher from New York. She is editor-in-chief of Saalt Press, an collaborative publishing initiative focused on working with creatives of colour to desseminate critical and provacotive printed matter, as well as the host of *Saalt Press Radio*.

WEDNESDAY

1. humpday
2. maslov's heiarchy of needs
3. burnout
4. healing the mother wound
5. it's as if i could just float away
6. hyperproductivity can feel like a panic attack
7. overstimulated in the city
8. can too much coffee stop the heart?

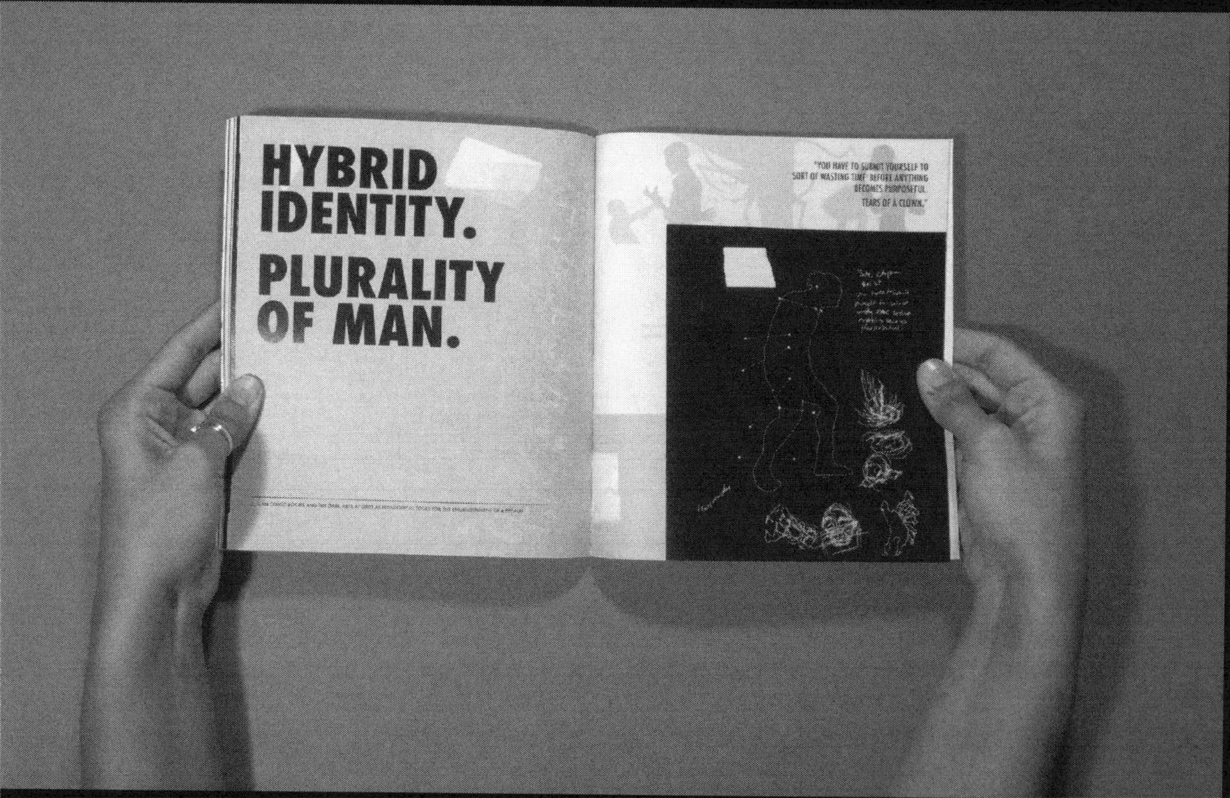

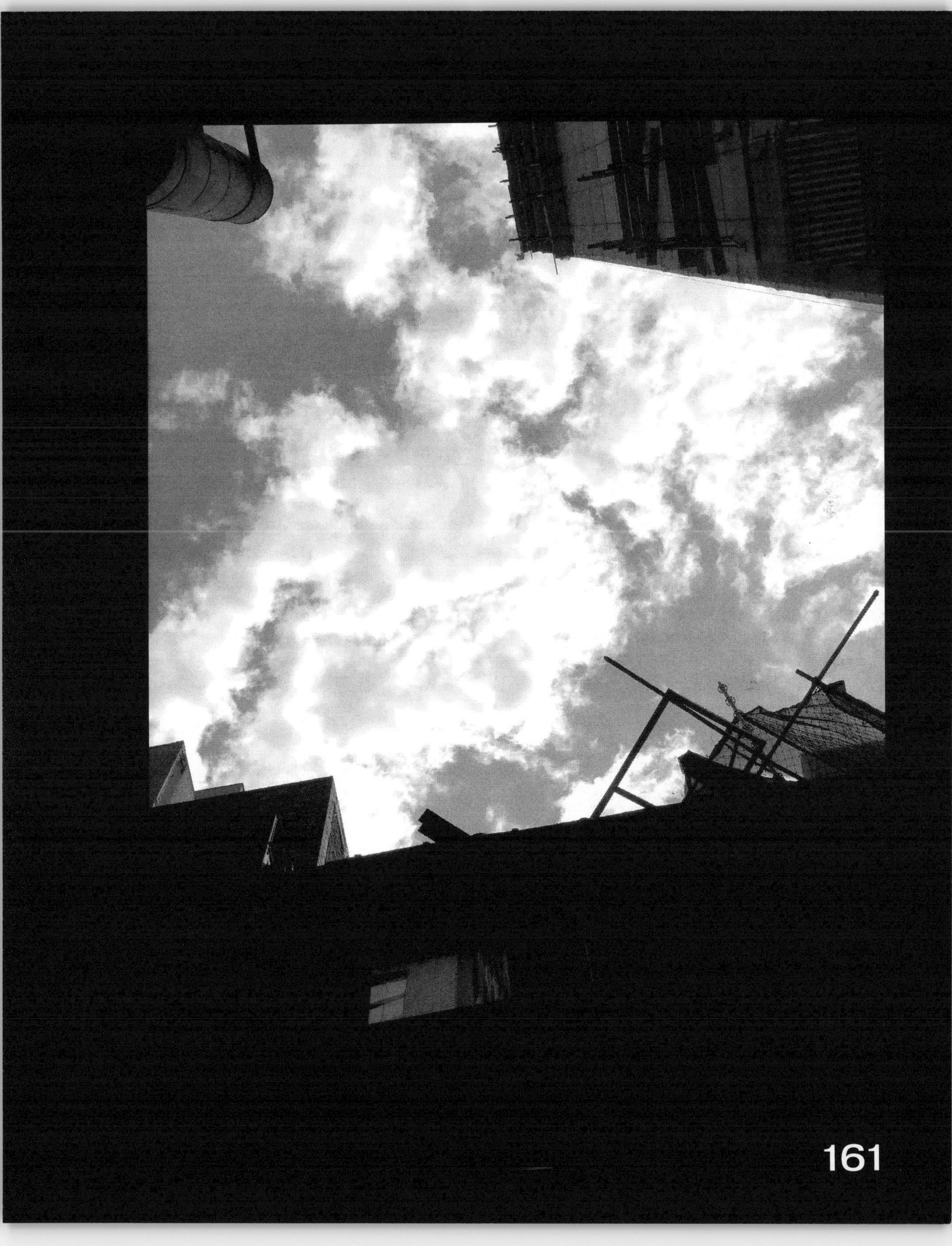

THURSDAY

1. after work shenanigans
2. margaritas and thrifting
3. curry goat and soca
4. all my friends have 401k's
5. graduate school(?)
6. should i move back home?
7. my art is indecisive

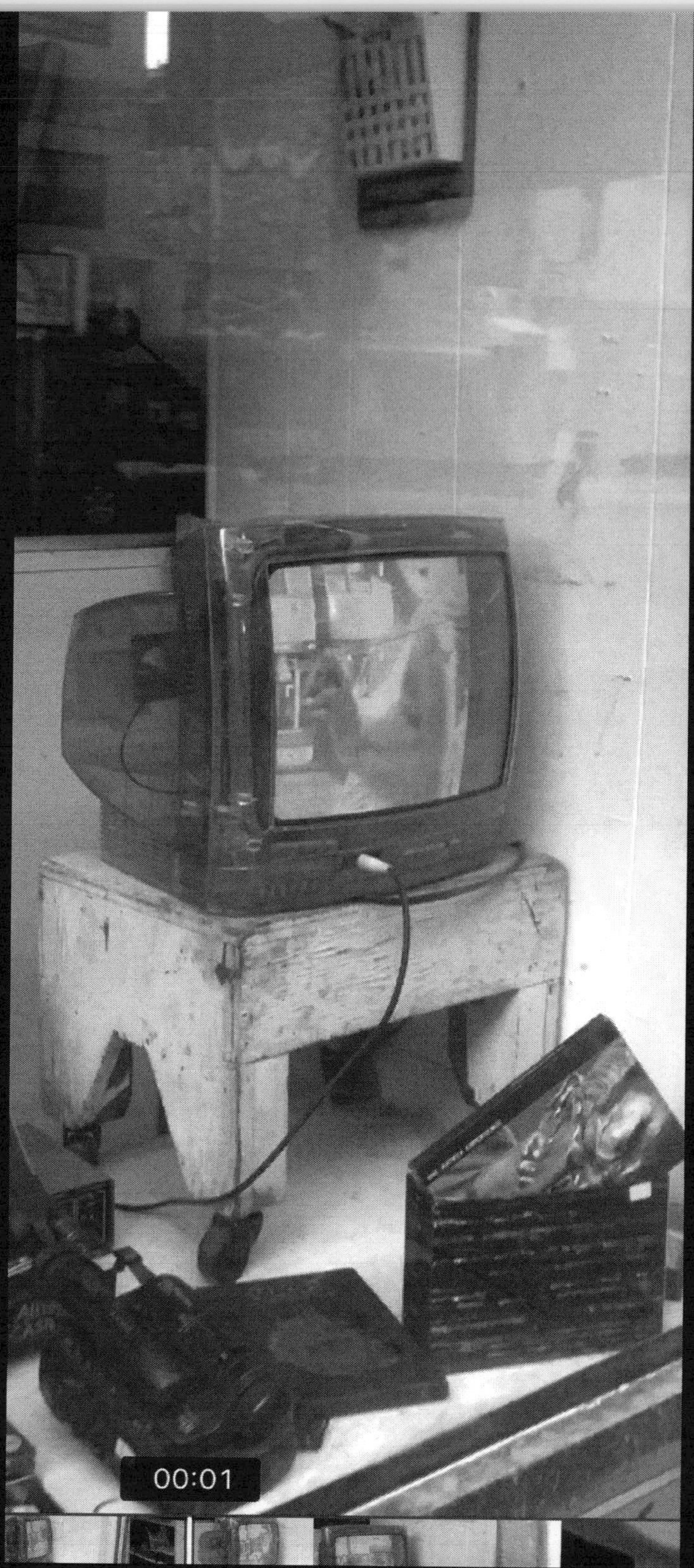

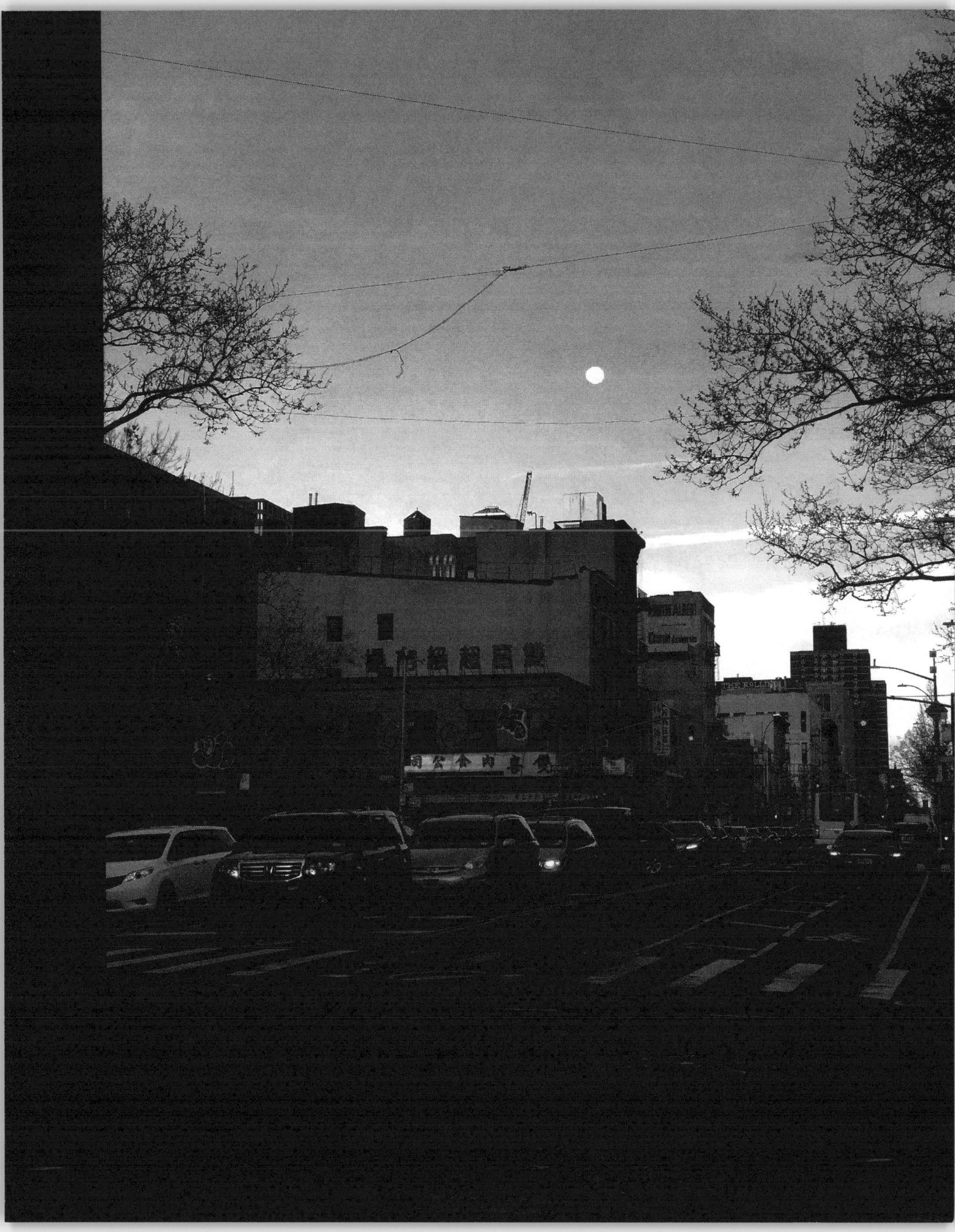

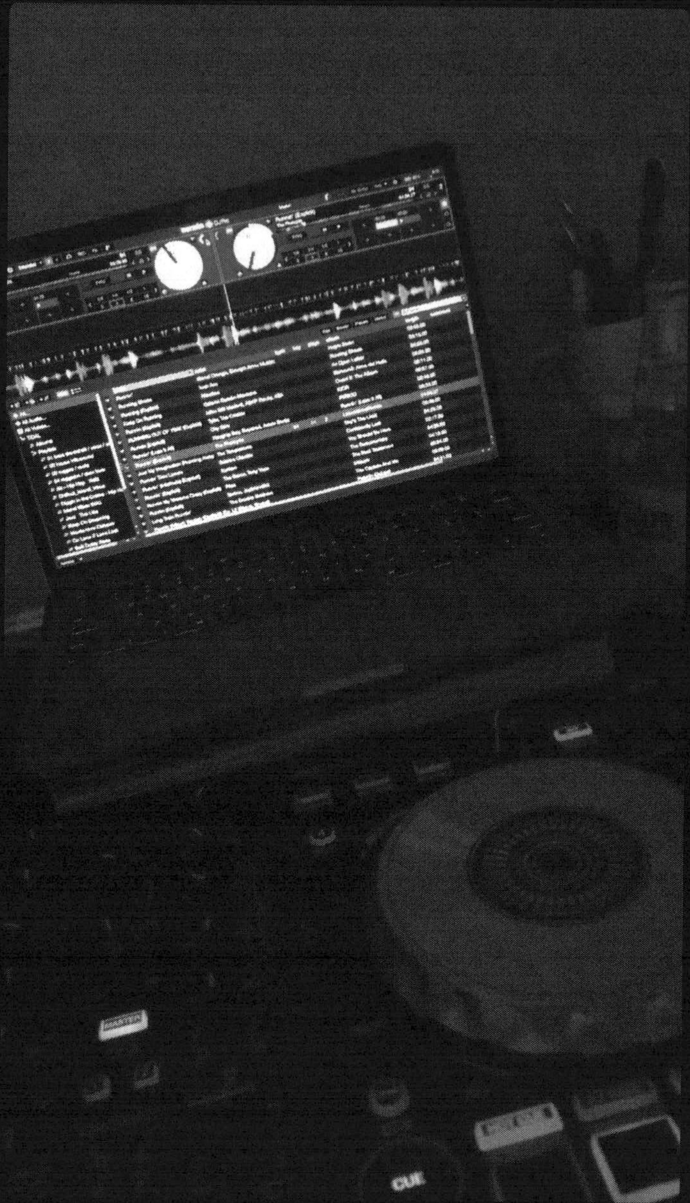

FRIDAY

1. four day weekend
2. mami chula social club
3. conac and popcorn
4. accountability meeting
5. five hour practice set

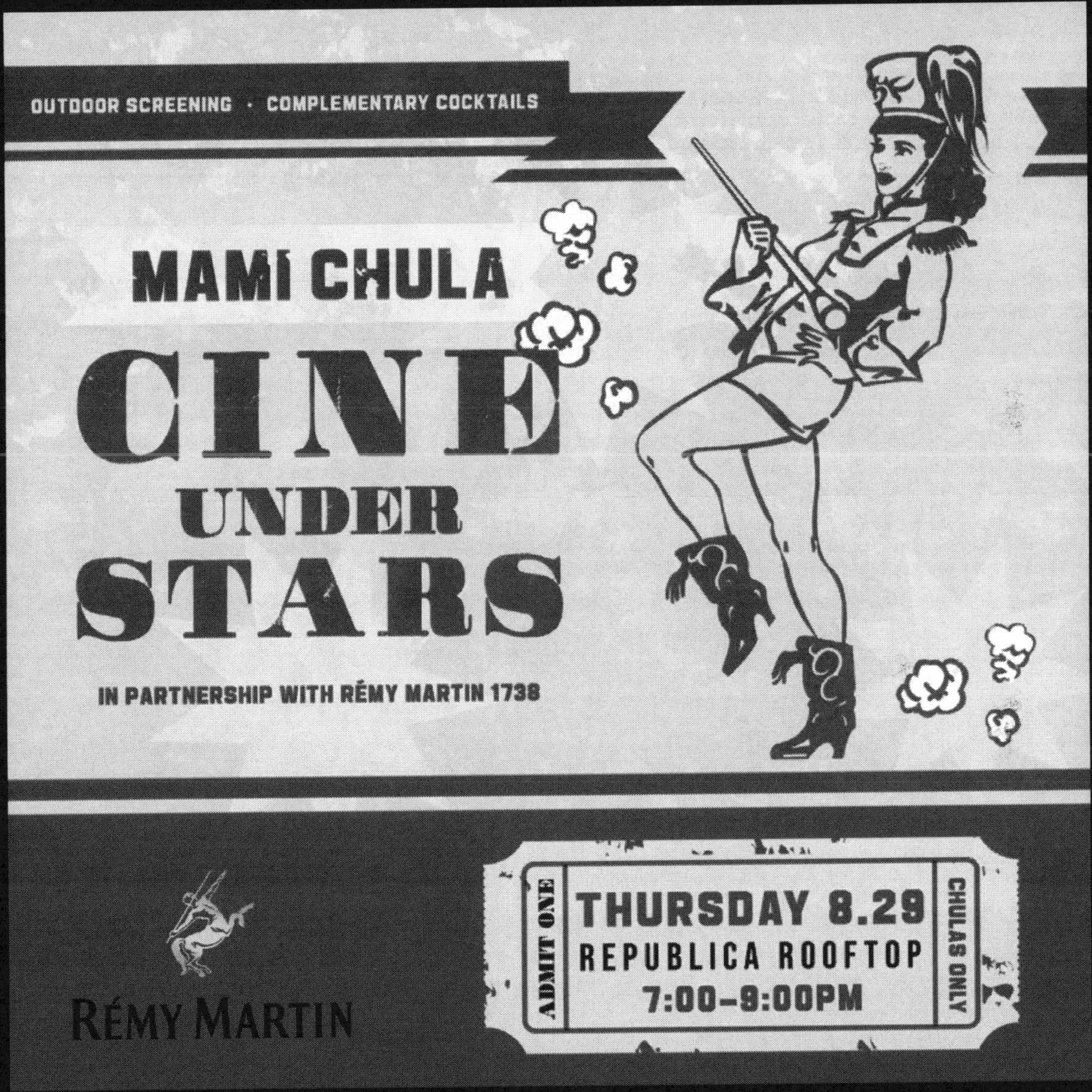
OUTDOOR SCREENING · COMPLEMENTARY COCKTAILS
MAMI CHULA
CINE
UNDER
STARS
IN PARTNERSHIP WITH RÉMY MARTIN 1738
RÉMY MARTIN
ADMIT ONE
THURSDAY 8.29
REPUBLICA ROOFTOP
7:00–9:00PM
CHULAS ONLY

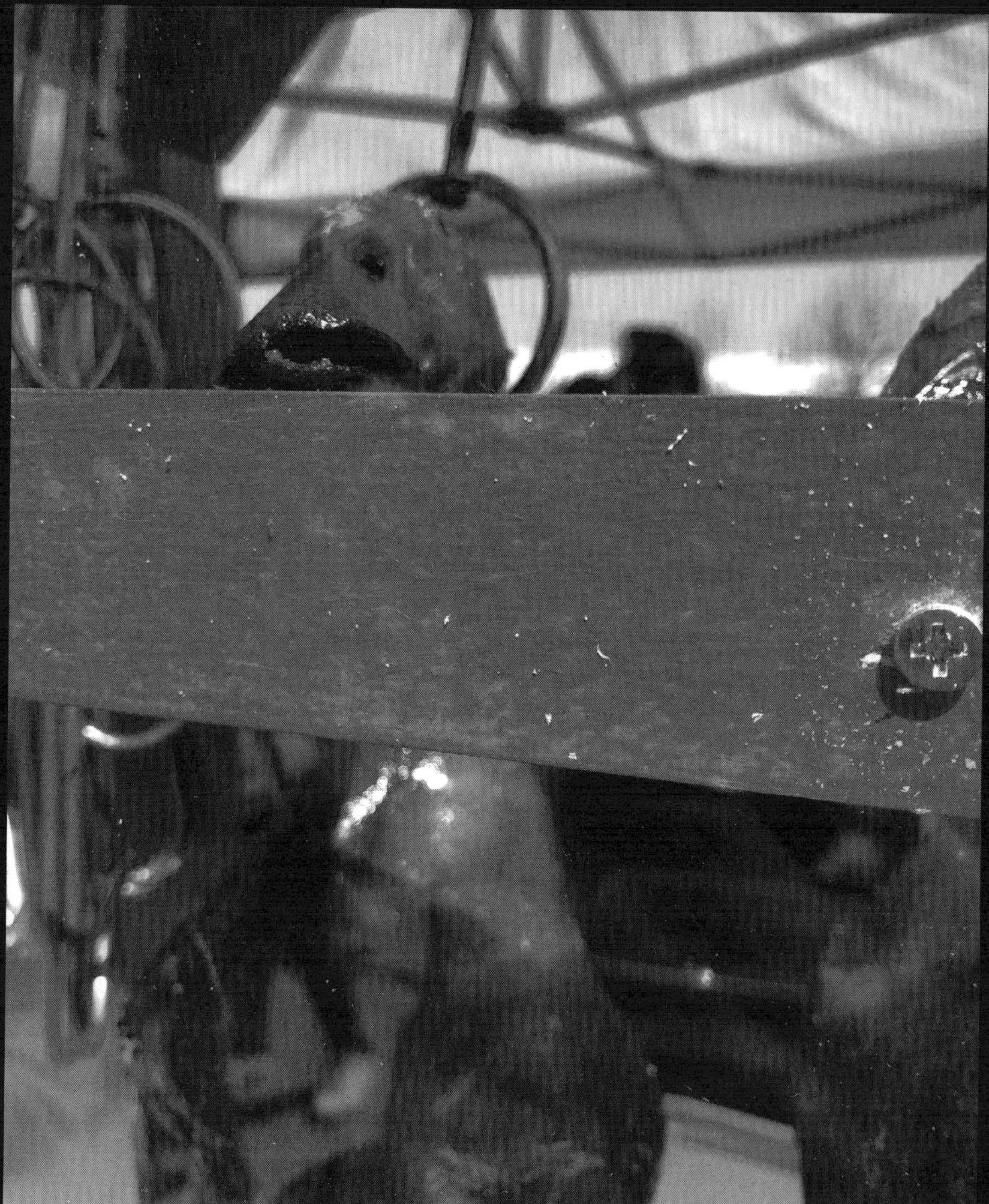

SATURDAY

1. peking duck
2. just to get out of the house
3. resentment for brooklyn
4. [re]counting dollars
5. doing nothing is productive
6. frosé
7. 78˚F
8. should i check my email?

SUNDAY

1. [re]organizing
2. dusting and emails
3. a tenative to do list
4. contemplates the void
5. contemplates faking my death

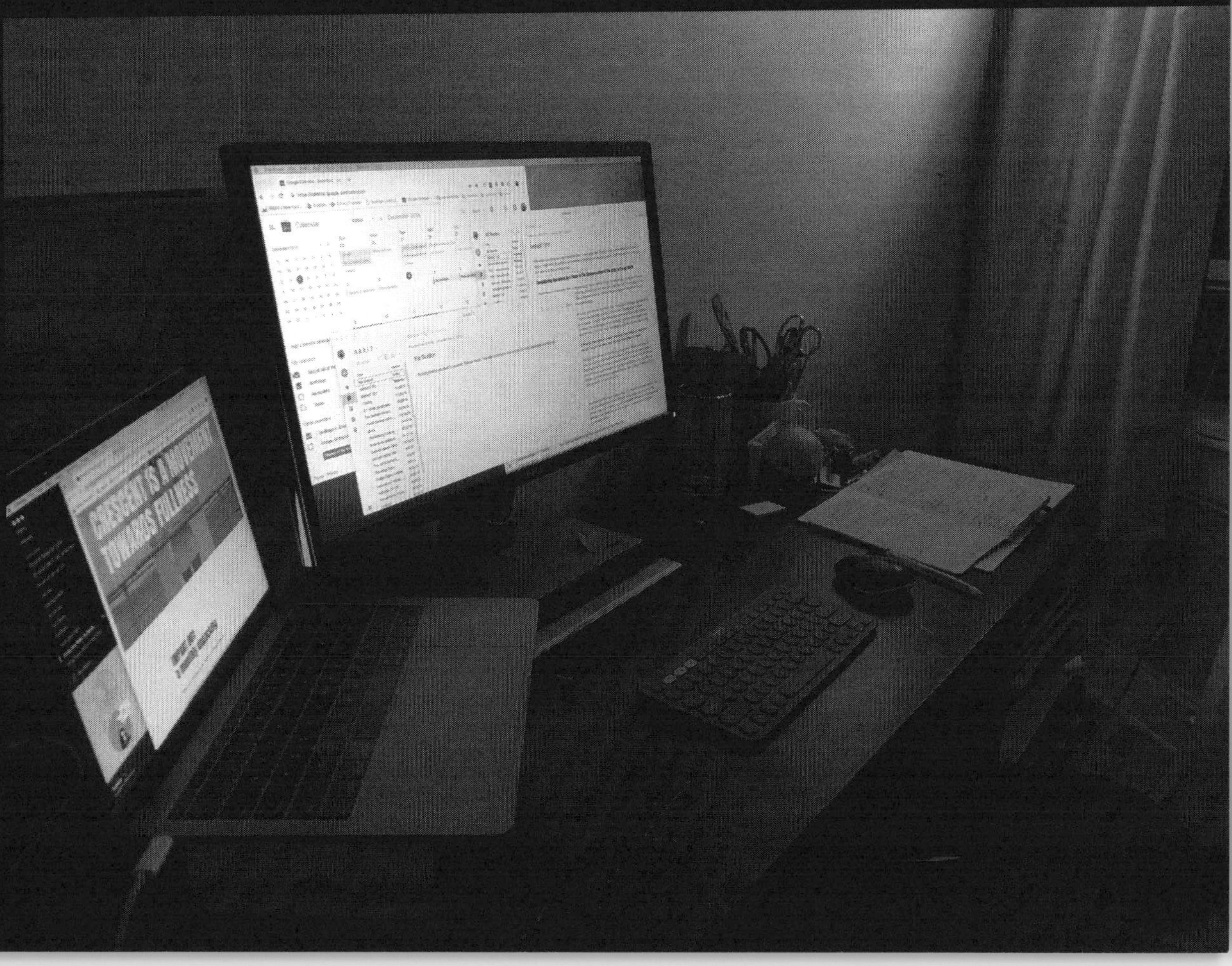

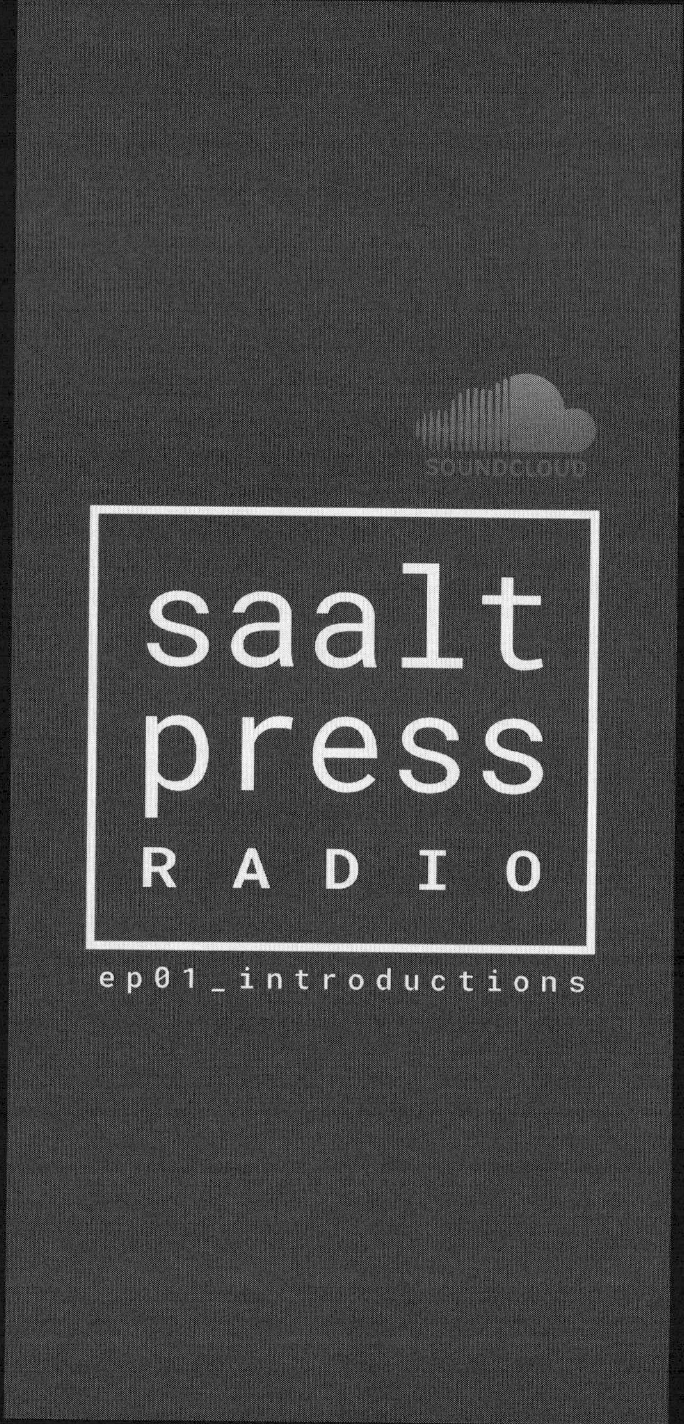

MONDAY

1. launch saalt press radio
2. "speak up"
3. experimental radio waves
4. activate the throat chakra
5. "im sorry i cant hear you"

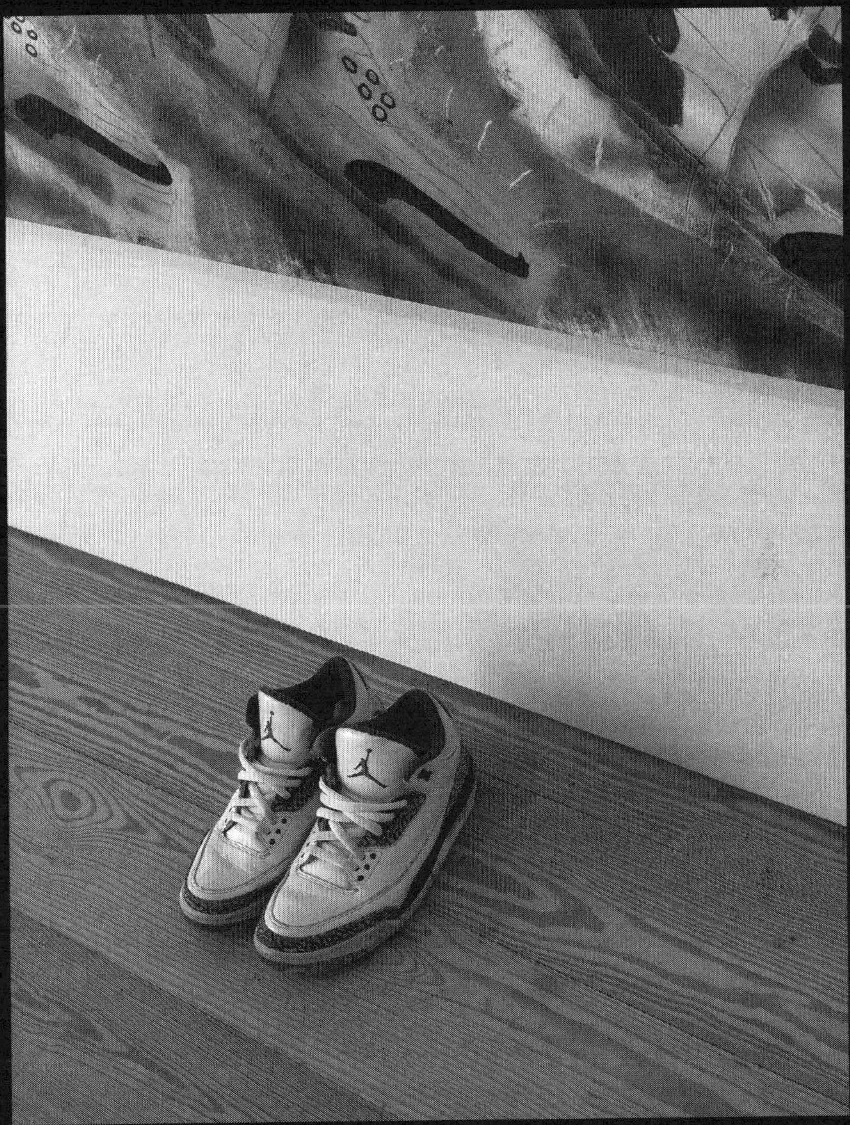

TUESDAY

1. laundry
2. plesantly surprised by whitney biennial
3. wearing white as self care
4. crippling imposter syndrome

irina tarsis

is an art historian and a practicing attorney in Brooklyn, New York. Her practice concentrates on disputes related to ownership of visual art. Founder and Director of the Center for Art Law, she conducts provenance research and consults on art law matters such as title disputes, copyright infringement and fair use, artists' rights, restitution, authenticity and provenance research.

NOTICE

The following information may be legally privileged and confidential. If you are not an intended recipient, please inform me of the error and delete all copies. Unauthorized reproduction or dissemination is strictly prohibited.

WHAT DOES AN ART LAWYER DO?

What does a typical work day or a typical work week in the life of an art lawyer entail? Read contracts, go to court, and sit in on mediation sessions. Call a Ministry of Culture in Eastern Europe, hold a Skype meeting with a client in Western Europe, have lunch with an attorney from France, spend hours in the Frick Research Library, run from the Surrogate's Court at 31 Chambers Street to the Supreme Court at 60 Center Street, negotiate with a gallery to host the next art law mixer (no, it is not a singles event), respond to inquiries from clients, journalists, students and family members all unrelenting. Compensation (negligible) aside, there is never a dull moment in my life, between organizing events, conducting research and writing and representing clients' interests. Even as some of the most successful art lawyers, such as those on the "Art World's Most Powerful Lawyers" list, negate the very existence of this practice area and describe our work as simply representing arts-related clients in different transactional or dispute resolution issues, even though more and more art law questions and opportunities — courses, lectures, case law and legislation — emerge on a daily basis.

I went to law school knowing that I wanted to be involved in art law, in some capacity, either as a practitioner or as an academic, as a rainmaker or as an advocate. Little did I know then that even in this niche field, specializing would be a good idea. At the first day of our class orientation, in response to "Who knows what they will do after graduation?" my hand was the only one in the air. Even though everybody laughed and I was assured that my goal would probably get coopted along the way, for the last eight years I consistently gravitated back toward art law courses, internships, programs, topics, projects, opportunities and clients. While some insist that there is no such thing as art law, I learned from experience that there is plenty of art law to go around.

Those who aspire to practice art law may wish to specialize in various areas such as tax (museum donations, wealth management and inheritance) or cultural heritage law (curbing illicit traffic in antiquities, protection of cultural property during armed conflict, enforcing import/export restriction on trade in endangered species). They may anticipate drafting and enforcing contracts between artists and non-artists, resolving legal issues related to museum management, sorting out copyright matters and other intellectual property rights and remedies, policing and enforcing art market transactions, facilitating restitution of stolen property and pursuing forgery rings and other illicit activities involving works of art.

In law school one of my more skeptical professors asked "well, if there is art law, is there also what, donut law?" Well, come to think of it, if there is Sports Law and Entertainment Law, why not art law?

We have case law: De Sole v. Knoedler Gallery, LLC, 974 F. Supp. 2d 274 (S.D.N.Y. 2013) (breach of warranty and fraud); Cariou v. Prince, 714 F.3d 694 (2d Cir. 2013) (copyright infringement) ; In re Salander O'Reilly Galleries, 453 B.R. 106 (Bankr. S.D.N.Y. 2011) (bankruptcy law); US v. Portrait of Wally, 105 F. Supp. 2d 288 (S.D.N.Y. 2000) (restitution and immunity from seizure); Rogers v. Koons, 960 F.2d 301 (2d Cir. 1992) (copyright infringement) ; Autocephalous Greek-Orthodox Church v. Goldberg, 717 F. Supp. 1374 (S.D. Ind. 1989) (cultural heritage law); Matter of Rothko, 43 N.Y.2d 305, 401 N.Y.S.2d 449, 372 N.E.2d 291 (1977) (fiduciary duties and estates issues) and hundreds of thousands of others.

We have legislation: Visual Artists Rights Act of 1990 (VARA), Native American Graves Protection and Repatriation Act of 1990 (NAGPRA), The Endangered Species Act of 1973 (ESA), Immunity from Judicial Seizure Statute of 1965; import restrictions on antiquities from 2016 back to 1983, see for example Convention on Cultural Property Implementation Act, state laws governing nonprofit organizations and percent-for-art legislative efforts, state arts and cultural affairs laws governing relationships between artists and galleries and much more, not to mention the perennial efforts to pass a federal resale royalty bill (see, American Royalties Too (ART) Act) or allow artists to take fair market value deductions when donating their own art to museums (see, Artist-Museum Partnership Act)).

While there is no Ministry of Culture in the United States per se, there are plenty of regulations affecting our creative industries. Thus, as a founding director of the Center for Art Law, I thought it prime time to introduce an independent nonprofit initiative to promote art law information-sharing and to bring together creative people, both artists and attorneys, students, collectors, professionals from the ancillary industries by offering valuable and educational information exchange and relationship building.

After this long opening statement, for the sake of this exercise, any given work day for me (part art historian, part practicing attorney and always a dedicated advocate for expanding the nexus between law and the arts) may look something like this:

DAY 1

a courtroom peek at the first day of the Knoedler trial;

DAY 2

eventful;

DAY 3

concerns consignment law and a typical dispute arising out of an artist-gallery relationship;

DAY 4

and the efforts involved in restituting
art works looted during World War II;

DAY 5

Art Law Blasts

DAY 6

Irate/Defrauded Collectors v. Knoedler Gallery et al,

The first civil trial - against the now defunct - Knoedler & Co Gallery started on Monday January 25, 2016, the date which conveniently coincided with the start date for the Center for Art Law's spring Interns. For the following weeks, as much time as possible would be spent at the Thurgood Marshall Federal Courthouse. Starting the morning with going through the metal detectors, depositing all electronic devices with security and regretting not having a computer to comment about experts and evidence ushered before the jury in real time, followed by mid-day and evening updates about who took the stand and what questions were asked on direct and cross-examinations. Calls to clients between the morning, lunch and afternoon breaks. Finally, working throughout the night drafting and editing articles for publication on the Center for Art Law website.

Today, on the first day, there is jury selection, reserved glances exchanged by attorneys representing plaintiffs and defendants, assessment of the contingent observing the proceedings, and curiosity about the court illustrators hard at work capturing the shades of suits and faces of the key players. Jury selection is slow, and while most would-be jurors are hoping to be excused, the presiding judge Paul G. Gardephe repeatedly admonishes his fellow citizens that but for a valid excuse he would not release people from their civil duty. The trial is expected to last no more than four weeks.

The cautionary tale of Knoedler's demise, the longest operating art gallery in the United States that shuttered after more than 160 years in business for selling forgeries is a great case study and a legal primer on insurance law, corporate governance, criminal law, law of contracts, civil procedure, evidence and trial advocacy. The De Sole case involved an affluent couple that purchased a work of art from Knoedler, wrongly believing it to be a Rothko. They were not the only collectors to fall victim to the forgery ring that used Knoedler's reputation to sell dozens of art works to the newly minted "Mellons" and "Rockefellers."

At every stage of the trial, from the jury selection to the opening statements and the witness examination the case was an excellent teaching opportunity, not to mention the use of shadow jury, confidential negotiations, and posturing. The trial generated great interest from the art trade, the media, and art lawyers - seasoned, junior and future -- all sitting in on the proceedings, hanging on to every word and question and eager to find out what the penultimate director of the gallery knew when she accepted dozens of forgeries on consignment from a little know then and an infamous now dealer out in Long Island.

Two and a half weeks into the trial, as the date for the key defendants to take the stand kept being postponed and new damaging evidence (emails, letters, lists, depositions) accumulated, the case settled. Gregory A. Clarick, the lead litigator representing De Soles, would later make the top 10 list of the Art World's Most Powerful Lawyers.

DAY 2

Art Law Community Day

Tuesday calendar promises another busy day...and a busy summer if today is of any indication of what lays ahead. A midtown meeting with my future co-counsel to discuss our evidence and litigation strategy, followed by a lunch-time conference call with the executive committee of the New York State Bar Association, and ending with the finishing touches on the complaint that is being filed tomorrow and the evening meeting of the New York City Bar Association with a special guest speaker, one of the experts from the Knoedler Trial.

These Bar Associations (not to mention the New York County Lawyers, American Bar Association, American Society of International Law and other professional organizations by and for lawyers) have members who love to talk shop and attend continued legal education (CLE) programs on related topics. The next art law program, "Legal Primer for Artists: Leasing Commercial and Residential Space & Dealing with Tax Issues" co-organized by the State Bar Committee will take place at the New York Foundation for the Arts in Brooklyn, across the street from the Center for Art Law offices on June 9, 2016.

As for the New York City Bar Association's Art Law Committee, their summer public event is entitled "Fraud in the Contemporary Art Market: The Lessons of the Knoedler and Johns Scandals." It is scheduled for the Meeting Hall on Wednesday, June 15, 2016 from 6:00 to 8:00 p.m. Note to self: add both events it to the calendar for June and save the date for our next art law mixer on July 19th.

DAY 3

Artist - Art Merchant Relationship of Trust

It is typical for art lawyers to represent artists who after having consigned their artworks to a gallery experience difficulties getting compensated from the proceeds of the sales, despite their best efforts to enforce the terms of a consignment agreement (if there is a written agreement) signed by the artists and the galleries. I just finished drafting a complaint to be filed with the Supreme Court for one of my clients, an artist, who is ready to sue the gallery. In this particular situation, the gallery owner has returned one out of every four calls I make and has not agreed to a payment schedule or a complete accounting of the works by my client in the gallery's storage.

Under New York Arts and Cultural Affairs Law works of art consigned to galleries by artists and proceeds from the sale of these works are supposed to be kept in a constructive trust. Specifically:

Whenever an artist or craftsperson, or a successor in interest of such artist or craftsperson, delivers or causes to be delivered a work of fine art, craft or a print of such artist's or craftsperson's own creation to an art merchant for the purpose of exhibition and/or sale on a commission, fee or other basis of compensation, the delivery to and acceptance thereof by the art merchant establishes a consignor/consignee relationship as between such artist or craftsperson, or the successor in interest of such artist or craftsperson, and such art merchant with respect to the said work, and:

(i) such consignee shall thereafter be deemed to be the agent of such consignor with respect to the said work;

(ii) such work is trust property in the hands of the consignee for the benefit of the consignor;

(iii) any proceeds from the sale of such work are trust funds in the hands of the consignee for the benefit of the consignor;

(iv) such work shall remain trust property notwithstanding its purchase by the consignee for his own account until the price is paid in full to the consignor; provided that, if such work is resold to a bona fide third party before the consignor has been paid in full, the resale proceeds are trust funds in the hands of the consignee for the benefit of the consignor to the extent necessary to pay any balance still due to the consignor and such trusteeship shall continue until the fiduciary obligation of the consignee with respect to such transaction is discharged in full; and

(v) such trust property and trust funds shall be considered property held in statutory trust, and no such trust property or trust funds shall become the property of the consignee or be subject or subordinate to any claims, liens or security interest of any kind or nature whatsoever of the consignee's creditors. NY Arts and Cultural Affairs Section 12.01 (a).

Even if a gallery declares bankruptcy, artists' interests are protected and artists must be able to recover their works and proceeds before all other creditors. Galleries that violate the terms of their consignment agreements may be held criminally liable. The silver lining for artists who cannot pay legal fees under the New York law is that "[a]ny person who has been injured...may bring an action...to enjoin such unlawful act, to recover his or her actual damages, or both. The court may award reasonable attorneys' fees, costs and expenses to a prevailing plaintiff in any such action."

DAY 4

The Restitution Principles

In countries whose citizens were despoiled during World War II, claims involving Nazi-era looted art and cultural valuables become increasingly difficult to resolve the further East they extend. While over forty countries signed the famous 1998 Washington Principles, agreeing to seek "fair and just solutions" to questions involving looted art, countries like Poland, Czech Republic, Ukraine and Russia have remained very reluctant to address restitution claims in earnest. Having lost vast national collections and libraries, they subscribe to the thought that individual claims are inconsequential. Possession of tangible property and good faith purchases after the War are more important in these countries than a valid pre-War legal title.

Nevertheless the mores are changing and while Ukraine is seeking to distance itself from its neighbor to the East, I am working to recover a family portrait from a regional Museum in Ukraine to the heirs of the Holocaust survivor who is depicted in this very painting. Her portrait was commissioned in the late 1920s from a local artist and hung in the family home until the family, together with hundreds of other Jews from the Hungarian speaking town were deported to Auschwitz. By 1945, the family home was emptied of all property: furniture, books and paintings. A few years later, unbeknownst to the family, the portrait was purchased for the newly formed local museum in the town where it was once painted and then lost. In his 90s, one of the cousins of the original owner decided to pursue the restitution of the painting.

In preparation for my upcoming trip to Ukraine to raise the issue of restitution in private meetings and also in a public lecture, the subject of which is looted art and established restitution processes, I am also meeting with members of the State Department and with Ukrainian government officials.

Letters are being sent to nonprofit organizations and private individuals, hard copies are soon to follow in English and Ukrainian addressed to the newest Minister of Culture, Yevhen Mykolayovych Nyshchuk, in office since April 14, 2016. There is a 7-hour time difference between New York and Kyiv. Juggling the frequent changes at the Ministry of Culture, not to mention in the Ukrainian Parliament, national holidays and time difference proves to be a challenge when tasked with arranging calls and meetings in addition to reaching a consensus regarding the legal status of a work of art.

Perhaps it is time to retain a local attorney to facilitate communications between myself, the Museum and the ministerial staff.

According to Ukrainian law on cultural valuables, generally, objects such as this portrait held in state museums are not subject to deaccessioning or to export. We are in for a long uphill battle, which will resume tomorrow and next week, and will go on for months to come. Incidentally, a Ukrainian painting which was looted from a Kyiv museum in the 1940s, was recently consigned for sale to an auction house in New York. Perhaps the two displaced works may be swapped, like some war prisoners.

DAY 5

...because you can never have too much art law

Our electronic Art Law News Blasts (the "Blast" or "Newsletter) have been produced by Center for Art Law since about 2010. It takes weeks to prepare each Blast. While new articles are being proposed, drafted and edited by law students or practicing attorneys, information gathering and processing occurs on daily basis. Blasts are free, for now, and they include a calendar of events listings, recent developments in the news and art law gossip, summarized opinions and pending cases and announcements on noteworthy publications Center for Art Law headlines.

Sending Blasts are not an exact science. We want all of our subscribers to read each newsletter but "open rate" varies from week to week, and from season to season. Blasts started appearing in mailboxes on Monday mornings, we then tested the Tuesday afternoon reading cycle and opted to push deadlines and mailings to Wednesdays and Thursdays. Lately, Blasts have been hitting mailboxes on Fridays later and later in the day. The content gets better and longer, the readership is growing.

Depending on the time of year, and our writers, the Blasts turn out to be either bimonthly or monthly occurrences. The purpose, as always, is to keep track of art law events, publications, cases and newsworthy material. Issues are sometimes dedicated to lighthearted or significant events. For example, one of our summer 2015 issues was entitled "Celebrating Life" acknowledging the recent passing of two very influential art lawyers — John Henry Merryman in California and Charles Goldstein in New York. Merryman, long-time faculty member of the Stanford Law School, was the author of the important treatise on art law entitled Law, Ethics and the Visual Arts. Goldstein, of counsel with Herrick Feinstein, was the President of the Commission for Art Recovery, who became an effective advocate for Nazi-era looted art recovery efforts after a successful career as a real estate attorney.

Today we are sending our latest Blast; it happens to be the April 1st. We decided to ride the April Fool's theme for our title , similar to what we did with the March 15th (Ides of March) issue two weeks ago. A four-person team is in the office, working on finalizing the content before we hit the send button at the close of business day. By 2:00 p.m. we have generated numerous April Fools - worthy jokes related to art law...however, it is no laughing matter. Many esoteric jokes are rejected, such as those about bitter protracted art law cases being settled or bills with 0% chance of passing being signed into law.... at the end, one joke sticks: "Knoedler Gallery to reopen." At 2:41pm it appears on our Facebook page. with the header BREAKING NEWS. We end up naming today's issue "APRIL FOOLS ART LAW RULES" and superimposing Jeff Koon's blue gazing ball on top of Richard Prince's "Graduation" collage from the Canal Zone series.

Why not !?

christina dibiase

is a NYC-based artist and writer. Most of her creative energy goes into her website, *The Aurora Archives*, where her interest in wellness and beauty lives. In the matrix, her time is currently spent in an office.

MONDAY

When something isn't working, do something else. After two-plus years of job searching and only having internships to show for it, I'm annoyed to say the least. I have accepted the competitiveness of NYC, but it's time to make a change as bitterness is settling in and I don't need that in my heart. Monday, I started interviewing for jobs as a barista again. I genuinely enjoy making coffee and the job seems to embrace me as I am. I am feeling the release of the idea that it's not a "career" and the fact that my salary won't make sense for living in one of the most expensive cities in the world is old news anyway. On a positive note, a job that lets me use my hands creates balance for when I go home and work on my website, the passion project I actually care about. Which brings me to my next point.

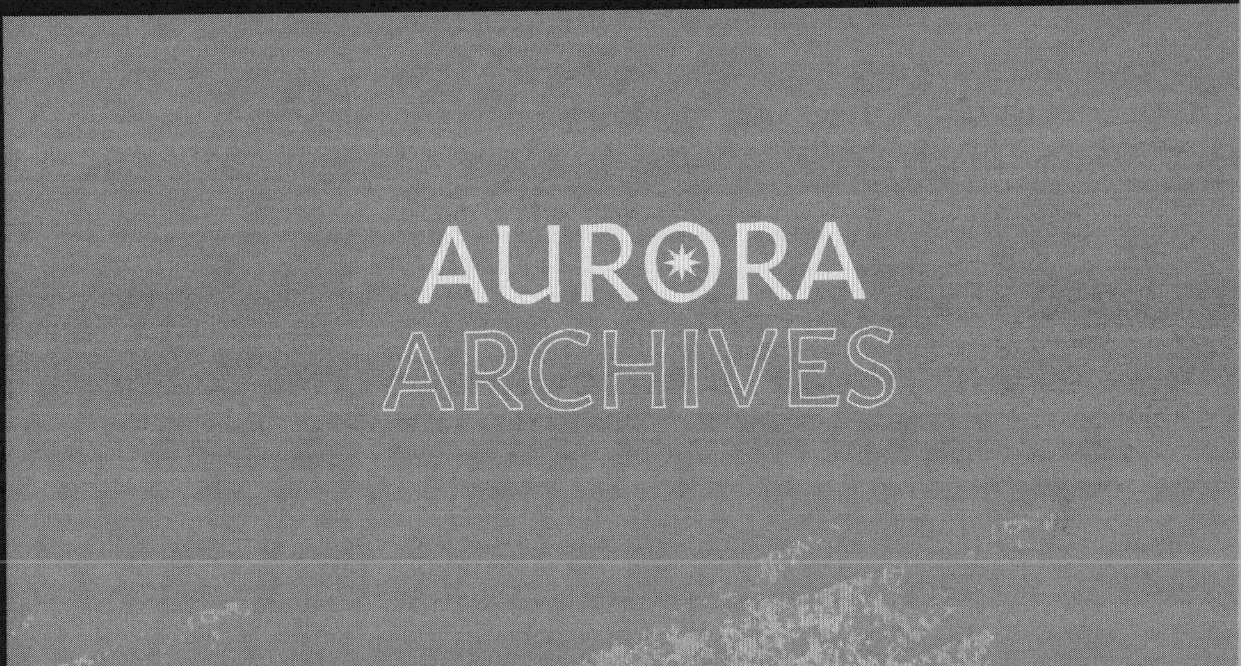

a simple promo for my website.

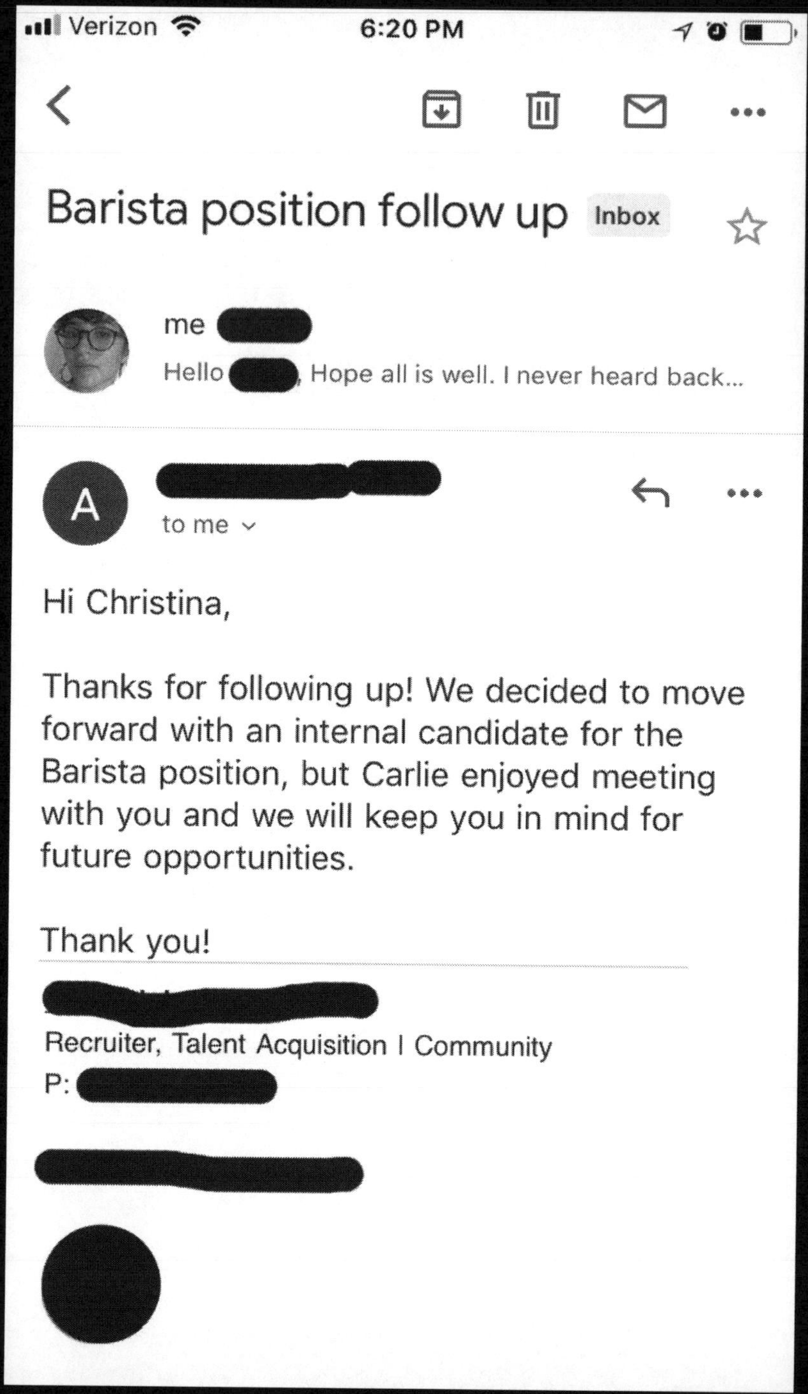

i really got my hopes up about this particular job, onwards and upwards.

TUESDAY

Money will always stress me out unless I learn to let it not. Tuesday, I saw this video on Youtube where they had dozens of people of all different income brackets express their money stresses. Those making $15,000 a year were scared of the possibility of never having money and those making $1M a year were scared of losing it. I understand that circumstance changes everyday so I may as well remind myself to let go of the burden that's resting in the pit of my stomach.

WEDNESDAY

Sometimes nothing happens. Wednesdays are good for that. Sometimes nothing changes and as long as it doesn't last an unsettling amount of time, it's fine. Maybe it's a good opportunity to connect with friends, pick up my dusty guitar, or just embrace the nothingness and stare at a good wall. Refresh to return to my self-inflicted artistic responsibilities.

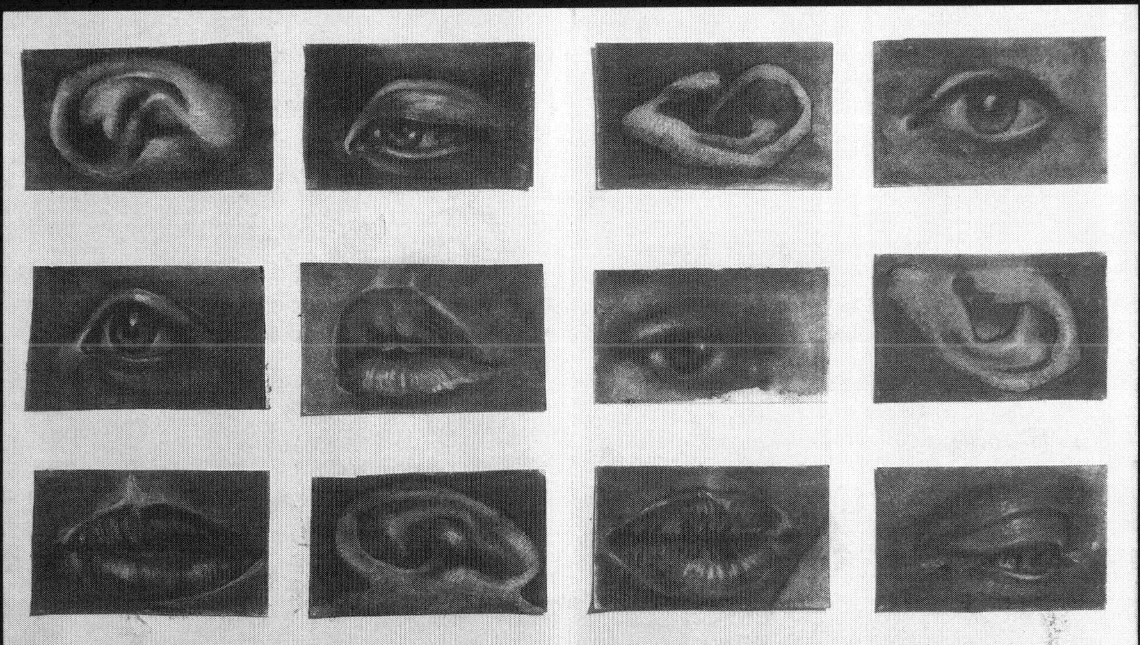

charcoal drawing, 2019.

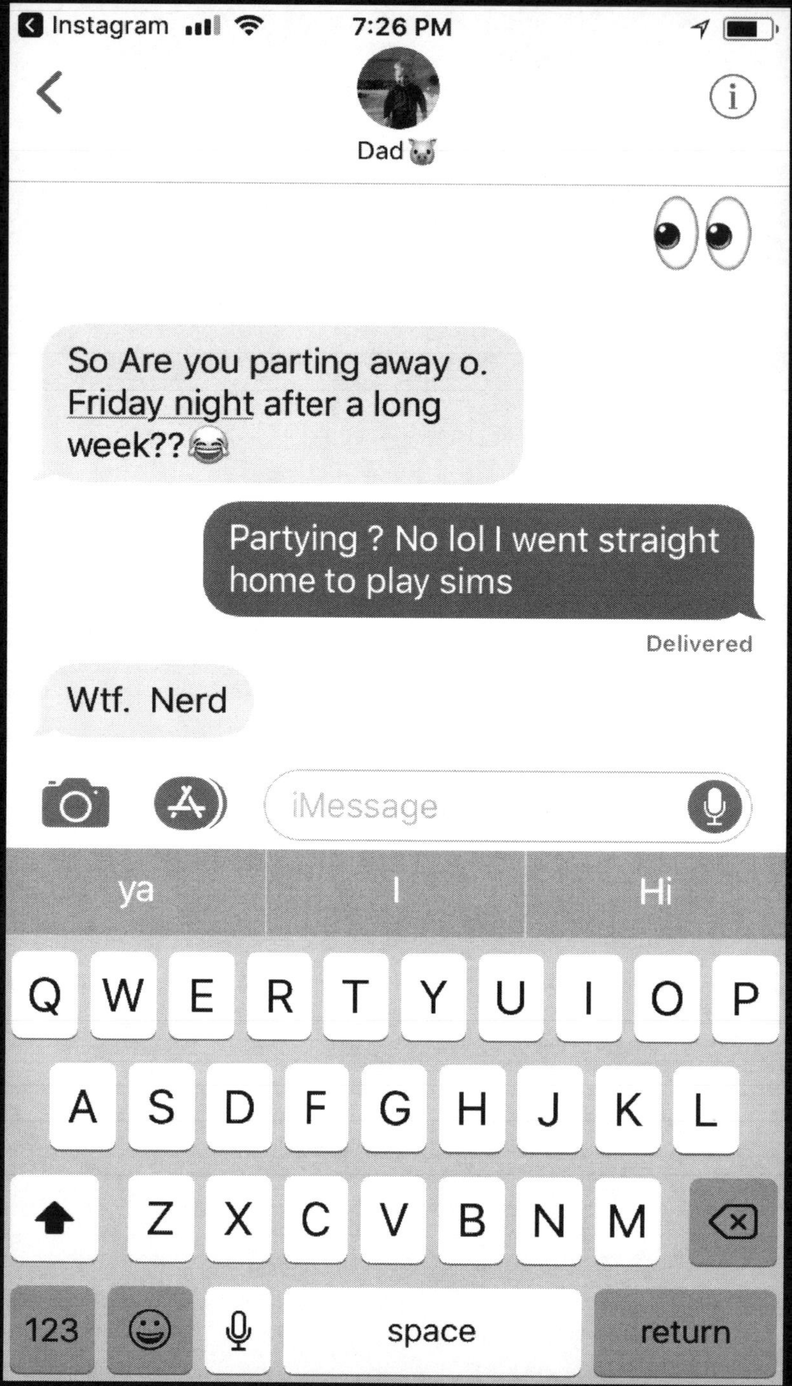

not an uncommon conversation between my dad and I.

THURSDAY

Sometimes too much happens all at once (emotionally). Some days, the feeling of being stuck at a spiritually dull office job catches up to me. When the unsettling nothingness of stagnancy becomes overwhelming, my personal projects help me maintain a semblance of my sanity. Now is a good time to light a fire under my ass (as my dad likes to say). With the previously mentioned website, I decided I'll never appease all my fears and doubts, so fuck it. We are doing this now or never and if it ends up going nowhere, I am at peace with that. Thursday is when I announced that I will be launching within the week. No going back.

FRIDAY

Cats are a blessing. Friday, I had to give up one of my friends and I know she's okay but I miss her. After multiple job rejections, crying at work (more than once), and saying goodbye to my baby, it was not a particularly happy week. But Kida and I had a heart to heart and she told me to flow through the motions of life with ease and grace, and so I shall. And through these trying times, I'll give my love to the two cat babies I still have left.

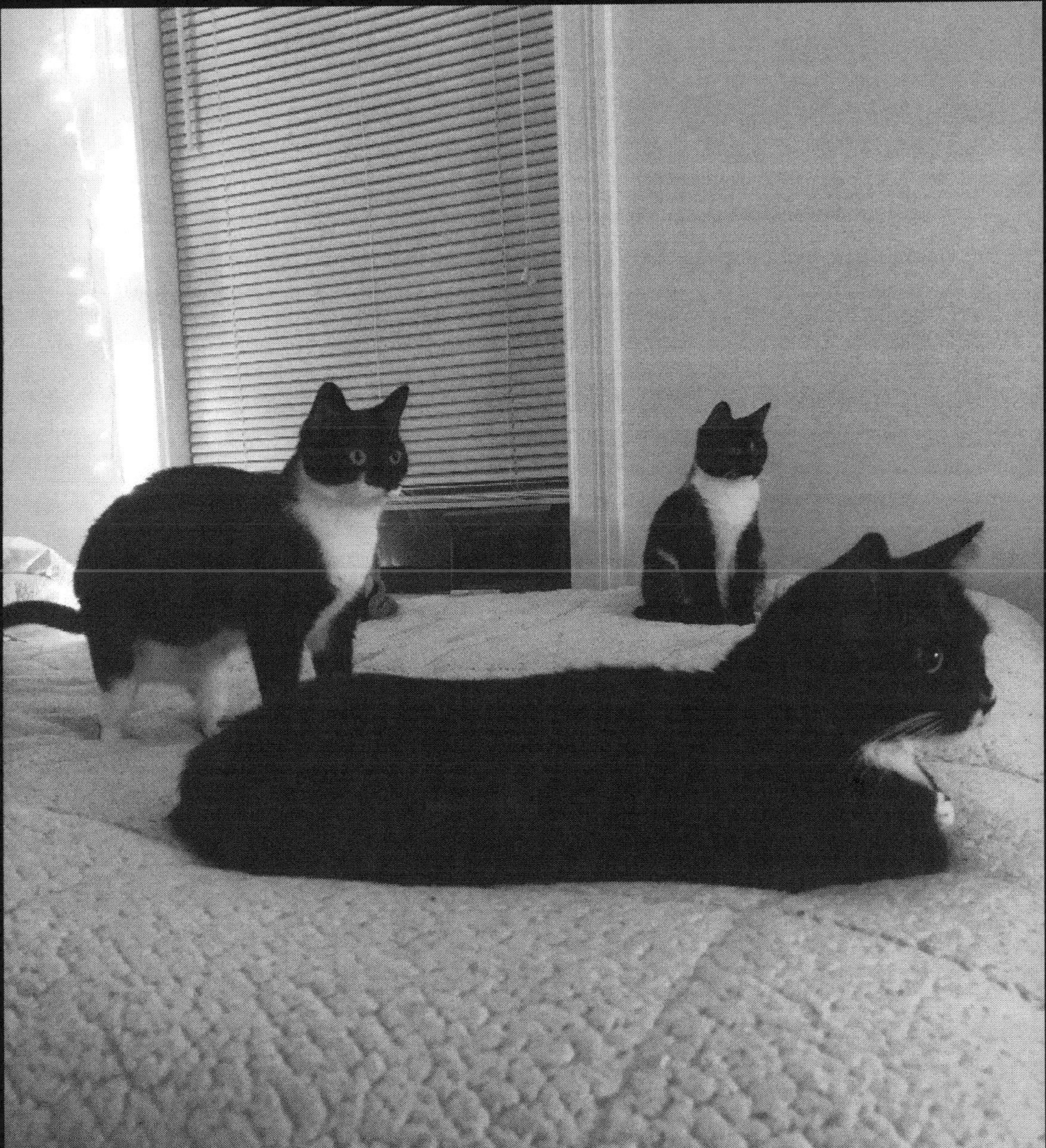

Kida, Fela, and Yaya—the whole gang looking like the cover of an Aventura album.

fernando galán

Is the editor and director of the international art publication art.es.

MONDAY

As the well-known Spanish saying so aptly puts it, "after Plácido Domingo (quiet Sunday) comes bloody Monday..." ARCO (Madrid's art fair) opens on Wednesday. And I'll meet face-to-face with all the gallerists who haven't paid for their subscriptions or ads appearing in the magazine...if the moment of waking is terrible every day, having to fight the temptation to turn over and continue sleeping and the obligation to get up and step into the real world, this Monday is worse... I'm going to end up having to put a coffee machine on the night stand with a tube directly inserted into my mouth, so I can have a quick cup of coffee in bed and gather strength to face the day...

TUESDAY

The second rude awakening of the week. My feet are already aching from wandering around ARCO yesterday during installation to deliver the magazine by hand to exhibitors who are friends or subscribers and/or have ads in this issue. The printer has performed another miracle: a week ago they couldn't guarantee that the new issue (we're up to 66-67 now!) would be here for the opening, which is tomorrow, but in the end they got it to the stand yesterday. One less thing to worry about. But how many others are there?

WEDNESDAY

Today I do have to get it together quickly, get up and be at the stand by 11. Even if I didn't get to bed until 5 in the morning, preparing unpaid invoices and working with my team until 1 am to leave the magazine at every stand so that all the exhibitors will find a complimentary copy in the morning as a gesture of welcome. Everyone will be at the opening as if they'd slept for 10 hours, smiling like they have no worries in the world.

THURSDAY

I went to the opening and nothing disastrous happened. Or am I still dreaming? On the contrary, praise for the new issue of art.es was unanimous. Of course, being the inauguration, I went from one end of the fair to the other while avoiding looking in the eyes all the exhibiters who I need to collect long-overdue payments from. I'll have to begin that task today. And the question I ask myself every year: Will I have time to actually visit the fair this year?

FRIDAY

This morning I barely have time to think in bed and review everything I have to do. I ended up falling back asleep. Sleeping only five hours a night during the fair is terrible. The public can't imagine how exhausting these fairs are for the exhibitors, who spend eight hours conversing the whole time with people who pass by the stand, some more friends than others. It's true though that various happy reunions make it all worth while. And business, of course. But spending eight hours without seeing the light of day and surviving on cookies and chocolate make you lose all sense of time.

I started tracking down the people who owe me money. One gallery, who subscribed with a handshake in 2008 when we coincided at Art Dubai, and who never gave me his bank info because every year at ARCO he begged me to request them by e-mail but they never answered, couldn't think of any better reply (after eight years) than that he wasn't receiving the magazine... And I know from my correspondent in his city that he is. But I'm a gentleman: as soon as he told me this I tore up the invoice in front of him and said, "I never argue about money and you don't have to pay for what you didn't receive."

SATURDAY

Well, it looks like good news prevails. Yesterday the director of a Portuguese museum passed by the stand and told me that she had been wanting to subscribe to the magazine for some time now. She not only bought a subscription, she ordered every back issue since the first one because the few she had she wanted to keep at home. And she paid everything right then and there, before receiving the entire back catalogue. There are a few similar gratifying cases, but pursuing delinquent debtors makes me ill. The former correspondent for Morocco, Abdallah Karroum, who left the post when he was named director of the Arab Museum of Modern Art in Qatar, also visited the stand. The magazine's success, like that of almost everything in life, is not determined by the number of computers we have, nor the level of technology, but by the human factor, the quality of the people behind it, on both a professional and human level. And I'm happy to say that I've almost always had a good eye for choosing the personnel: I've lost more than 10 correspondents because they were named directors of museums or similar posts.

SUNDAY

I can't believe that today is the last day of ARCO. On the one hand, time at art fairs passes ever so slowly, and on the other, quickly. Yesterday I once again went to see a gallery owner who is one of our biggest debtors: four years of continuous ads without paying, beginning five years ago. Unperturbed he claimed he didn't owe me a cent. I told him that my lawyer had wanted to send a letter of execution for some time now but that I had wanted to wait until we had the opportunity to settle the situation in person and with good will on both sides. When I added that the entire case was registered in the e-mails we had sent each other at the time, he seemed to lose his apparent indifference... Then he said that it was a bad moment to talk because there were a lot of people at his stand and that fairs were for selling. I asked if he preferred that I write him a friendly letter the following week including all the relevant documentation proving his debt and he replied that he thought that was a good idea. And that he'd answer immediately.

Incidentally, the Editor's Letter in this last issue was titled Art galleries and crooked dealers. Of course, I dedicate more space praising instances that deserve praise than in denouncing shameful ones, because there are far more positive cases. Though for me, just one shameful example is one too many.

artemis potamianou

is an artist and curator who is currently based in Athens. She is the curator of Art Athina Contemporaries of International Contemporary Art Fair of Athens since 2012 and Director of Platform Project @ Art Athina 2013-2014.

LOOK, LISTEN, LEARN... IT'S HISTORY

The work «Look, Listen, Learn, It's history...» places the spectator in an almost scopophilic game of viewing a collection of the artist's personal objects from her adolescence, creating a mental keyhole for the sake of the exploration of a personal diary and of what that means. The spectator is invited to reconstruct a utopian and, at the same time, nostalgic universe, by means of her own associations and perceptions. The reading is personal each time.

Musical bits, photographs and slides, books, create the coordinates of a microcosm made of the artist's personal "trophies", in an installation that refers directly to the work of Joseph Kosuth Information Room (Special Investigation, 1970) as well as to the work of Christo and Jeanne-Claude.

The installation attempts to deconstruct the art object's process of production in order to reconstruct it with the spectator as participant in a sharing and collaborating role, thus transforming a strictly personal process into a channel of/opportunity for communication. A u-topia is thus suggested: a place full of promise for optimal understanding and interaction between the creator and viewer but, simultaneously, a place that is non-existent.

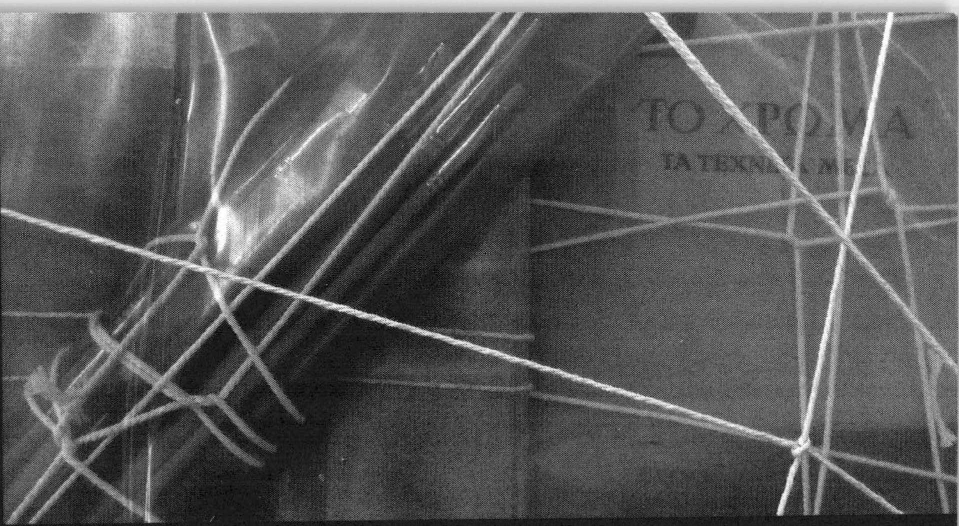

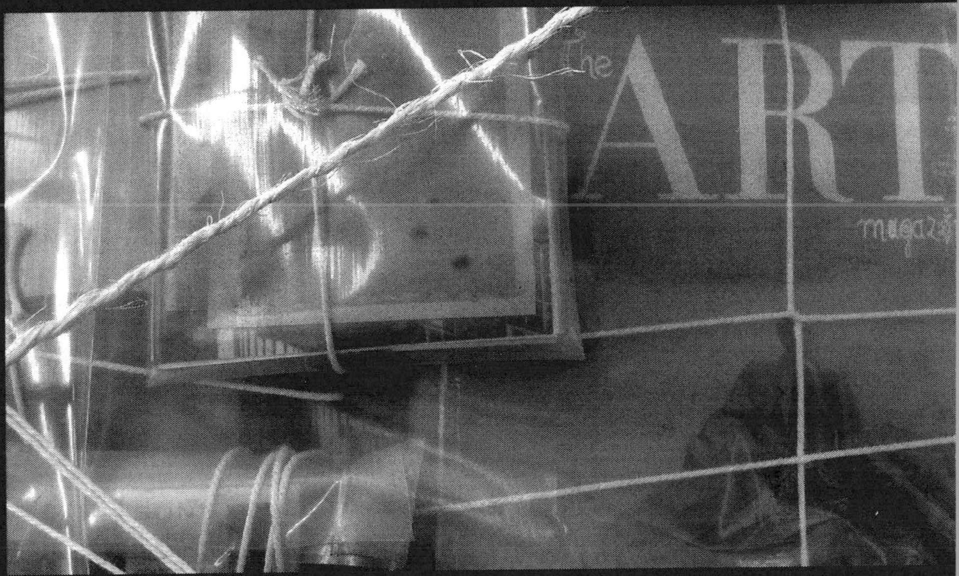

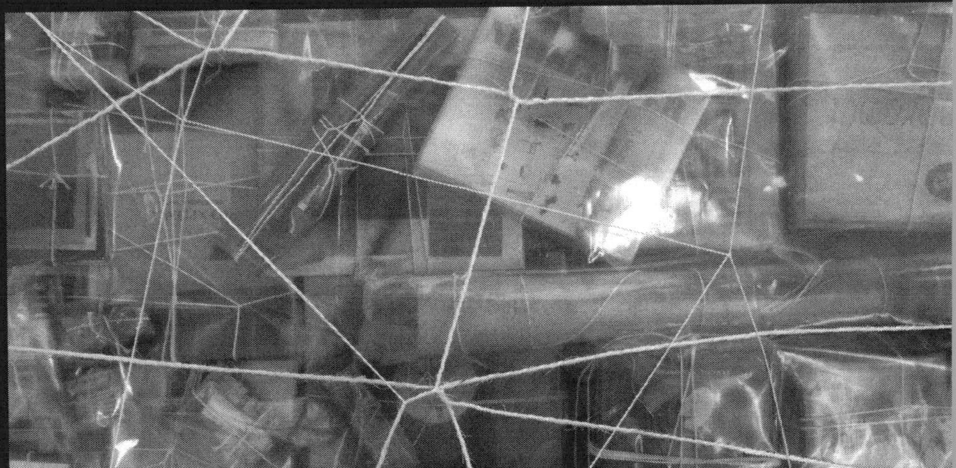

203

renee royale

is an independent curator, artist, and writer. Her goal is to provide alternate ways of experiencing art, utilizing innovative methods and modern technology to break down socioeconomic and institutionalized barriers for a more equitable, authentic art world. By presenting art in a myriad of ways from intimate encounters to public installations to social media, she seeks to diversify the relationships we have with art.

Someone called me an art purist yesterday. After much self reflection I have to admit, there may be some truth in that statement. At 29 I have created one of the largest independent platforms for black art, collaborated with museums, curated multiple shows, given talks, managed other art social media platforms and yet...I am totally dissatisfied with the art world.

People laud my accomplishments as if much has changed in the past 20 years. Art for art's sake was never the purpose of art. To maintain a state of elitism for the sake of exclusion is a disservice to arts and to communities all over the world. Art was always supposed to be for the people. I lament feeling like a victim of my own success. What good is art if it's only for a select few? What good is an artist when your social media following and social clout mean more than your actual skill? What makes a curator when a piece of paper, elitist connections, or the right viral trend can net you a show, devoid of true substance and intention? All the art world did was shift trends. Artwork centering around identity is in, Black art is in, controversy is in, the list goes on. Everyone acts as though the art world is breaking barriers for actions that should have been taken over 20 years ago. Art was about being ahead of the curve, not following or maintaining it. Tangible issues, such as fair compensation (I.e., residual income), innovative ways of immersing art in communities, full transparency of museum practices (and their boards - not just the trending big oil/pharma members), all still have to be tackled. We need a true art revolution, and until then I will never be satisfied with my work.

stephanie jeanjean

received her Ph.D. in Art History from the CUNY Graduate Center. Her field of specialization is postmodernist and contemporary art, with a focus on the relationship between reality and fiction, narrative structures, social construction, hyper-reality, and semiotics. Jeanjean is also an active independent curator and writer, frequently writing for cultural magazines and newspapers.

THIS MONTH, I AM HANGING BY A STRING

This month, I taught 64 hours of classes in 5 different courses, at 3 different universities, in 2 disciplines, and in 2 languages. In addition, I regularly lectured at one of the big New York museums. To add up—the hidden part: prep. work, grading (when applicable), and various ½ and day-long trainings and meetings at museums.

Yet, I did not see much art shows again, missed out a lot. I read about some of them (the ones that were written about, eventually...). Some I really hope I had seen or will see before they close, and I am not far, but moving too fast, too much, always having to go... And, then, the little I saw was not transcendenting, which is not unusual. I did couple of studio visits, met couple of motivated artists; the work was not sensational. As for the news, it is art world business as usual; despite the "Panama Papers", nothing is really happening out there or out of ordinary. Unless it is the antic site of Palmyra retaken, and the Roman theater preserved. What a statement of the timeless spectacular power of imperial aesthetics, conquering even the iconoclasts, who used the theater to perpetrate public massacres and spectacularize death!

I have to write... There is one piece for an edited book, due 6 months ago, that I wrote it in my head 3 times already and did not put it on paper yet... When? I taught 13 courses this past year. Now, with everything going on that fast, maybe what I had to say is not relevant anymore, I have to write it again, why does it still matter? I also have to continue making regular progress toward the completion of this book I am co-editing, for the end of the year. Too rarely I can actually sit for hours at my computer to do this work, even less with my mind free from tasks, duties, assignments, or other late correspondences...

This month, I graded 100 student papers (1-3 pages each) and 70 midterm examinations; I also caught 3 cheating with their cell phones...

Results are poor, few did really good, but very few. The overall average is low, low interest, low contribution, low involvement, and low (self) esteem. How can pretending artists disregard art that much, art of the past, art produced by others than themselves, art that mattered and matters to others beyond the artists or the moment when it was made? How to activate the millennial? Is that a question?

Making references to early video works by Birnbaum and Nauman using surveillance, last class, I turned the classroom videoconference capability on, for a little while, and had them face their images on the large screens, just long enough to have them reflect on the uncanniness of the apparatus and to confront the representation that they'd like to have of themselves.

Did this work? Then, surprising, surely alarming, earlier this month, informing them about performance and body art and making references to their context of emergence, I came across that they—all my undergraduate students this semester—had never heard about May 68. Recent history already swept away from collective memories. Even if it was deep and life changing for those who participated in it, for the ones who were not there, born later, except I guess a few "eccentrics", curious, nostalgic, wandering minds, May 68 does not meet any referent — it is neither communicated as knowledge by family, education, nor society. What else have they not heard about? Has it been replaced by anything else, if any? We cannot reinvent the wheel continuously...can we? Most of the folks I am speaking about here are also old enough to vote in next year's presidential elections, and the race is ugly and really concerning, as we write.

I am not allowed to vote...

Who am I? I am called an "alien non-resident with extraordinary abilities" and with too much work (paid, underpaid, and unpaid), a lot of unnecessary worries and not enough stability and support. I am currently on grace period for immigration. Because of an administrative mistake shortening my visa, I had to expedite a new application with premium services (and 3/4 of my savings). I have 3 lawyers at work and the entire process is stressful and absolutely terrifying. Hopefully, I'll hear back soon that my request went through, and that I can continue this life (which I like, nevertheless) next month. Until then, I am hanging by a string...

holly crawford

received her Ph.D from the University of Essex in Art History and Theory, B.A and M.A. in Economics in addition to M.S. in Behavioral Science from UCLA. From 2004-2006, Crawford was a non-clinical Fellow at NYU Medical School Psychoanalytic Center. She is a member of AICA-USA. She is also the author of *Attached to the Mouse*, *Critical Conversations in a Limo*, and *Artistic Bedfellows*. Crawford is and artist and art historian specializing in contemporary art.

ART—HERE, THERE AND EVERYWHERE

Let's party!
It's in the cards
past, present and future
build, paint and fix
hire and unfortunately fire, and here we go again
email and social media
your project here
and my project there
openings and closings
websites,
new websites
welcome to my party

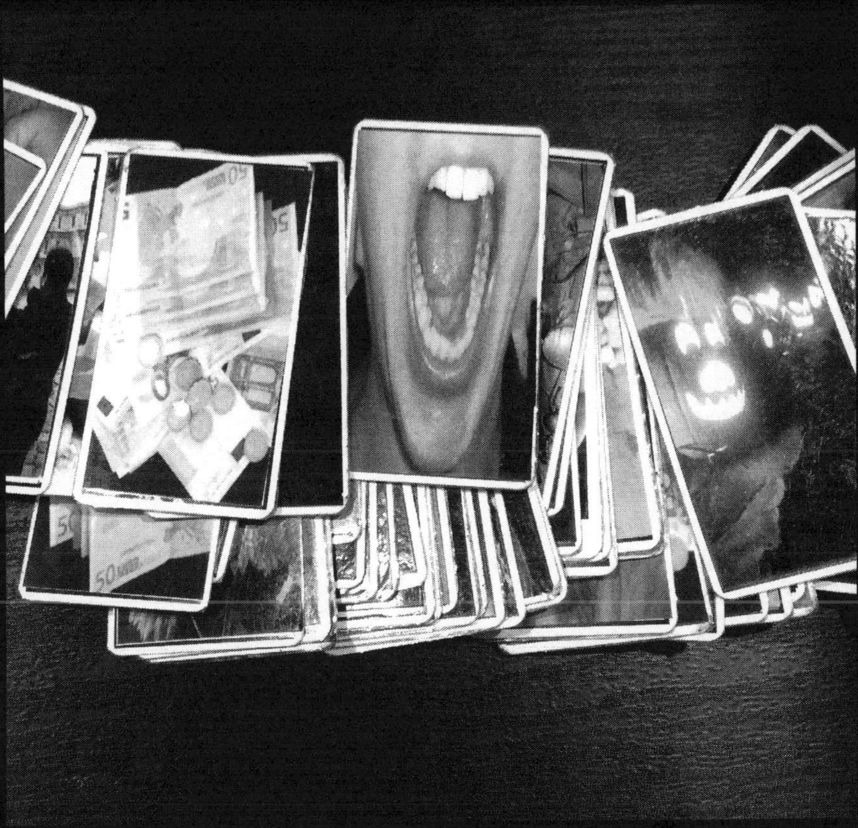

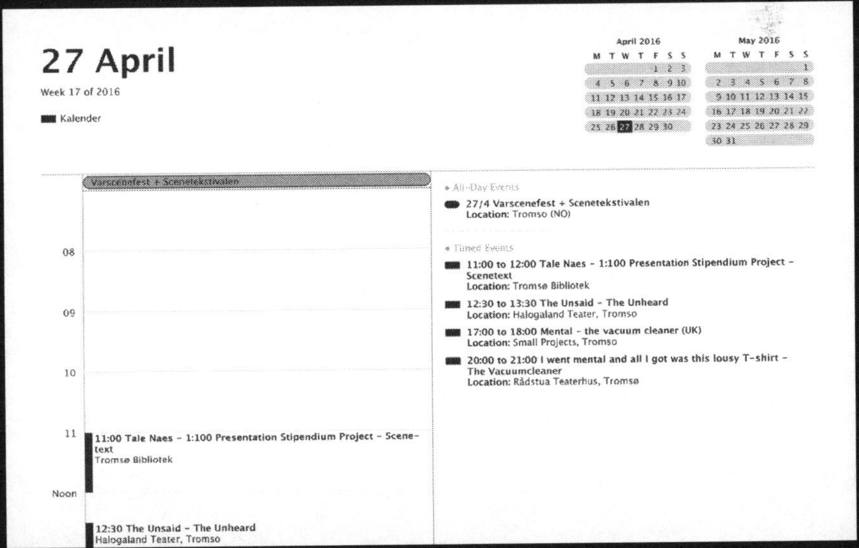
27 April
Week 17 of 2016
Kalender
April 2016
May 2016
Varscenefest + Scenetekstivalen
All-Day Events
27/4 Varscenefest + Scenetekstivalen
Location: Tromso (NO)
Timed Events
11:00 to 12:00 Tale Naes - 1:100 Presentation Stipendium Project - Scenetext
Location: Tromsø Bibliotek
12:30 to 13:30 The Unsaid - The Unheard
Location: Halogaland Teater, Tromso
17:00 to 18:00 Mental - the vacuum cleaner (UK)
Location: Small Projects, Tromso
20:00 to 21:00 I went mental and all I got was this lousy T-shirt - The Vacuumcleaner
Location: Rådstua Teaterhus, Tromsø
08
09
10
11
Noon
11:00 Tale Naes - 1:100 Presentation Stipendium Project - Scene-text
Tromsø Bibliotek
12:30 The Unsaid - The Unheard
Halogaland Teater, Tromso

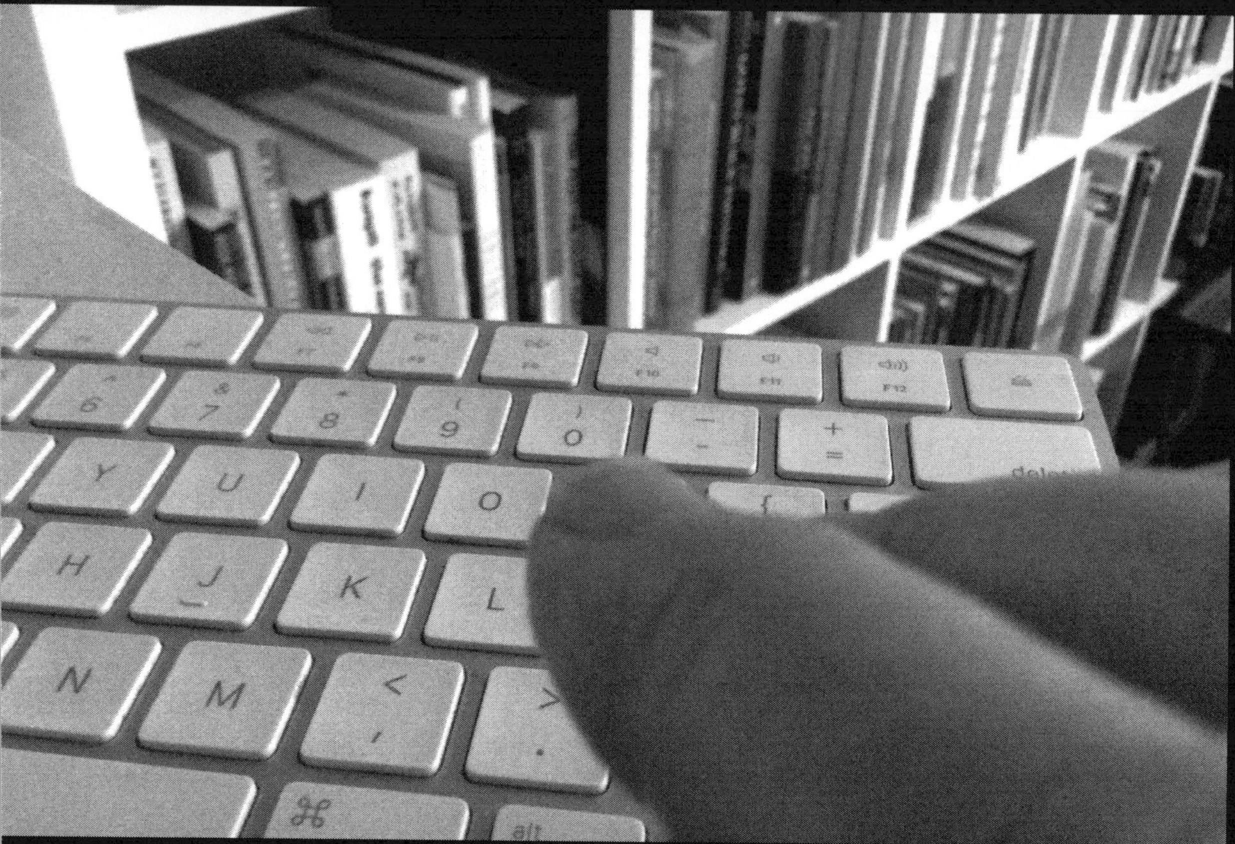

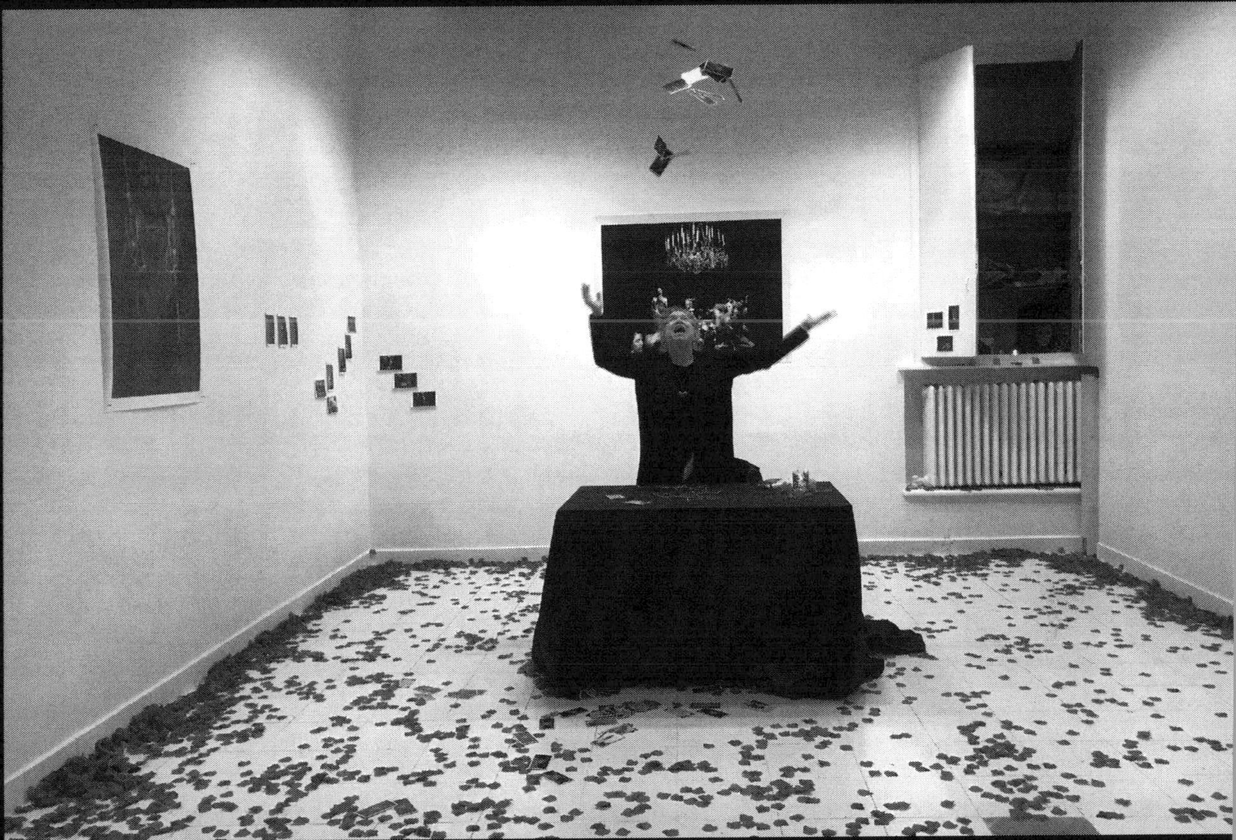

linnea west

is a freelance writer, blogger, and curator with a passion for the visual arts. West received her Master's degree in art history from The University of Georgia in 2015. In 2012-3, she researched contemporary Hungarian art and national identity at the Ludwig Museum of Contemporary Art in Budapest while on a Fulbright grant. She has written for the blog *Art Ravels: Arts and Culture Unwound*. With a focus on contemporary art, the blog is a reflection of the wide exposure to the art scene in New York City and more recently in Budapest, Hungary and Athens, Georgia (USA).

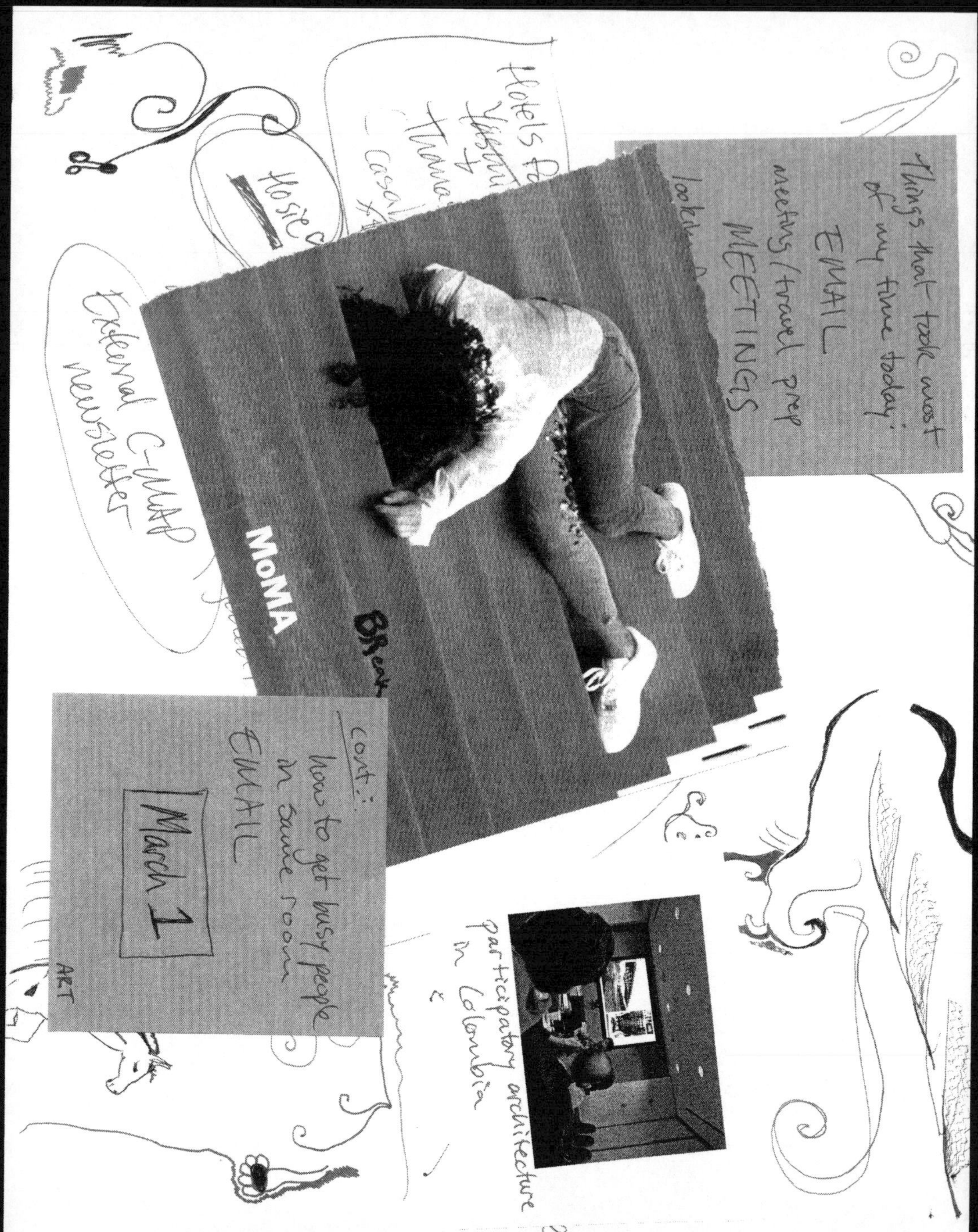
Things that took most of my time today:
EMAIL
meetings/travel prep
MEETINGS
External C-MAP newsletter
MoMA
cont.:
how to get busy people in same room
EMAIL
March 1
participatory architecture in Colombia

GALLERY VISIT on a Monday afternoon…

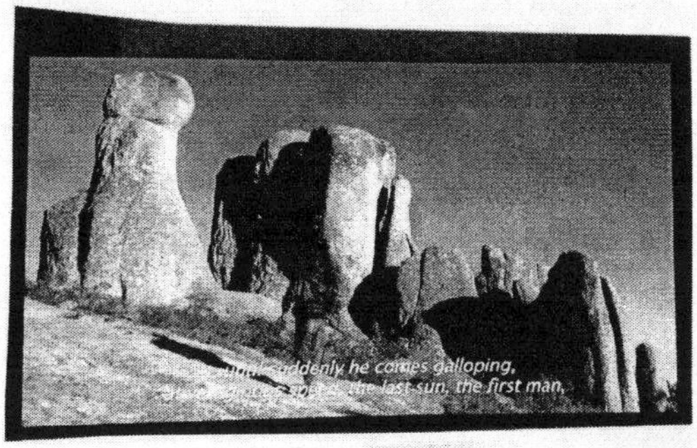

Antonin Artaud

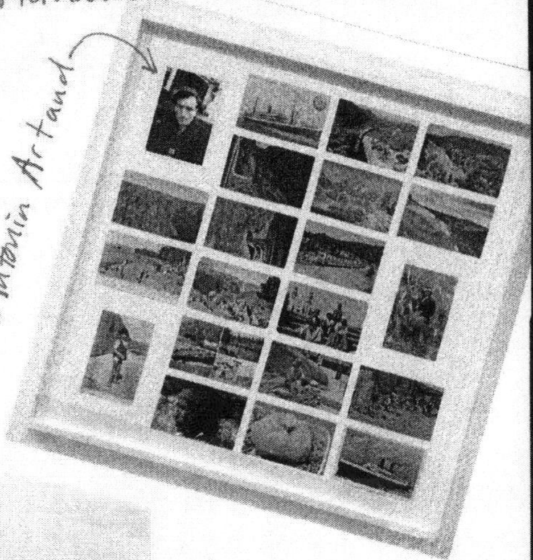

madness, Artaud, heroin addiction, the implacable Mexican desert, organs + straight jackets

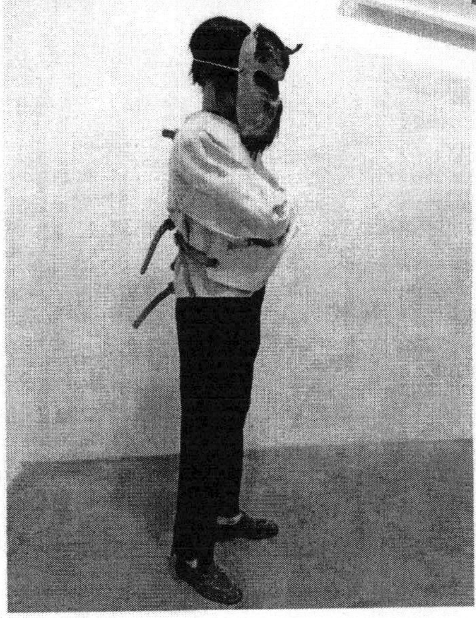

"Javier Téllez: To have done with the judgement of God" at Koenig + Clinton

//////////

~ My program at MoMA often organizes gallery or museum visits to see works of particular interest to the group - here Venezuelan artist Javier Tellez examines the personal history of Artaud and the contemporary reality of Northern Mexico in a new film. Encounters like this offer staff a chance to engage w/ new work, often creating new relationships + connections.

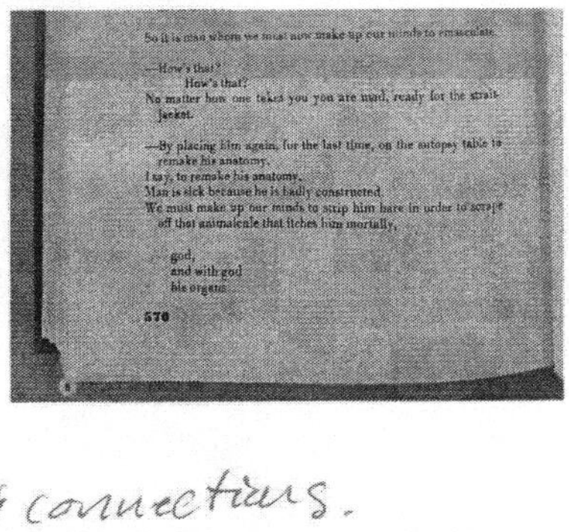
So it is man whom we must now make up our minds to emasculate.

—How's that?
How's that?
No matter how one takes you you are mad, ready for the strait-jacket.

—By placing him again, for the last time, on the autopsy table to remake his anatomy.
I say, to remake his anatomy.
Man is sick because he is badly constructed.
We must make up our minds to strip him bare in order to scrape off that animalcule that itches him mortally,

god,
and with god
his organs.

576

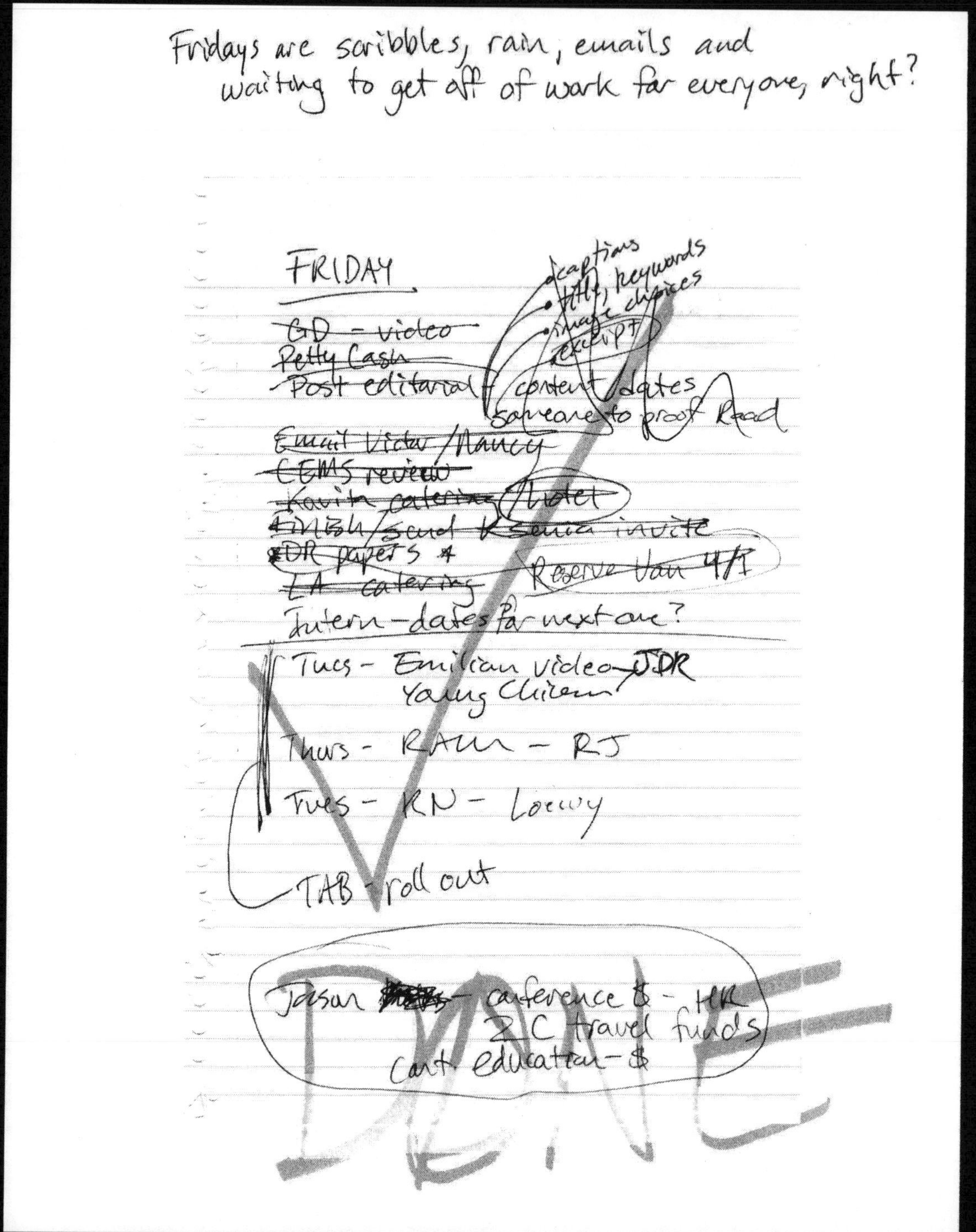

Fridays are scribbles, rain, emails and waiting to get off of work for everyone, right?

FRIDAY

GD - video
Petty Cash
Post editorial - content dates
captions
title, keywords
image choices
excerpt
someone to proof Read
Email Victor/Nancy
CEMS review
Kavita catering/Hotel
Finish/send K Senica invite
JDR papers $
LA catering
Reserve Van 4/7
Intern - dates for next one?
Tues - Emilian video - JDR
Young Citizens
Thurs - RAM - RJ
Tues - KN - Loewy
TAB - roll out
Jason - conference $ - HR
2C travel funds
cont. education - $
DONE

~~publish Forbes on Czech AG~~
~~do monthly Analytics~~
start Raqol →
Thursday ~ from the Archives

institutionalized institutional critique...

?

> The museum is a colossal mirror in which man contemplates himself, in short, in all his aspects, finds himself literally admirable and abandons himself to the ecstasy expressed in all the art journals.
> —Georges Bataille, *Encyclopaedia Acephalica*, 1929–30

Over the past decade, major museums in Cairo, Copenhagen, Detroit, Doha, Kuwait, London, New York, and other cities have installed or reinstalled their collections of Islamic art. The results have attracted bouquets and brickbats in equal measure. Some of these museums house collections whose origins lie in nineteenth- and early-twentieth-century intersections between antiquarianism, commercialism, and orientalism. Others, especially those in the Gulf, house collections of more recent vintage, whose acquisition over the past two decades has infused the market with a giddy frisson of excess seldom previously associated with Islamic art.[1]

This reinvestment of Islamic antiquities has been paralleled by the development of Middle Eastern franchises of museums such as the Guggenheim and the Louvre in Abu Dhabi, and the global emergence of an extensive array of galleries and museums dedicated to showcasing the modern and contemporary art of the Middle East. These range from small commercial galleries and private spaces in cities such as Beirut, Cairo, London, New York, and Ramallah to national institutions such as Doha's Mathaf: Arab Museum of Modern Art, whose opening in 2010 signaled the role of the Gulf region in the vanguard

of these developme… and foundations fo… and contemporary… East, Europe, and t… art is enjoying an o… and study (both in… global modernism… sorships, the writi… ment of curators t… Museum in Londo… New York.

These develop… ground of tumult… Middle East, from… through Israel's 2… the Arab Spring,… tatorship in Egyp… against a brutal… by the very petro… their cultural infr… political violence… sected, with dis… the Museum of… of Islamic art, w… nated outside t… entirely destroy… prize artifacts (f…

"Staging Traces of Histories Not Easily Disavowed" —Finbarr Barry Flood

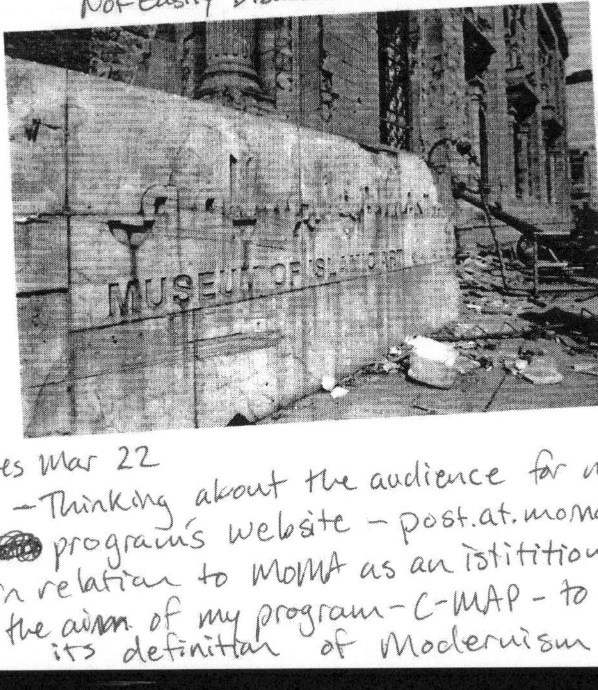

1 Damage to the Museum of Islamic Art, Cairo, after a bombing across the street on

Tues Mar 22
—Thinking about the audience for my program's website – post.at.moma.org – in relation to MoMA as an institution and the aim of my program – C-MAP – to expand its definition of Modernism

3/24/2016 IMG_8942.JPG

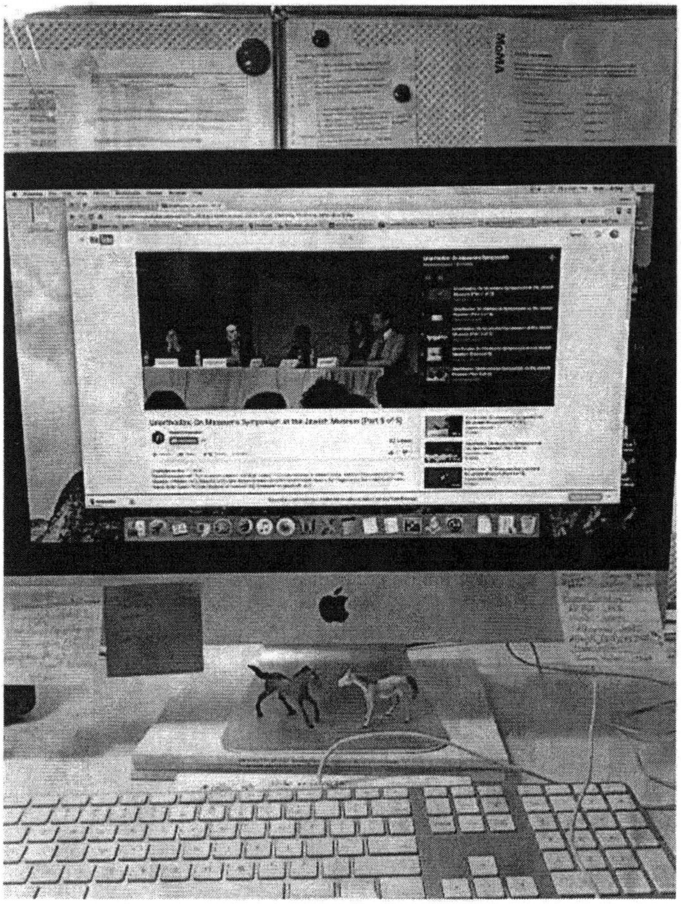

MoMA "the elephant in the room"
"ocean liner of a museum"

Its the end of a relatively quiet, meetingless's day and I'm having a meta-moment watching a video of a panel discussion to see how it discusses my program (C-MAP) and its about the changing structures of the art world + the museum.

So, watching a video on the role of the museum while journaling about my experience working in a museum.

https://mail.google.com/mail/u/2/#inbox/153aa94088c21fec?projector=1 1/1

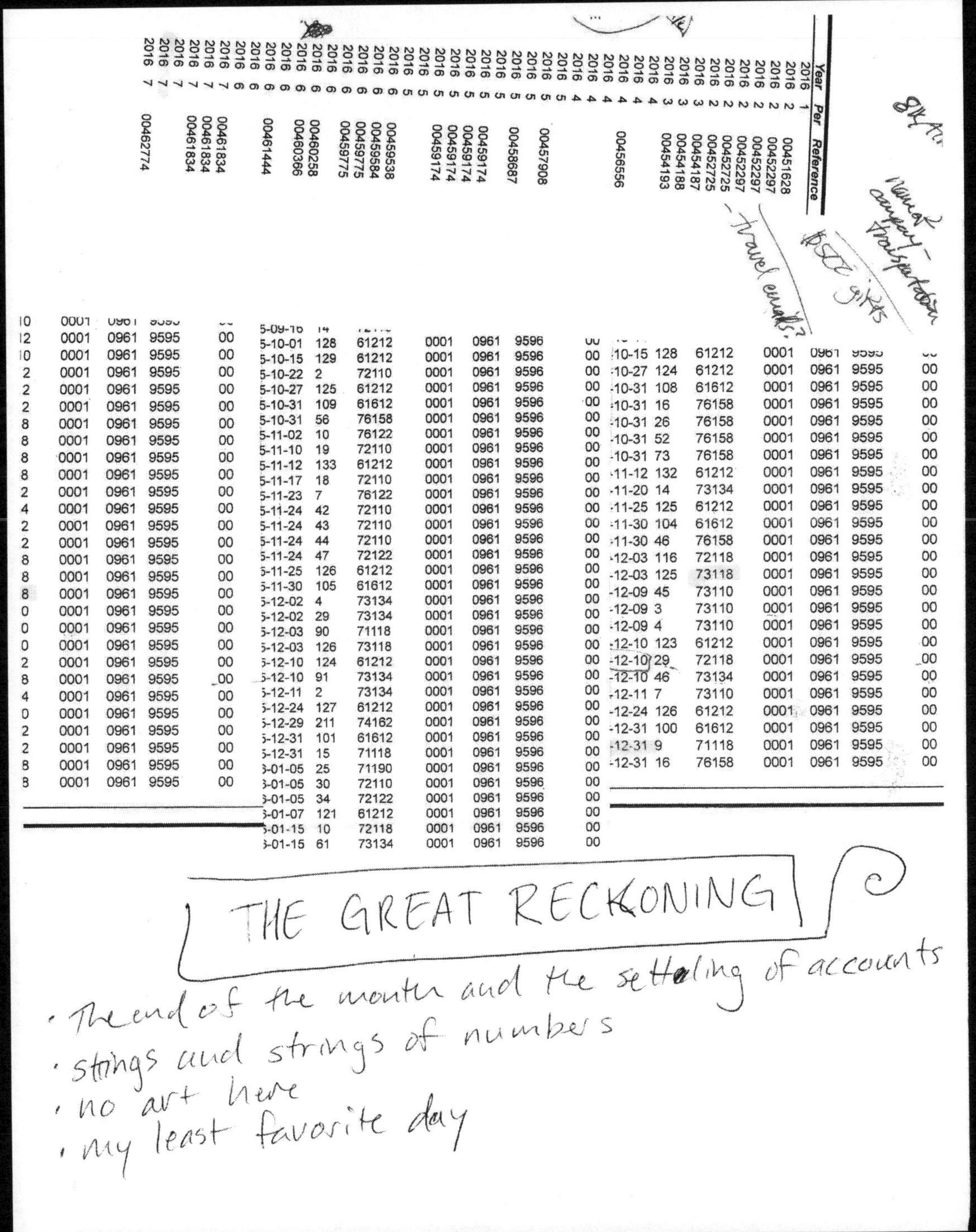
THE GREAT RECKONING
· The end of the month and the settling of accounts
· strings and strings of numbers
· no art here
· my least favorite day

April 1, 2016

In an effort to democratize and demystify the art world in New
engage in a week long journaling project.

We are interested in exploring the day to day of living with art. What is it li
City on a daily basis? What is it like to traverse the varied and expansive art ve
the form of a travelogue of the New York art scene or it might be more diaristic.
perspectives, approaches and mediums to convey this week long engagement.

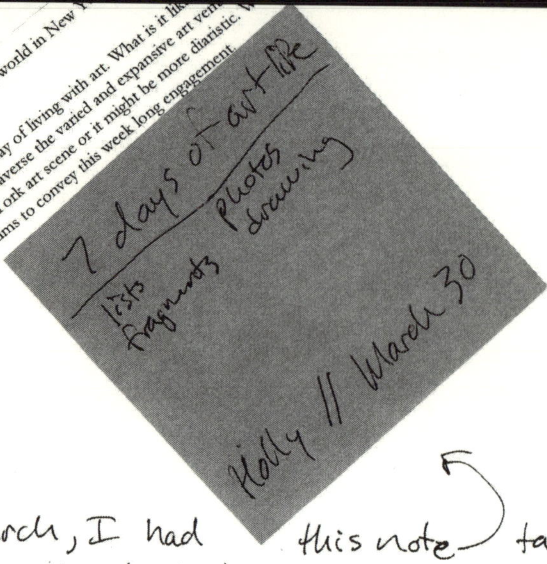

For the month of March, I had this note tagged up in my cubicle. I just started a new job at the Museum of Modern Art and consequently this idea of how I navigate the art world was very much on my mind, as well as the role of my program within the institution and in a broader context. Therefore, I thought it would be easy to describe seven days of my art life. Instead I find myself presenting a series of interrupted fragments. They are non-continuous scraps of daily life that felt significant to me. Perhaps it will be easier for you to interpret them.

Looking at them in retrospect, I see them as part of a larger picture, in which administering a program is the kind of office work that could take place anywhere, where the museum structure presents challenges as well as incredible access, and where art is typically an absent presence—recalled and referred to but rarely physically there.

—Linnea West

mary valverde

is an interdisciplinary artist, professor, and writer based in New York. Valverde teaches at Hunter, Brooklyn College, & Cooper Union School of Art and has lectured at institutions including Stanford University and Long Island University's MFA departments. Valverde is Commissioner (Sculptor seat), of the Art Commission / Public Design Commission of the City of New York, since 2015. She received her MFA at the University of Pennsylvania in 2012 and her BFA from the School of Visual Arts, NY in 1999.

Influence

Art asks questions

It obsesses and makes compulsive inquiries

It disrupts and invites examination

It amplifies the suppressed and illusive

It unpacks and tries to decipher qualities and patterns

It makes connections and you synthesize with it

It becomes your instrument

It amplifies your ideas

It influences

The opportunity to mentor is a great privilege, and as a professor I recognize the importance of my role to lead the minds of (young) impressionable people. I stand in a room as the authority and my job is to share and explain what I know and make it accessible to groups of people with varying capacities and exposures on the subject of art. My approach is very broad and often I feel like it is my job to make sure that all my students can enter the conversation on their strengths, be it academic, creative, experimental, methodical, critical or argumentative.

I tell my students that you are your own best resource. Your lived experiences are valuable because those experiences mark a specific perspective and vantage point from which to present ideas. You make choices and formulate value systems based on those experiences. Whether you put forth ideas, issues, positions, or intentionally reject, disagree, and abstain from ideas in your work, it is a position. You have made a choice.

BLOOD

My family was bigger than the standard nuclear family. The indigenous embrace of extended community as family was a quality that transcended migration. Your Tios and Tias were not always blood related and your cousins could be bestowed by close association or by who had a hand in their upbringing. In the late 60's and early 70's amidst the political tensions in the US came a surge of immigration to New York from Latin America as an effect of the growing disparity in many countries . My family was part of that movement north. One at a time they came out of desperation and stayed together in support of each other. They traveled across miles of water to save the families they left behind.

The lower east side of Manhattan was where most of my family settled in first. They later branched out to Harlem, the Bronx, Brooklyn, and Queens when they could afford to. Even so, growing up in the 70's & 80's still was very insular and we found ourselves frequently at each other's homes for birthdays, holidays and the occasional trip to Orchard or Rockaway Beach. My Tias were second mothers and my cousins were siblings. Today it is still the same.

LOVE

There were very specific values ingrained in my upbringing. Our system was unlike my peers, which effectively caused me to be a bit gullible and idealistic. The results of which are still unregrettably felt. In my family I saw love. Real love was generated daily through acts of uncompromised dedication. We could rely on each other. We knew that outside the safe space of our homes, the rest of the world did not operate that way. Despite this fact we lived with an unyielding optimism and embrace the belief that all we needed to succeed was the vision and structure, to worked in the right direction.Those were different times. Our parents were able to shield us from so much through a strict, traditional upbringing, heavily based in fear of wasteful distractions and possible failure. Catholic guilt worked.

My dad reminded us that he did not go to medical school as he had once dreamed of, instead he made sacrifices. In this country he was still able to make use of the high school diploma he received in Ecuador and the broken English he learned in New York City to offer us a life without similar sacrifices.

For a long time as a little girl, I saw my dad who stood 5'3" as the strongest man in the world because he seemed to always work so much. My father left the house at 6am and got home 12 hours later. Usually 6 days a week, and sometimes 7 when we needed something else at home. My mother lead the home base with seamless mastery. Traditional food from scratch, meant she was double-dutching from the kitchen, the laundry, our school, and babysitting her friend's children. Even though it always seemed like each of them spent their days in a nonstop hustle of daily tasks and small accomplishments, it felt good. I sometimes like to remember that time with a nostalgic eye. I pretend it was perfect and easy and that we were the rulers of our own world. With adult retrospect, I look back in awe of their resilience and strength and wished that I had been a more studious, and less rebellious child. I could have made it easier on them by not challenging almost every rule they made. Those very rules I fought later became the roots of my own family values. I pray every day that they know how indebted I am to them. I owe them all my success.

INFINITY

I adored my father as a little girl. It was not a regular love. I had an unconditionally passion for him and it always presented itself viscerally and emotionally. I am guessing I felt free to love him that way because he accepted my love without question as truth.

My parents turned on the lights and radio early in the morning to start the day. The radio static and loud commentary along with the smell of hot coffee and warm bread triggered my involuntary reaction of thumb sucking and a closed-eyed, slow shuffle to the kitchen table. I met my dad there while he chewed his food with closed eyes and slow breaths. My father always looked like he was charging up and praying at the same time. My very short legs climbed up on the only other chair in the tiny kitchen table and I settled in, head on the table and fingers still in my mouth. My mom never disturbed our ritual. It allowed her to focus on her own. She was too busy packing the home made lunch she made earlier that morning.

My father finished and put on his ski hat, jacket, and put his backpack on his shoulder. I always followed him to the door and the elevator where my mom lifted me up to the round elevator window so I could wave bye to him. I ran to my brother's bedroom which faced the front of the building. I climbed atop of the window sill and stuck my head out over the window guards to yell, "Bye, Papi!" He would look up at me and wave. I'd watch him until he disappeared behind the cars and trees that lined our block. He spent so much of his time away from us but, he always came back home, and made us whole.

SACRIFICE

My mom was the middle child. Like a true farm girl, she loved to ride horses. Her mother died very young and my mother was raised by her dad and spent many years in a school guided by nuns. Her older sister was the wild child and her little brother was the comedian of the family. My mother acted as the responsible one. She took the fall for all of their misbehaving and settled on a role of caretaker from a very young age.

One of my Tios bartered with some friends of his to help him pick my mom up from the airport on her arrival to New York. He convinced his friend that she was such sight to see, "a big fine, beauty". What my uncle didn't know was that in the months leading up to her arrival, my mother had gone through tremendous struggle. My mother had recently become a single mother of two. She was confronted with the inability to care for her children even with help from her family. She made the difficult choice to leave Ecuador and make the journey to the States without her children. My mother doesn't like to talk about it. I know why. As a single mother, I know well that feeling of desperation. If you ask her about the choice she had to make to leave my eldest brother and sister behind, she pauses and becomes very emotional. Speaking about that trauma and the effects it had on her children still make her cry. At the airport arrival area, my Tio's friend was clearly disappointed when my very thin mother walked towards them. My Tio found himself apologizing to him, and now wanted to make sure my mother was fed. It was a long while before my mom recuperated her weight. When she did the universe had my parents meet. They made a great team. My older siblings eventually made it to the States with their own children which brought solace to my mother.

SENSES

When I was really young I would spend time with one of my Tias. She had no children of her own but, that did not stop an ongoing joke about who's child I was because we looked so much alike. Tia was much younger than my mom and she would indulge my childish requests. Her apartment was in the same neighborhood as ours and sometimes we would sit and eat cookies or go to the park together. She would tell me stories about her pet squirrel and cat, her sisters in Ecuador, and the warm coastal sun she missed during the cold New York winters. Tia lived in a cozy studio apartment that had just enough room for her reams, tin of buttons, thread rolls and sewing machine. She taught me to sew buttons and make even stitches. She moved slowly and was modest with her voice. Tia seemed to be very sensitive to sound and taste and the textures of individual swatches of fabric she touched. Her gestures seemed highly selected as if she could feel them at a higher frequency than everyone else. I never understood how she kept herself so calm all the time. I was a shy child so, perhaps she enjoyed my silence. When we did talk it always felt like very thoughtful discussions on the specifics of random life occurrences. Her best stories were the scary ones about premonitions, deja vus, and ghosts. She told me to practice remembering my dreams and I became obsessively aware in them. I have found answers in my dreams from time to time.

SACRED DIAGRAMS

Every child is an artist. Every artist is sensitive to their world. This sensitivity causes us to obsess. We funnel our obsessions and sensitivities into actions, sometimes producing art. We draw, dance, play music, write, sing, or experiment. I have asked myself about this phenomenon. Why did the universe give us this ability and the urgency to use it? How do we explain this need to create connections and understand the world outside of our own existence? We continue to question and consider our time and our space in hopes to make discoveries. In science we look for proof to explain occurrences and anomalies. In art we proposed question that art understood without quantifiable answers.

Math is another love of mine. I don't know math, music and art to be separate. They are all visceral arts that can be described diagrammatically, and presented both physically and conceptually. Their qualities are not bound by the physical. Each of them can be experienced and presented in all dimensions. Also, I add love to my list of visceral arts.

peter frank

is an Associate editor for Fabrik Magazine and former Senior Curator at the Riverside (CA) Art Museum. He has served as Editor of *THEmagazine Los Angeles* and *Visions Art Quarterly* and as critic for *Angeleno* magazine and the *L.A. Weekly*. He contributes articles to numerous publications and has written many catalogues for one-person and group exhibitions. Frank has taught at many major universities including, Columbia University, Tyler School of Art, and UC Irvine, among others.

So here is a page representing a week in the life. The last week in January 2016, to be exact. The latter part of the week, especially, brims with gallery openings and similar events (that weekend normally sees a concentration of art fairs here in Los Angeles). I don't — I didn't — attend most of them, but I made sure I knew about them all so that I could determine which had to be attended, which were good ideas to attend, which I'd enjoy attending, which I could attend were I nearby at the right time, etc.

The information is all entered into my copy of the Museum of Modern Art's 2016 appointment calendar. I've been notating in MoMA datebooks — with very few years excepted — since my mother first gifted me one while I was still in high school.

lane cooper

received her MFA in painting from the University of Alabama as well as her MA in Art History. Cooper is a full time professor at the Cleveland Institute of Art.

CONTEXT

I live in an inner-ring suburb of Lakewood, Ohio. I teach at the Cleveland Institute of Art. I inhabit and am in love with my 1908 home that I bought cheap because it had been foreclosed on. My studio is two converted bedrooms. I sometimes use the basement as my woodshop. I would like to put a $100,000 into restoring the house and pimping out my studio but that seems unlikely in the short term. I am mostly a painter. I sometimes sell a piece here or there. I have been "in art" for so long I'm pretty sure I'm out of touch with other forms of reality.

As an artist I'm a member of the art world's version of the 99%. I am not a "star" - whatever that means — let's face it to be famous as an artist is like being the most important person at a lint collectors' convention. Art fame mostly means that other art folks know who you are. Personally I rankle when others cast aspersions on the intentions of art world luminati - "oh they're just in it for the fame, the money." Yes, well - good luck with that.

Whatever role one inhabits being an artist is a job in many ways like any other - you clock hours and hope to at least break even. For most of us it will never mean the kind of things that the larger culture might understand as success - but it is a profession that offers something more than work and survival. The ongoing practice of engaging a project destined for failure - the constantly reaching for what is out of reach - the looking - the thinking - the "after" conversations - the "before" conversations - the filling up and drawing down - provides a being here - a putting one in the moment - that I would not exchange for any other way of being. So here are my 7 Days .

MONDAY, MARCH 21

Wet kitty noses
sketchbook/journal -
what needs doing? - 3 more paintings before the show opens on April 1. Work on the 2 bigger ones and the 1 smaller. Leave those really big ones for after.

SCHOOL

meeting at noon - no time to shower - 2 hours in the studio before heading out. Mix the colors. How many colors - never enough variation in the value. Really that purple next to that green? Why don't I like cobalt blue? It looks dusty - hard.

Look for keys -what the hell did I do with my keys? Why can't I train myself to always but them in the same place? - head to school - sit through that meeting - rally thoughts - yes - what needs doing for the student spring show - who's doing it?

After meeting - 2 hours in the school's shared studio - working on the small one - repainting that gun that's too big.

CLASS

5 to 10 pm - students presenting on their work - I am trying to offer thoughtful, helpful insights - I am trying not to crush spirits - I am trying to be honest. "There is no try, only do." They are so afraid. I wish I could beam it into their heads - see it for what it is. Don't worry about how I or anyone else sees you or your work. You're ok. Just have a conversation like any other. Let it go. Go on. My mother used to say "Do the best that you can. Pat your foot and then go on."

Rain check on the after class drink.

HOME TO STUDIO

an hour to paint - microwave that Lean Cuisine Butternut Ravioli - glass of Cabernet. Bed.

TUESDAY, MARCH 22

Fur balls waft by - the house needs cleaning. Wash the disgusting dishes; terrify the cats with the vacuum. 2 hours in the studio before school. I'm constantly picking fur off of tape. Is it a good idea to put glitter on that? People are going to think this is stupid. Maybe I should ditch that little glitter painting. I should try to finish 4 before April 1. Can I really finish 4? That means starting a new one. Another woman with a gun? People are going to think I have issues. It's obvious though - it's over the top. It's clearly noir gunplay not real - trust people more.

Where are my keys? - I should take a shower - I'll take one tonight - I'll go run at the gym after class. I'm libel to have a blood clot from sitting still so long.

CLASS

A different group of students - this time presenting on long dead artists. Who, what, when and where. No one has a thesis - oh well. It's entertaining and they at least have enthusiasm for their subjects.

GYM

Thin young women in Uggs and puff jackets - older women who look like me - please don't look at me - really this is where you have to stand? Running is like painting. Constantly the conversation inside - how far? How fast? What is that pain? Should I stop? Am I winded? No, I can go another mile.

HOME

Avocado on a salad - glass of cabernet - I should be painting. I shouldn't have gone to the gym. Set the alarm for 6:30 am - I will need to leave the house tomorrow by 7:45 to get to school on time.

WEDNESDAY, MARCH 23

Alarm - kitties - fur on all my clothes - what to wear? Shower. No time to dry hair. Will I ever learn to get dressed any faster? The paint covered hoodie and the too short jeans. Old running shoes as footwear. Gawd that midriff spread is killing me.

SCHOOL

I'm teaching Foundation Drawing - I just want to sit and draw with you. Can't you learn just by me drawing next to you? Is there some way I can make real work in this class? "Sorry the head on that figure is too big. Think about proportions. Look at the material - what qualities does the material have?"

Artist talk at lunch - a sandwich. I love listening to other artists but I'm also thinking about what I need to be doing. I need to be painting. The gallery for the show is big and I really need to make some more pieces.

Back to Foundation Drawing. Reset the room. Tonight is open studios. We paint in open studios - anyone in the school can paint with us. Tony - my colleague - plays some mad tunes. I paint a woman with a gun. Really - green and brown? I keep tinkering tinkering with what I'm painting. I look at the photo and then back at my painting - every comparison reveals the wambly nature of my image. I wish I could be like Alice Neel - all character and fearlessness. I don't leave until almost 11 pm.

I stop by the grocery. I'm almost out of cat food. Enough to last until the weekend.

HOME

Glass of cabernet and bed.

THURSDAY, MARCH 24

Two hours in the studio before school. I bite the bullet and start the new one, a woman with flowers instead of a gun.

Lunch time meetings you are sucking my soul.
Afternoon - I should be reading papers but I am talking about art and artists with Karl and Erin.

CLASS

Earnest young people talking about long dead artists. How will you survive if you don't learn to speak loud enough to be heard? I know you're afraid. We're all afraid. Don't be afraid. We're just people and what's the worst?

HOME—STUDIO

I get lost in making the painting. Right now all I want to do is make tiny paintings and get lost. I'm listening to Sherlock shows I've watched a thousand times. I finish around midnight. I microwave Lean Cuisine. Cabernet.

FRIDAY, MARCH 25

Ping - a text - "Happy Birthday!" Crap — it's my birthday. 2 hours in the studio before Paddy Johnson's talk. Audible books — Radiant.

Paddy Johnson's talk - I think I'm in love. "You're coming to dinner right?" "I'm coming. Text me where and I'll meet you. I have a meeting after the talk." I leave during the questions. Just enough time to make my therapy appointment.

THERAPY

Yes I'm still coming to terms with the death of my sister last year. My only sibling and our parents are both gone. No - I don't think I'll ever come to terms but yes - I'm doing well right now. Things are going well - I'm making work that I like. (Honestly I only truly feel ok when I'm making work.)

HOME - SHOWER

Do I own anything nice? The phone rings. Do I have time - it's my beautiful niece Kaylee - I have time. "You're too sweet. No I haven't had time to check the mail." The box on the porch - chocolate, chocolate - chocolate for days. Cards and sweet notes. Texts with cake emojis.

DINNER

For once in my life I'm on time. Colleagues and friends with Paddy Johnson at the center and Turkish food on the table. "Sure, I'll have a mojito." On the edge of the conversation but luckily more than enough good folks to chat with - these are the perks people. Baklava with candles and singing and Barry picking up my check. I feel like Sally Field ("You really, really like me!")

Walk across the street to see Elmi's show. Wow - nice. The abstract work looks good. Congratulations!

HOME

Try to go to sleep.

SATURDAY, MARCH 26

In the studio - all day. Coffee first. Audible books. I'm going bankrupt on Audible books. Paint. Mix. Paint. Paint. Ugh - I need to go to the store.

Outside, as I'm leaving, Alice tells me her husband has cancer but it will be ok. (Please let it be ok.)

What do I need: masking tape, Thalo blue green shade, white - brushes. $20 for tape. $65 for paint. I need to pay bills. I'll look at that after the opening. My money is ok for once and maybe I'll sell something.

SUNDAY, MARCH 27

In the studio. All day. Paint. What color? Always what color? Why can't I get that right? Really that edge? It's blobby - it looks like a mess. The small one - I think that works. The blue is kicking but the green is puke. Will I get finished with that big one in time?

peter fankhauser

received his MFA at CUNY-City College in 2012 and has shown at independent and alternative spaces throughout New York City, including Judson Memorial Church, The Silent Barn, and TEMP Art Space. He lives and works in Omaha, Nebraska.

This is a love letter.

The much derided second person that inevitably asks you to consider the you I'm referring to is actually a me.

Just use your imagination.

You go to that opening and see that guy and mention the venerable institution for which you've tattered the seams running along "mid-life" and say things like "cultural collateral, cross disciplinary, politics of spectatorship" while lamenting trustee driven exhibition programming in a market that cycles around town heedlessly without crashing.

What happens when you make work for no one, rattling around alone in the dark? Secrets and hidden practices of anti-social art--no press, no documentation, no YouTube, no Vimeo, no web presence, no to language, no to writing and no to this?

And what about language? Can it amount to anything more than a life of things that were said too soon or not at all? Little remorses that constitute living; a language of regrets and "I really do love you's."

When you're 64 and dying of cancerous infestations or from coating your liver with cheap opening wine and Texas-sized margaritas at the after party, you walk into the water with pockets full of stones and hope there's someone to watch and completely understand. There. That's what it means to live with language. The meaning is losing. Everything else is courtesy.

You realize mechanically clopping through Chelsea on a Thursday, LES the day after, Bushwick the day after that, the universe is self-employed and feelings are fickle. They ebb and flow and you hope one day for reciprocal altitudes, but in the end, all you do is prepare for drought. Weather the changes.

After all, self-image is reflexive. You're seeing the sky while looking into the ocean. "Who you are" is a mirror that reflects a composite persona of assumed traits attributed to you by "who you aren't."

And you come to the conclusion the promise of a happy life slipped (slipped is sadder) along the fault lines of fragmented experience and compartmentalized disappointments that realign now and then to announce "I am not what you want."

You had blue chip dreams too. Or maybe a trust fund. You planned to win the lottery and live in a New York City hotel. That was enough--falling into privilege through circumstance. Isn't that living?

But instead you join the ranks of adjuncts and "working" artists to stack yourself willingly on the lowest rung of the ladder to compete.

Can you compete though? That question makes yours a man's world, accelerating at a man's pace.

Here is acceleration: on an episode of "Felicity," doe-eyed dreamboat Noel discusses his GF's new PC. It's cable ready, already outfitted (to paraphrase), when cable modems become available. Thanks 2000.

And so you think a little more about commodity culture and creative culture as indistinguishable not-so-reluctant evils and try not to be heartbroken all the time.

You decide it's time to go and adjust to the disappointment of packing away the last ten years in three medium Uline boxes with shipping labels that read your parents' Omaha address back to you.

You hop on a plane, distractedly asking internal questions about Bulimics with no gag reflex to avoid wondering whether you've jumped the gun.

Can erasure happen in jest?

Then your feet are planted, grounded again but how? And by which sun in which sky are you now oriented? Is that space--that wheeling space out front--horizon or sea? And was it inscribed onto this new location or were you in a railroad river town pulled under by the current all along? Shenandoah, Muddy Mo; Dickensian in a way (Emily, sorry Charles).

Transplanted and transient, you move through these stages of negative freedom. No fixed space, no market forces or elevator pitches. You stay fluid and I will too.

seph rodney

PhD, is a staff writer for *Hyperallergic* and occasionally writes for other publications. He created a radio show in London called *The Thread*, broadcast on Resonance FM from 2008 to 2011. He was featured in the Favorite Poem Project. Seph was born in Jamaica and lives in the South Bronx.

This past week every night I've resisted the urge to give up and go to sleep. I couldn't afford to. I have an editing job from a friend who has a small publishing house. She knows I'm a good and conscientious editor, but she's one of the few who know this. So, I can't turn down work. Three of the last seven days I've been working until midnight. One night I stopped at 12.45 am. The book I'm editing is a history on a particular nation's march toward modernism from the turn of the twentieth century. I don't want to give more away because the book is not written well, and if I bad mouth it, doing so may come back to haunt me. I sit and edit. On some pages there are so many things wrong I get angry. I wish that the writer had a better knowledge of English. I wish the translator didn't sound like her second cousin who is doing an English correspondence course after visiting Cleveland once for four days several years ago. Too many repeated clichés. Too many definitive articles. Too vague.

I'm in debt. I owe more money than I feel I want to admit. I can talk about the debt other than the education loans. I owe about $5,000 just on credit cards, plus about $7,000 more to friends. I found out yesterday that I have worked enough hours on this book to shed over $2,000.

In between chapters, my legs on a rolling, leather chair, my seat on my couch, a cup of mint tea, or a glass of gin with ice, I listen to James McMorrow singing. Each song sounds like a prayer, like something we would say to each other only in the deepest darks after sex, or after a scorching heart-to-heart conversation where we admitted things we didn't know were there to admit.

On a break, I go to Goodwill to drop off an old sweater I bought when I was in London and never felt comfortable, the slippers my ex-girlfriend wore around the apartment when she was visiting from the UK, a pair of trousers that don't fit anymore. I go the market to buy food. I buy a bottle of gin. I mail the rent check. I then come back home, go online and find that I have overspent the last few days. This means that I won't have enough to cover the rent check I mailed yesterday. On Saturday, I had deposited a check I just received for the catalog essay I'd written for a show of artists doing para-fictional work to open this month in North Carolina. It's not cleared yet, so I have $34.75 available when I go shopping for food. I transfer money from an account that belongs to my mother, knowing that I can put the money back in a few days when I get paid by my writing jobs, either Hyperallergic or the Harlem meet-up that is just starting up.

Luckily, in February I earn more for the editing project than the debt I had to pay off, so I will get $384.00 through Paypal today. I haven't earned more than $20,000 for the past ten years since I quit my job at Armani and moved to London to work on getting a PhD in museum studies. One year it was about $13K. Each year until I finished the PhD last year, I've told myself it will get better. This is the first year it looks like it may.

Last Wednesday, when I started to keep a record of my days, I went to the offices of Hyperallergic to work with them for the day. I'm not on staff. I'm only a contributor, but the boss seems to want me to be on staff, but either does not have the money or is unsure that I'm right for them, or thinks that I don't work fast enough. I suspect it's really a combination of the money issue and the question of how I will fit in—not that I won't. Rather the question is how. I'm contemplative. I like rigorous argumentation. There is a place for this on the blog, but most everything else is faster, reporting on what's happening now. I think about what has happened and what it means and that's an uphill climb because I have to pick my way over my own cluttered brain to get to sky.

Almost everyday I write. I write reviews. I write think pieces. I write about museums and what they are doing. I end the day at Hyperallergic around 4.30 and go home. I do my exercises when I'm home and changed. I sleep for two hours, get up and get back to editing. The day ends at 12.45. I eat. I stay up reading twitter and then crawl towards sleep, catch up with it and wrestle it to the ground.

Thursday I wake late. I do coffee, exercises and breakfast. Then I sit and edit. I hate this text more every goddamn day. I go to an opening in Chelsea. The gallery owner might one day be a friend. She is friendly to me. I might write about this show. The owner certainly wants me to, and the artist would like the press. I'm trying to learn how to like people even when what I do benefits them and threatens to make our relationship transactional.

Friday is the same as before. This time I have two openings to go to. The first is full of work of punk, raunchy, distressed watercolors of punk, raunchy, tatted-up women, posing for the artist, eating each other out, and generally looking autonomous, sexy and edgy. The artist gives me a nod when I walk in. I don't know him, so I don't go over to say hello. I walk the show and walk out. The second opening is one where I meet a friend I'm starting to like very much, Jeannie. She's fun and not afraid of me though she's a white woman and I'm a black man. I greet others I've met before. The work is about femininity and I think I want to write about it, because it's meaningful and I think I have something to say about it. My friend Nile shows up and we leave when it's time to go and get a drink before heading home to the text with its myriad inconsistencies and misspellings and awkward phrasing.

Saturday I go to Brooklyn to interview a woman who runs a small arts organization we want to talk about in an article for Hyperallergic. We meet and it's a good conversation. I take lots of notes. On the way home I buy some fish, parrot and kingfish. I have nothing like this selection in my neighborhood. After stopping off at Costco to get food for the week, it's more editing tonight. I was supposed to do some writing this weekend, but can't. Don't have the time.

Sunday I go to the gym to workout—my weekly session. I love working out, not so much for what I feel at the time, which is mostly just concentrated. But I love how I feel after: like I've done something good for myself and only for me, taking back some of the strength and presence stolen from hours sitting in a chair facing a computer. I'm grateful. I come home and edit. I go to sleep at 3.30 am

I wake up and know I have to do laundry, wash my hair, and get editing and writing done. I do three of these. Then I do some writing work for a huge design firm who hired me to work on a particular project involving artists and an enormous showcase as a global conference. The writing is not hard. I just have to set time aside and I do it. I do it gladly because they pay me real money and allow me to take my time finding things to write about for Hyperallergic. Only five chapters left to go after the editing marathon tonight.

Tuesday I meet with my therapist. We talk about me feeling that I don't have a right to desire the kind of woman I physically desire: tall, voluptuous, full lips, and dark hair. I know it's okay to want a keen intellect and an endlessly curious mind and an emotional sensibility that is keyed to recognizing injustice, but the physical part—that's what I feel is somehow not permitted, or marks me as superficial. I come home and check my bank balance, map out the rest of the week. I edit until I'm exhausted. I meet a friend for drinks. Two hours. I can spare these. I come home and cook dinner. I eat and write and edit.

I've been thinking a lot this week about a piece of writing I read about two weeks ago—a sports report. The writer, whose name I can't recall, talks about Stephen Curry, the point guard phenomenon for the Golden State Warriors who this season is astonishing watchers and analysts of the game. It's the first time in my lifetime we've seen a shooting guard as skilled and smart as Steph Curry—and he's small by comparison with most of the other men on the court. The writer says that everyone watches him because he performs small magic. Running up against men who tower over him, he "throws the ball over a mountain and into a cup." That stays with me because it's a simple but intensely effective image. I want that kind of insight in my language. Tomorrow I'm going to go to work to find it.

david raymond

is an artist, art collector, filmmaker, curator and supporter of the arts. He has been an internationally recognized collector of contemporary and vintage photographic works for over twenty years. David was a founding board member of Performa, which produces New York's performance art biennial and he is on the advisory board for the Manuel Alvarez Bravo Foundation. In May 2016, he co-curated the exhibition *Love, Devotion and Surrender* with Randy Shull in Asheville and is hoping to start a contemporary art center there.

Love, Devotion and Surrender preparations:

I moved to the mountains of North Carolina, close to Asheville in September 2012. I was pleasantly surprised by the depth of culture that exists here. It's a place with a very strong music scene, craft scene and food scene. Although there are quite a few makers that have taken up residence in the region, I was surprised by how little contemporary art gets shown. Apart from a few spaces and curators, not much was happening. I was fortunate to meet with a bunch of individuals that were thinking like me: Let's get something moving here. Two of them, Randy Shull and Hedy Fischer, a couple with deep roots in the art community here and myself decided to see if a contemporary art space could work here. We thought that a good beginning would be to do a show of video work and see the response.

Our hope is to show the community the power of contemporary art and use this as a springboard for other projects.

Randy and I decided to do a video show for our first show. He and Hedy, own a perfect space to do it in; 9,000 square feet with 30 foot ceilings. Firstly, we could borrow pieces without worrying about loss or damage as works could be sent via the internet or viewing copies could be sent. This was important as we were not curating the show at an "institution" or "gallery". The space does not have climate control and security is minimal for the moment. So, we chose some works from our collections and reached out to artists and dealers that we know with specific pieces in mind. The show, Love, Devotion and Surrender came out of this. The title of the show was borrowed from the 1973 recording by Carlos Santana and John McLaughlin, a tribute to John Coltrane. Yet here, the central themes splinter to merge the cinematic with sensuality, social media with spirituality, spectacle with alternative realities. The artists include: Petra Cortright (US), Clayton Cubitt (US), Jen DeNike (US), Nathalie Djurberg and Hans Berg (Sweden), Rafael Lozano Hemmer (Mexico), Jesper Just (Denmark), Shana Hoehn (US), Tony Oursler (US), and Bill Viola (US).

We are also fortunate that David J. Brown, a friend and colleague was available to assist us in putting our visceral selection into a cohesive context and wrote some amazing text to accompany them.

APRIL 22

Posted LDS announcement on Facebook

APRIL 24

Sent email with LDS announcement to my personal list

APRIL 25

Started receiving lots of positive feedback regarding the show from my email and Facebook list.

Looked for clear labels at Staples for wall labels. Couldn't find what I wanted. Had to order them on Amazon.

Shot some images for my Alice in Wanderland series with Emily, my partner and our daughter Paloma. It was the first time that Paloma has been in any of the images that we have shot. We now have a big Alice and little Alice!

MAY 4

Started to finalize installation of works. One DVD player is not working. Ordered another.

MAY 6

Intro labels and thank you list go up.

Further tweaking of works

Final wall installed

MAY 7

Installed two more works. Switched out the DVD player that was not working. Figured out the placement of 3 works that will be installed next to each other.

Reconfigured the placement of a couple of pieces.

MAY 9

Deciding on two possibilities for the display of the 3 part piece
Wine for opening delivered

A neighboring space offered to serve cocktails before our opening at our space.

Contacted by the entertainment writer from the Asheville Citizen Times to do a piece on the show.

Starting prepping for a video shoot for a documentary that I am working on that will take place on the 12th.

MAY 10

Got the 3 part piece installed. It looks amazing!! We also installed a piece that we have created a floating room for. A couple of final tweaks (getting the sound set up for a projected piece and final positioning of a smaller iPhone video piece) and we are ready to go for the Friday opening.

MAY 11

Finalizing the installation this evening. Wanted to wait for the sun to go down to see how the videos all translate in the space. There is also the question of sound spilling over from each piece that we need to address. Everything looks incredible except for a sound issue with a projected piece. Need to figure it out and fix it. Word is getting out about the show. We expect a good crowd for the opening. Randy has commissioned a local ceramic artist to make an edition of plates with Love, Devotion & Surrender on them to give to the first 100 people that attend to commemorate the event.

MAY 12

Spent part of the morning diagnosing and figuring out solutions for the audio issue. We'll be addressing it tomorrow early afternoon.

MAY 13

The show opened today. David Brown came up with a solution for the audio. It looks and sounds amazing. We decided to have people wait outside until about 30 were there. We served wine and a light meal. People used the plates that Randy commissioned and were told that they could take them home. Randy smashed a few to "launch" the space and open the show. We gave a brief talk with David Brown and then let everyone in. The space was silent, except for the sound of the artworks. People spent lots of time with the pieces. The amount of happiness and effusiveness was palpable. A few people came up to me and thanked me for moving here! Nothing like this had been organized in this region before. We set a new level and I hope that we can continue to do more and inspire others to. We did not leave the space until midnight. Not bad for a spot in the Appalachians!

daria hollowell

is an docent, adjunct teacher at the Timken Museum of Art in Balboa Park in San Diego.

Context

As a docent-in-training at the Timken Museum of Art in San Diego, last week was very rich. It started with the usual Monday two hour morning session at the museum in which the directors of the education program have both new and old sets of docents participating. For several sessions we have concentrated on the Timken's Russian Icon collection and learned so much about how it was collected, why the comparative rarity of Russian icons in western hands, and the context and significance of icons in the Orthodox Christian traditions of the East. A fascinating journey!

In addition, due to docent status, we have the privileged to access special lectures and tours, plus listen to lecturers who address either the Timken docents or members and docents of the San Diego Museum of Art. This week we had three such special lectures that were in that category:

On Wednesday, Dr. Katherine A. Schwab of Fairfield University lectured about combining archeology and artistic skill to recover figural compositions of the ninety-two metopes of the Parthenon in Athens. Her work is intended to reveal the "Invisible Parthenon" underneath the destruction of time, war and sabotage. Earlier, Dr. Marina Belozerskaya, Art Historian at UCLA, had lectured on how that damage had occurred.

On Thursday, once again, we docents were treated to a special tour of the current "Brueghel to Canaletto" exhibit in the SDMA, featuring Dutch still life paintings and views so representative of the Baroque age.

Friday closed the week with an invitation from the Docent Manager at the SDMA, to attend the SDMA lecture "The Journey of Buddhism from India to the Far East: A Story of Art and Religion." The speaker was Suzanne Cahill from UCSD.

So, art, its history, techniques and appeal were front and center in this south-west corner of the United States!

nancy lippe

received her BA in Human Biology from Stanford University and her Doctorate in Education from Fielding Graduate University. She currently lives and works in Colorado for the nonprofit organization Umbrella Arts and serves on several non-profit boards. Lippe is also an educator at Tufts University and UMass Lowell.

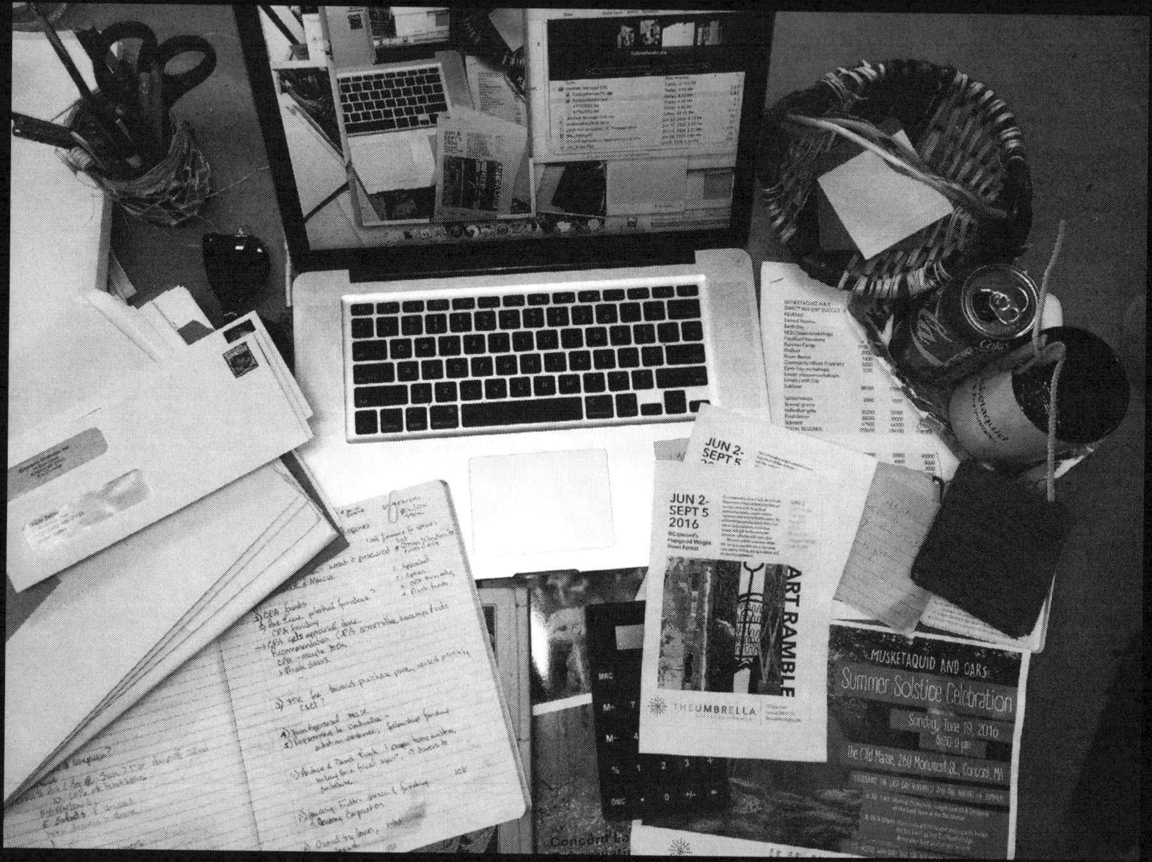
JUN 2-
SEPT 5
2016
ART RAMBLE
THEUMBRELLA
MUSKETAQUID AND OARS
Summer Solstice Celebration
Sunday, June 19, 2016

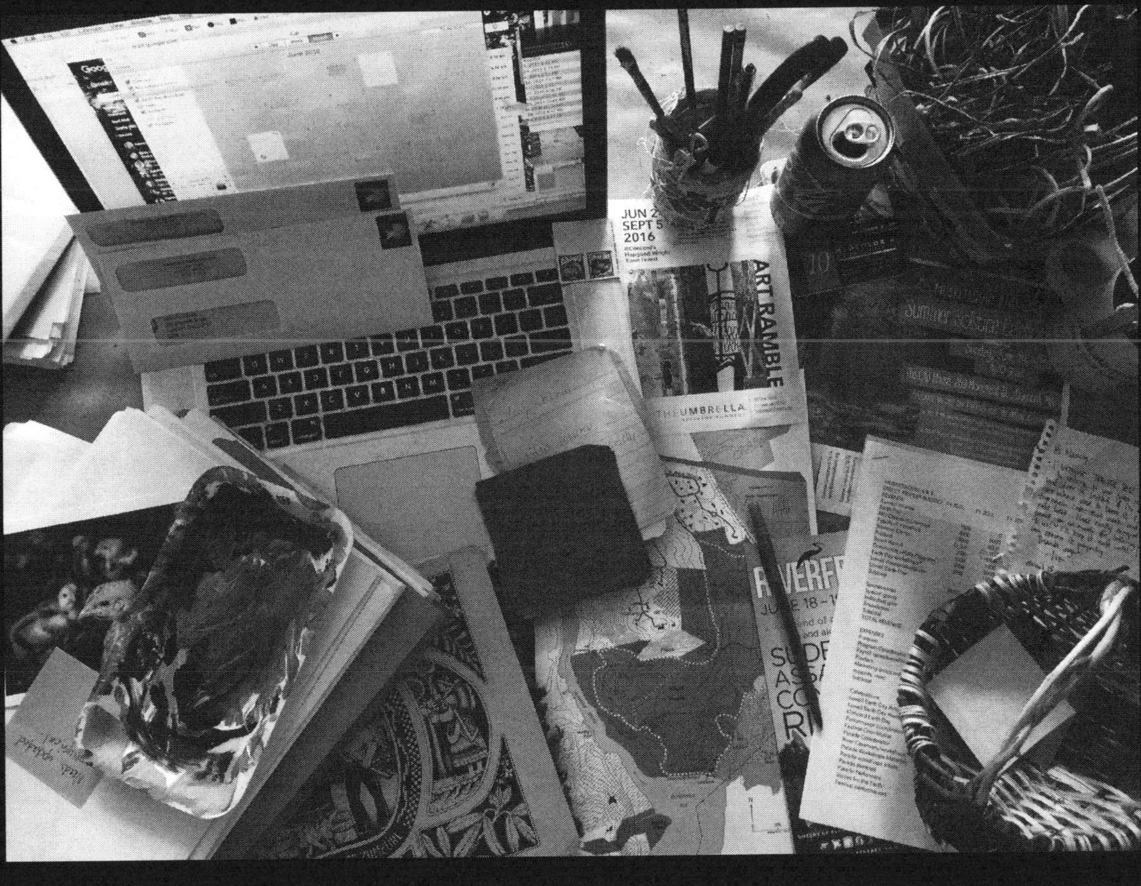
2016
ART RAMBLE
THEUMBRELLA

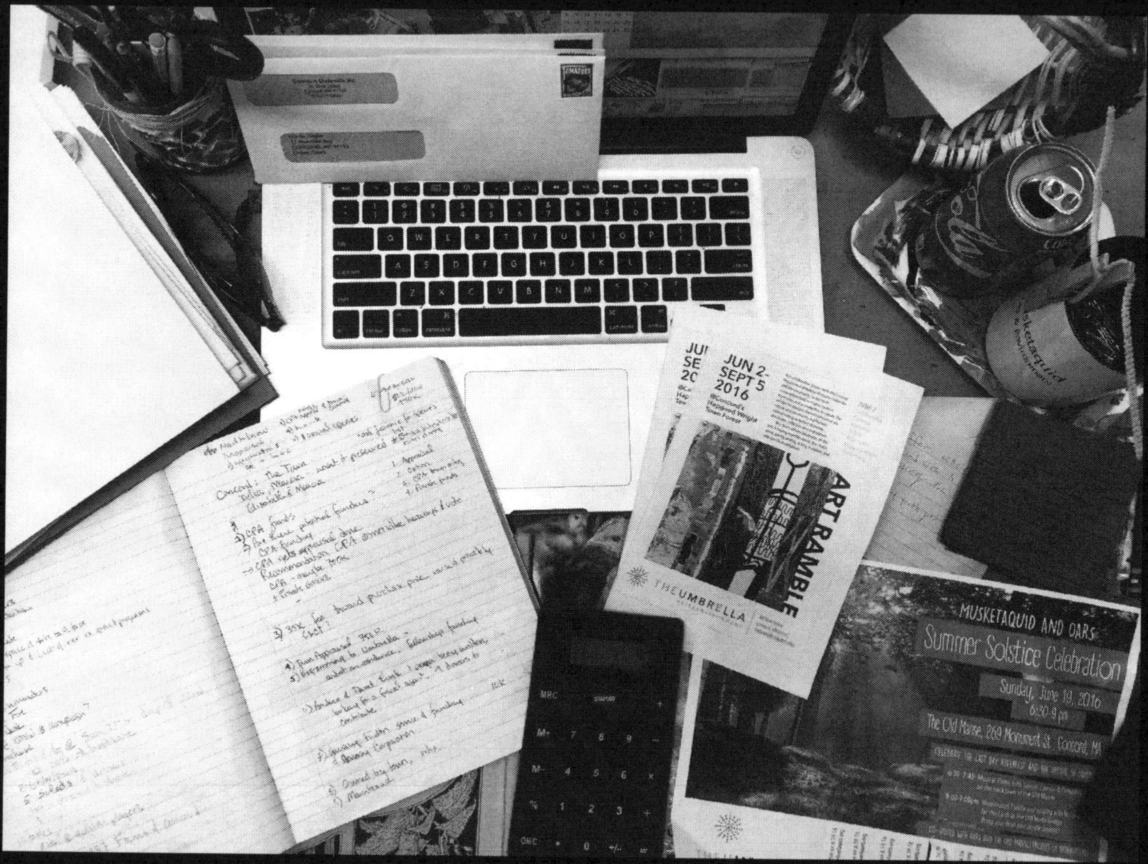
JUN 2-
SEPT 5
2016
ART RAMBLE
THEUMBRELLA
MUSKETAQUID AND OARS
Summer Solstice Celebration
Sunday, June 19, 2016
6:30-9 pm
The Old Manse, 269 Monument St., Concord, MA

natacha voliakovsky

(Buenos Aires, 1988) is a visual and performance artist. She's been selected to participate in prestigious educational programs around the world, including *EMERGENYC* at the Hemispheric Institute for Performance and Politics (NYU, 2019) and the intensive workshop in performance art at Venice International Performance Art Week (2018). Her work revolves around the concept of culture as a humanizing system and has created the Voliakovsky Performance Method, a series of training techniques for performance art. The artist's aim is to share the techniques she herself uses to prepare body and mind before carrying out a performance piece.

1

I coexist with fragments of my fat, vomit and flesh. The place I work in is also where I live, in Buenos Aires. I keep frozen fat extracted from my knees in my freezer, next to food and ice. Sculptures made of distilled fat on pedestals. Remains of vomit dried up on the walls. They're all works of art. I like to think that an already transformed part of me is all around. It feels like multiplying. Sometimes the smell of human decay is really strong, but I'm used to it.

2

Many Skype calls with mixed schedules that end up nowhere. Meetings for projects that will probably never happen. I write a huge amount of emails using an institutional language that doesn't feel like me.

I drink mate. The girls come to work. I put make up on and change clothes according to what event I'm attending, in order to look like "a female artist of my age". I have endless meetings with real people who come to the studio. We drink coffee, whiskey, we have dinner. Hours go by, we go to openings, restaurants; different places, different looks. Most of the meetings don't go anywhere, I have to keep working and looking good either way.

3

I train my body, my tool. I breathe, keep the air in, move in circles. I sit down and look at what surrounds me. I reflect on my next performance in order to design the right training for it. I figure it out during one of my 8 daily subway trips. I spread my legs and reclaim my territory: it's the everyday battle for public space. I'm screaming on the inside, my way of being present isn't a happy one. I try to be happy socially. It doesn't matter what happens on the way, I get out of the subway and arrive with my red lips and my hypocritical smile of self-improvement.

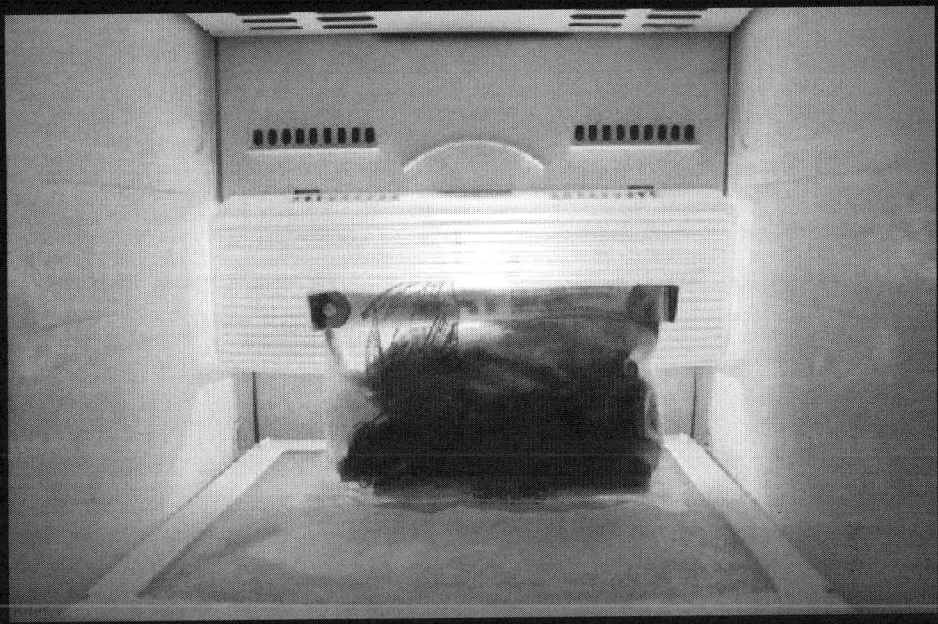

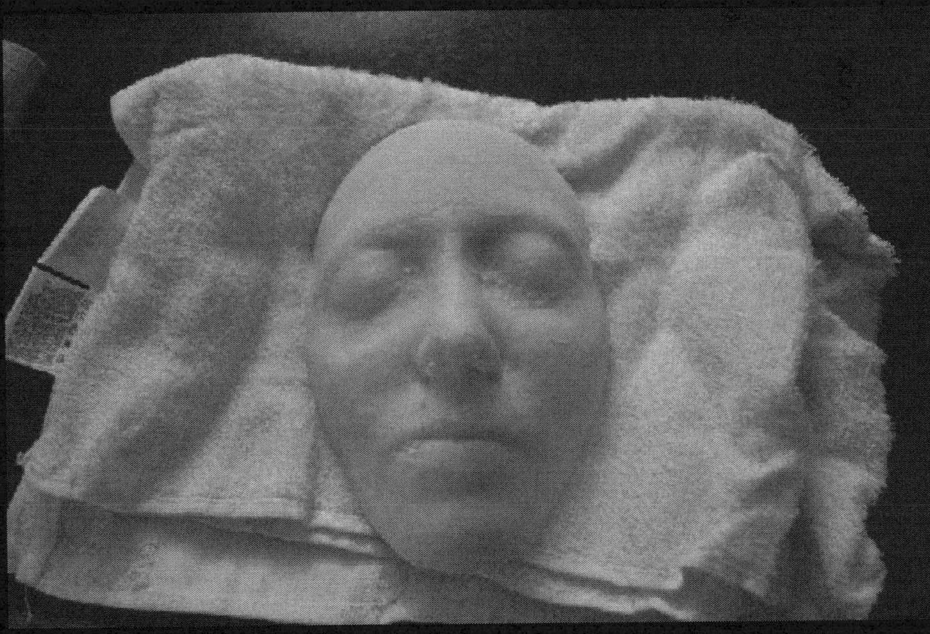

4

A film crew comes to my studio to shoot a documentary about my work. They've been filming for 5 hours, we don't know when it's going to end. It's distressing and amusing at the same time. Discussions follow, we analyze the work together. I feel it's the right moment to reflect on my work so I'm open to a debate with the crew. As if we were all part of the same thing and yes, we are.

5

Fat distillation. The place is flooded with a strong stench. We're all wearing chemical masks. Time is running, I have to move fast. Working with an organic substance is different than everyday materials. The mold is ready, so is the fridge, waiting to receive the distillation. Everything is recorded and photographed. At the end of the day I sit down and write the events. It happens differently every time. Then gallerists come and tell me I have to do more commercial work, that this is difficult to sell.

6

I'm going to the clinic today. I'm recording a surgery on my scalp, with local anesthesia, that will modify the appearance of my gaze. It doesn't hurt that much actually. I'm deeply focused, there are many people around me. I hear the sound of surgical instruments inside my skull. I hum a song from my childhood to cover the sound up. It seems it's going to last ages; the moment I think about it it's already over. Now bandages and more bandages. I take the cryogenic pieces of my scalp inside a surgical steel bottle and leave with my new face, now in pain.

7

I write down what I feel, what I think. I record and take selfies of my facial changes. I reflect. I start endless debates on Instagram. 500 people answer, some of them love me, others insult me. They tell me what I do is horrible. A girl looks into my life, she messages me using other profiles every time I upload something new. She is a stalker, one of many. I have to wait for her to get bored. I use this for my work. I make screenshots of things that matter to me while I recover from the surgery.

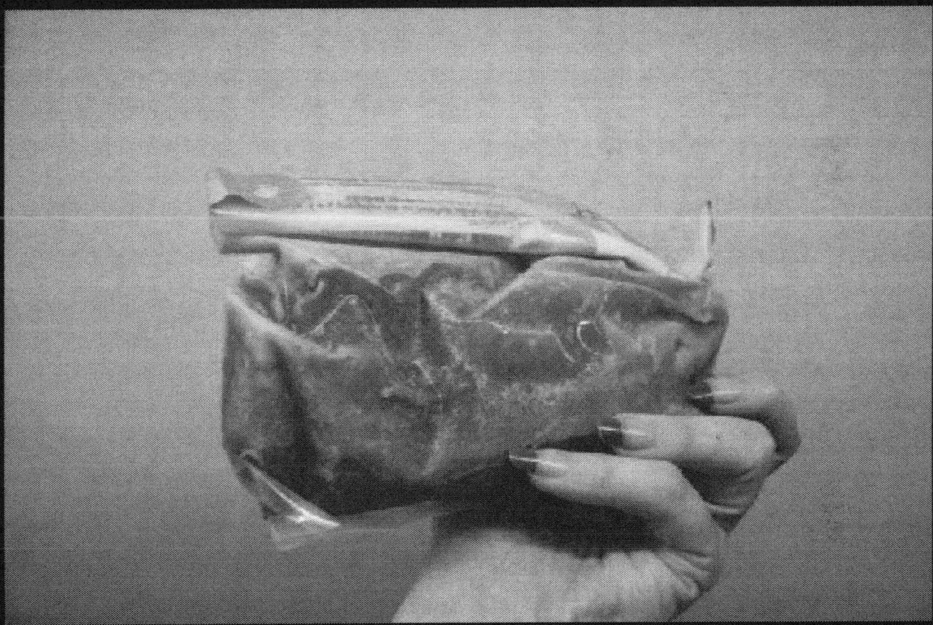

najir austin

is defined by his thought provoking lyrics and buttery flows, the New Jersey rapper combines infectious sounds with a fiery spirit. He reintroduces the familiar roar of an emcee, inviting the world into his imaginative landscapes persuading listeners to come face to face with their humanity. A graduate of SVA, the 24 year-old has already garnered notable attention in a short time with his debut song "Can I Call You" and a recent feature on an East Coast mixtape which received over 20,000 listens. Najir leads ORGANEYES, a mission based label focused on living life according to one's higher purpose. His highly anticipated forthcoming project is set to take him to new heights as he remains someone to watch in this new era of music.

This was the week leading up to my first performance at a festival as well as my first ever performance. Everything that I had done in preparation would finally be put to the test.

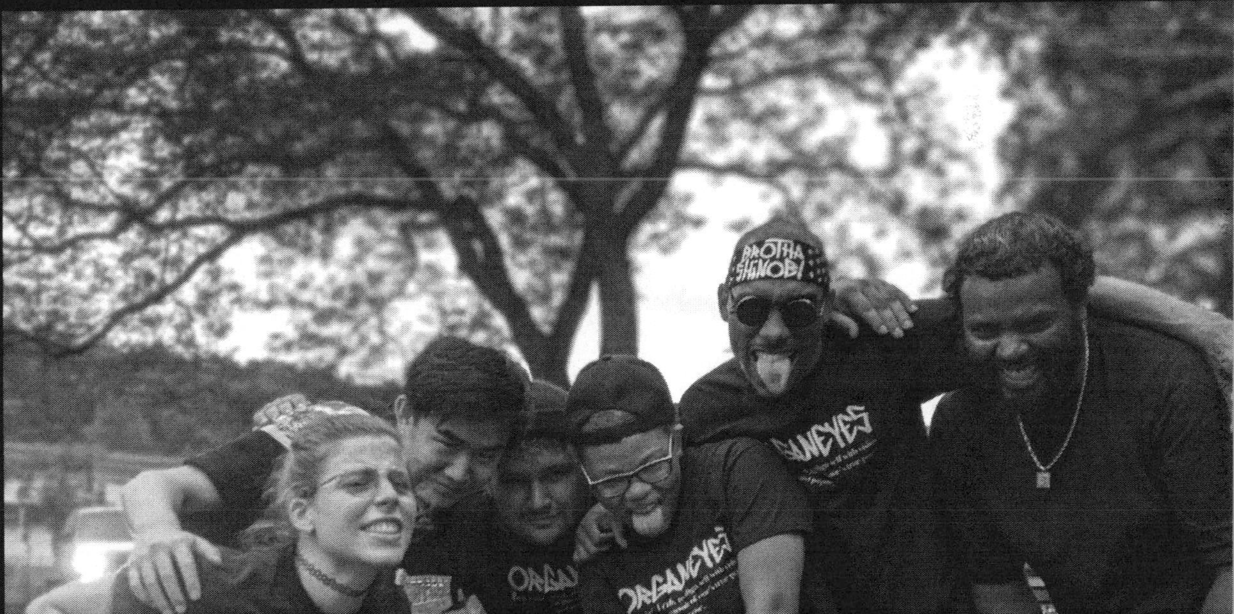

My crew who helped me put on the show, sell merch, document it.

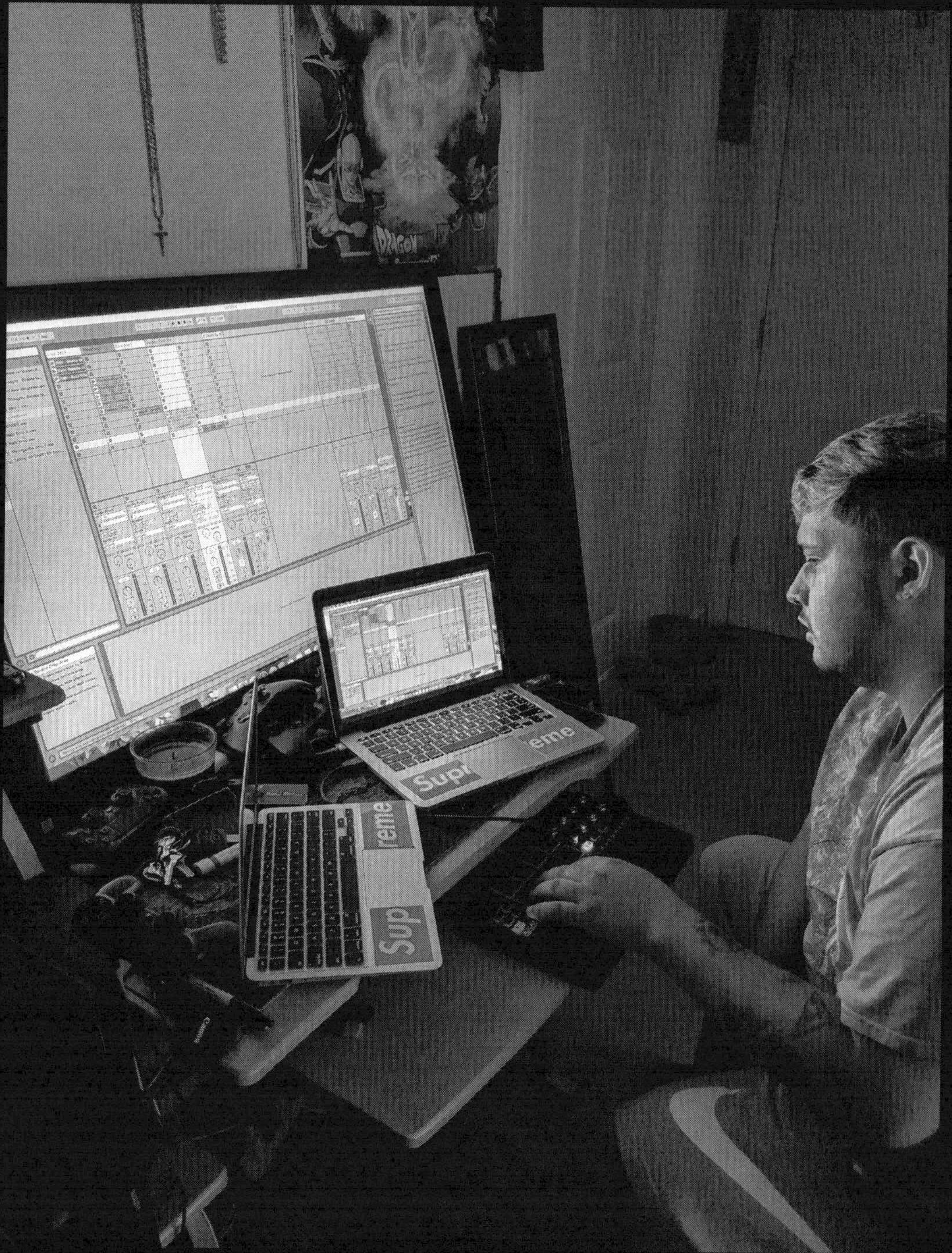

My DJ and I building the live set and practicing for the performance.

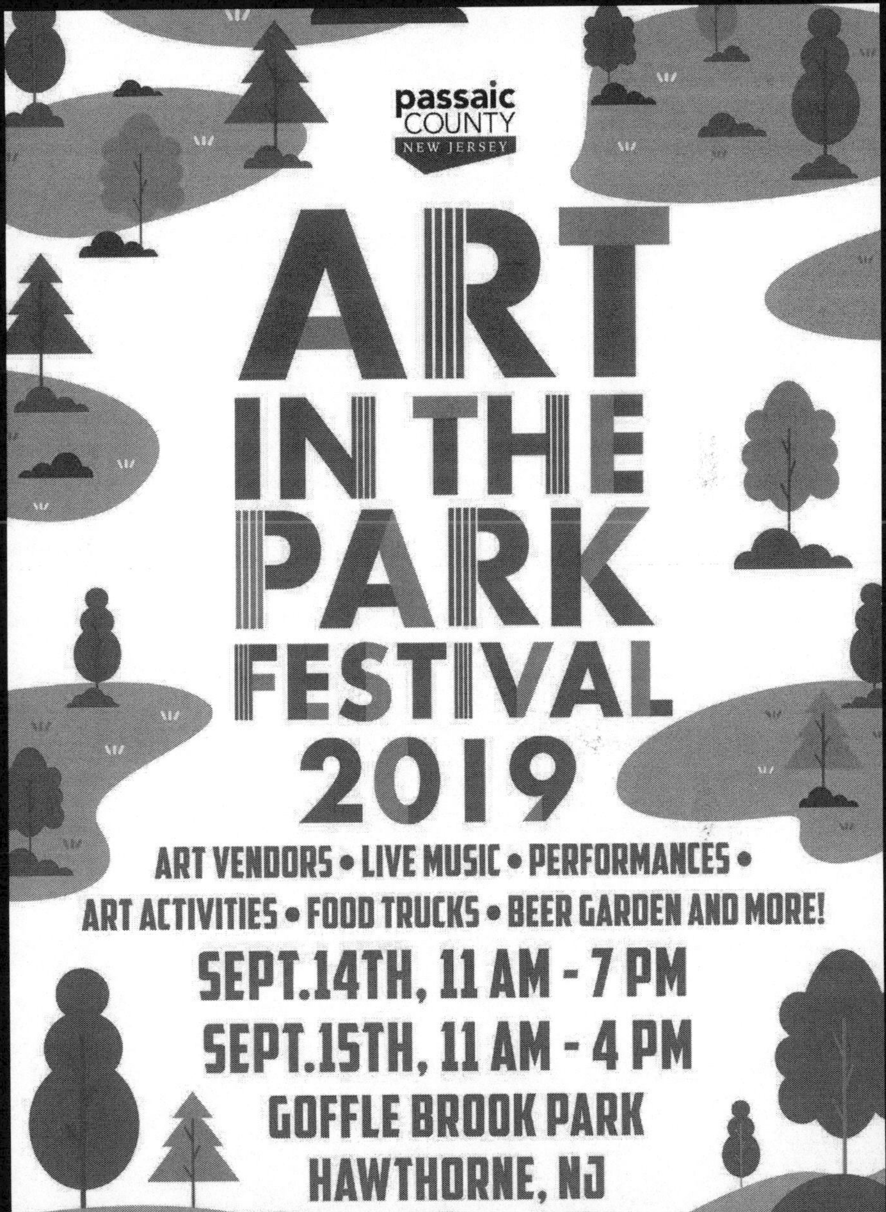

Nn ad made by the festival committee promoting my being on the festival lineup.

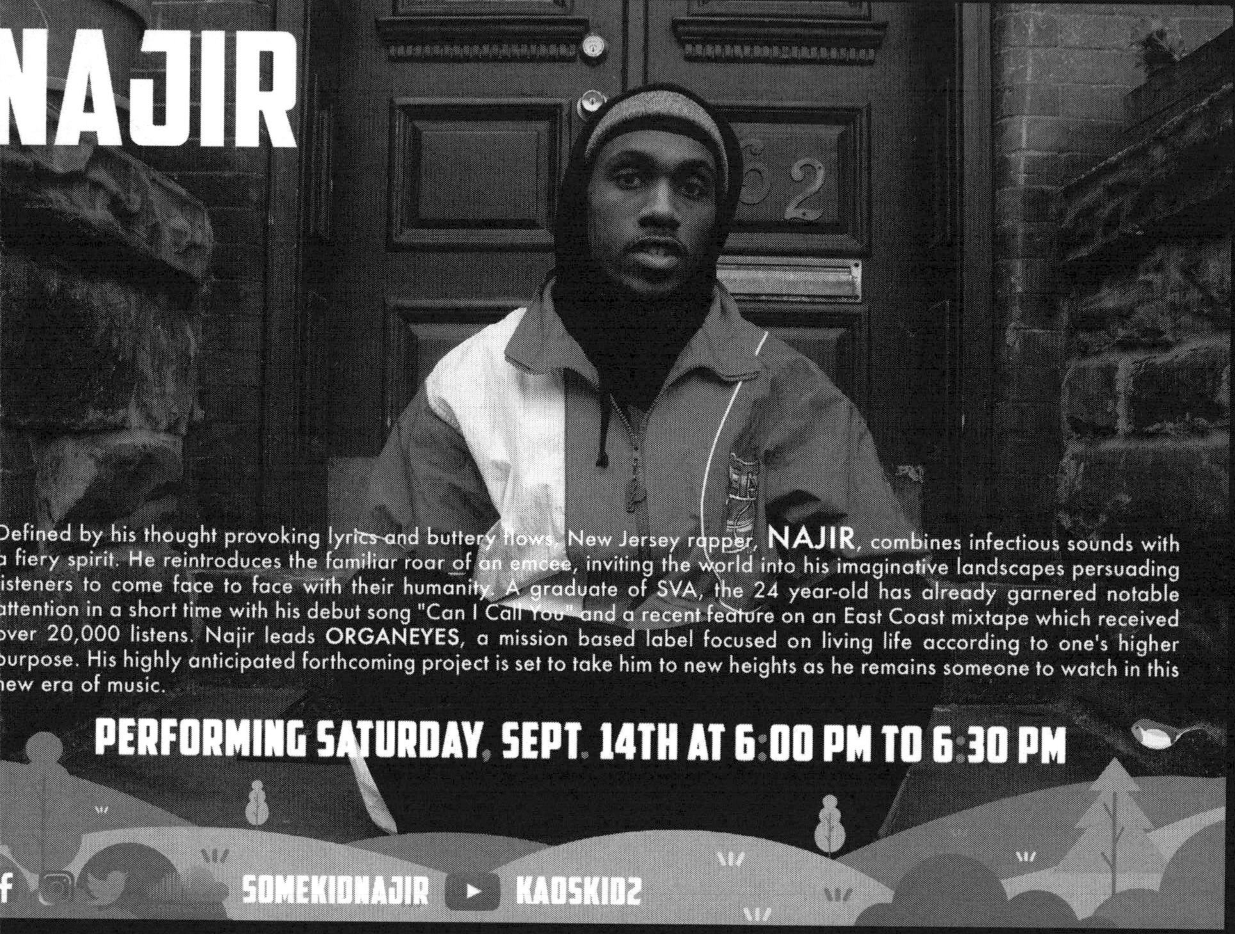

The festival poster I kept promoting all the way up to the day of the show.

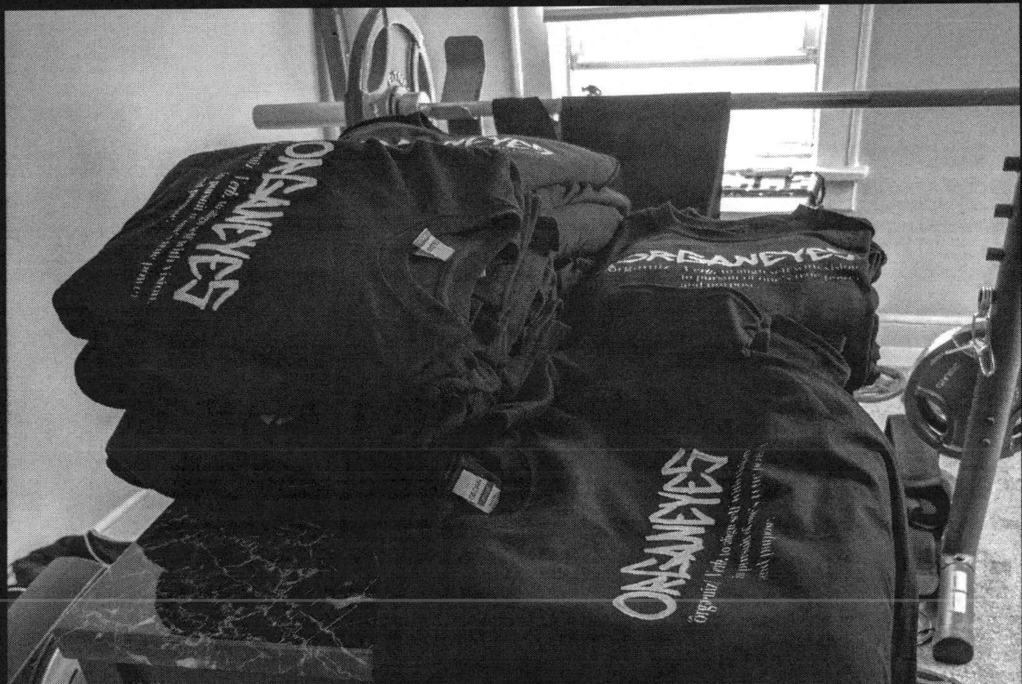

T-shirts a friend and I hand printed to sell at the show (these are still available. (Holla atcha boi, tell yo friends.)

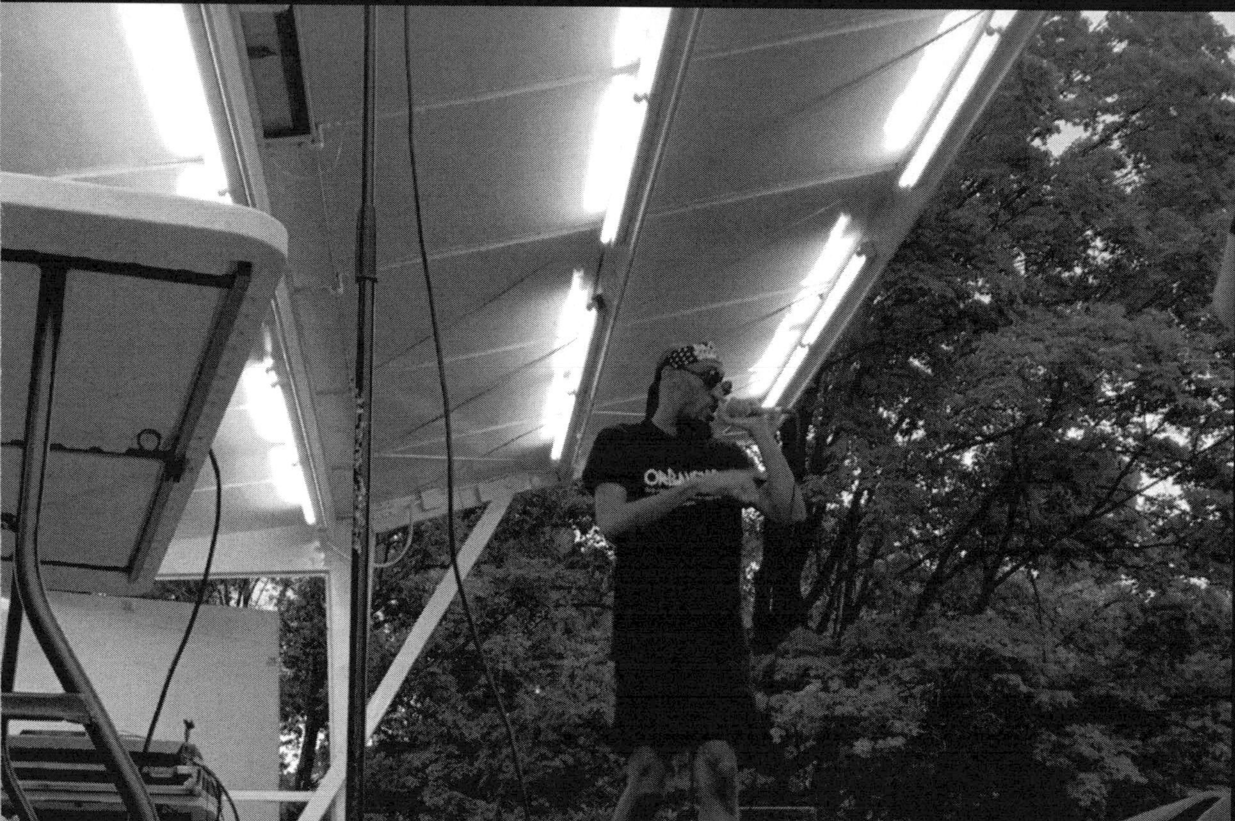

Me doing what I do on stage.

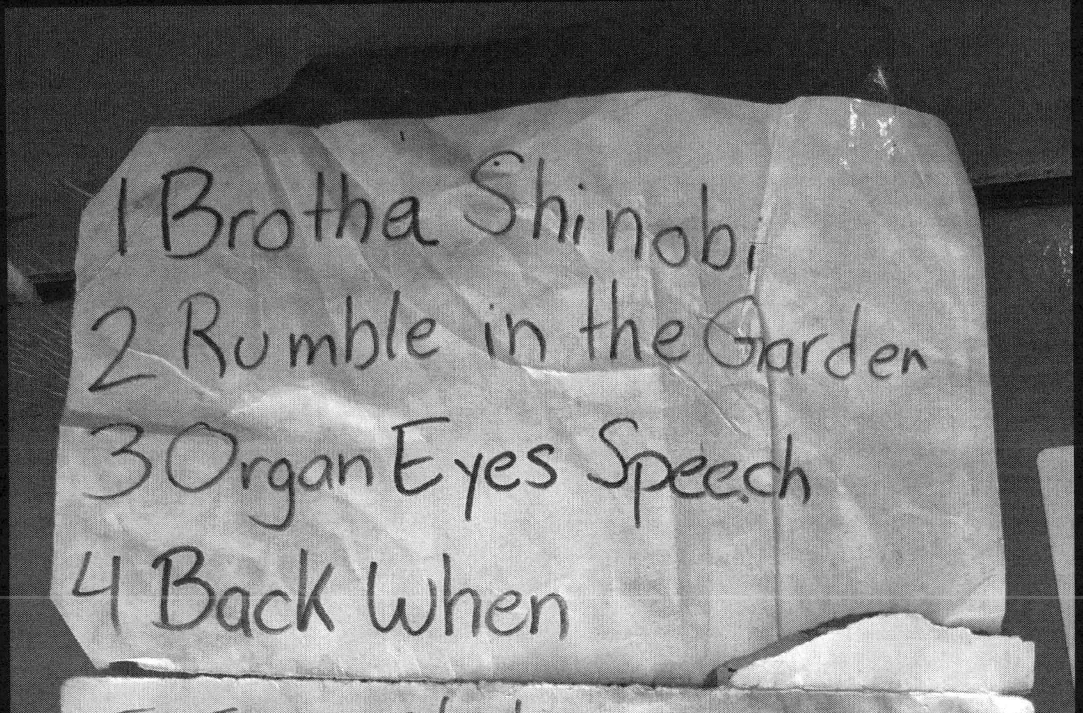
1 Brotha Shinobi
2 Rumble in the Garden
3 Organ Eyes Speech
4 Back When
5 Free Style
6 Stake your Claim
7 Jersey Club (Break)
8 Can I Call you.

john r. neeson

is a Melbourne based painter, installation artist, curator and writer. He has a PhD from Monash University and as a Samstag International scholar completed post-graduate research at The Royal College of Art, London.

My practice is three fold - studio based Still Life painting, site-specific referential installations (at 'not for profit' venues and artist residencies) and the daily photographing of Readymade Still Life. These three aspects of my practice run concurrent with each other over the course of an average week.

The Readymade Still Life is a curatorial project in which I habitually collect images of objects left on the streets by anonymous participants in city life. This daily process has resonance with the 19th century Flâneur and later the dérive of Debord and the Situationist International who strategized the conflation of art and life.

Now the networking capability of the smart phone and social media allow me to employ this strategy outside the conventions of studio practice and the 'white cube' exhibition, and enables the egalitarian reframing of these found objects as socio-political signifiers within the context of the 'readymade' and 'the still life'.

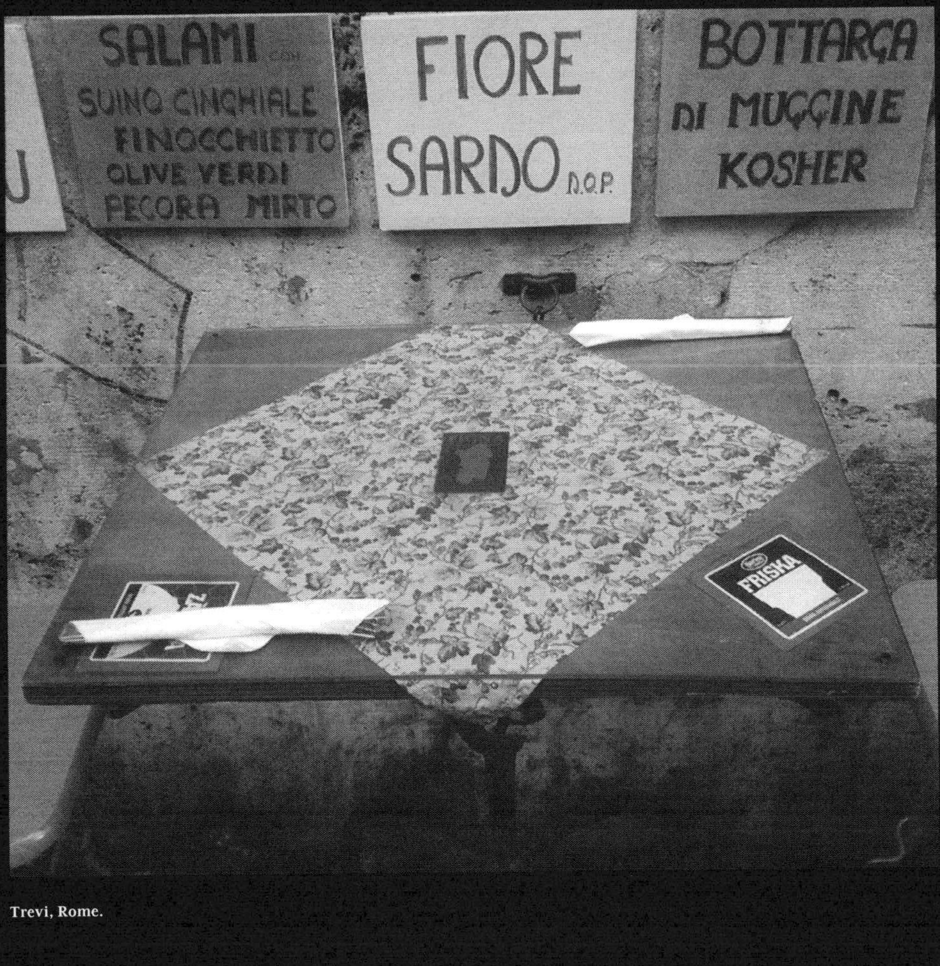
SALAMI
SUINO CINGHIALE
FINOCCHIETTO
OLIVE VERDI
PECORA MIRTO
FIORE
SARDO D.O.P.
BOTTARGA
DI MUGGINE
KOSHER
FRISKA

Trevi, Rome.

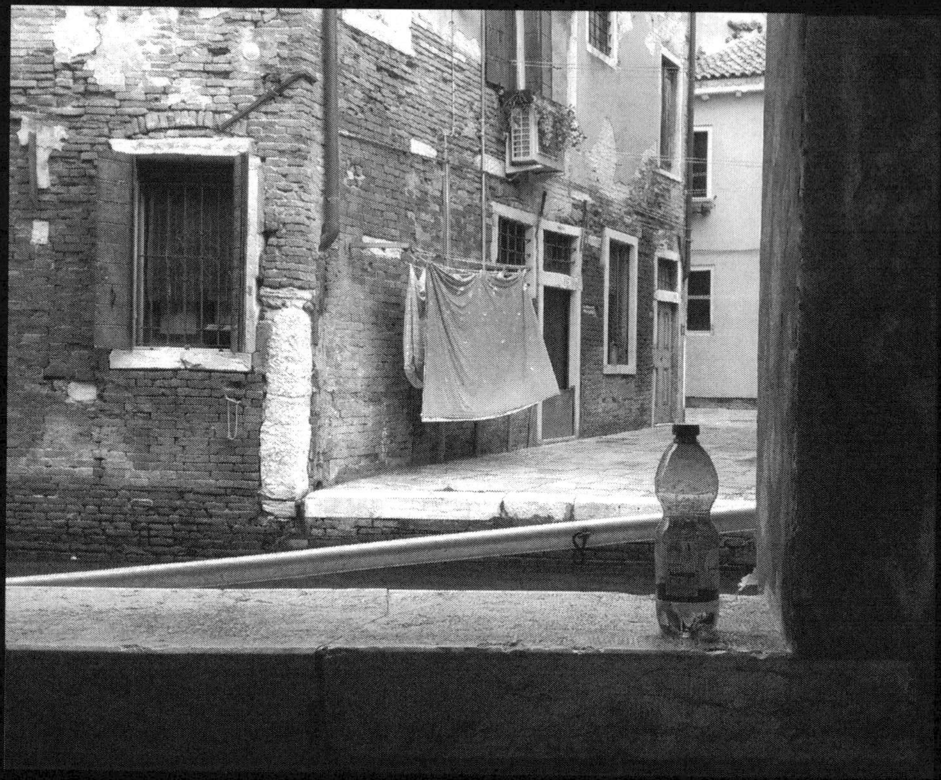

Castello, Venice

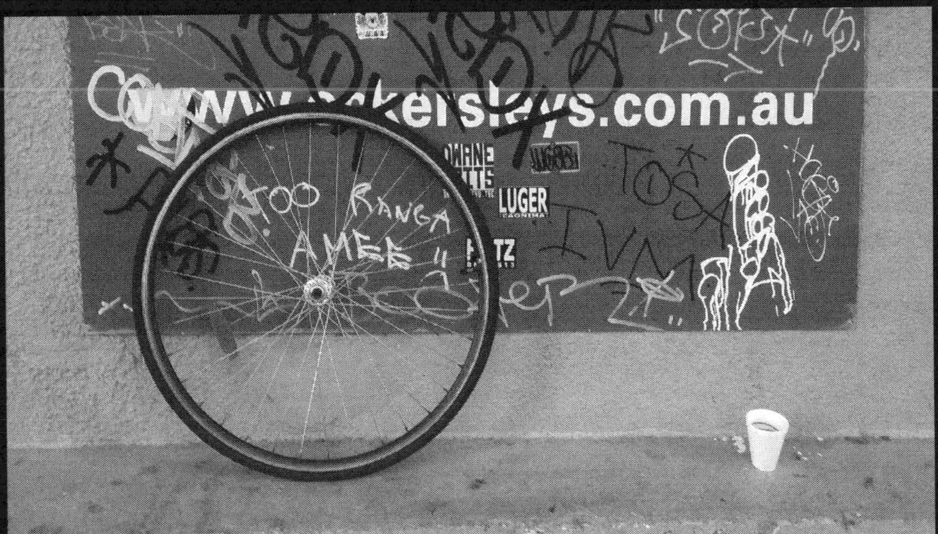

CBD, Melbourne. 20/06/2016

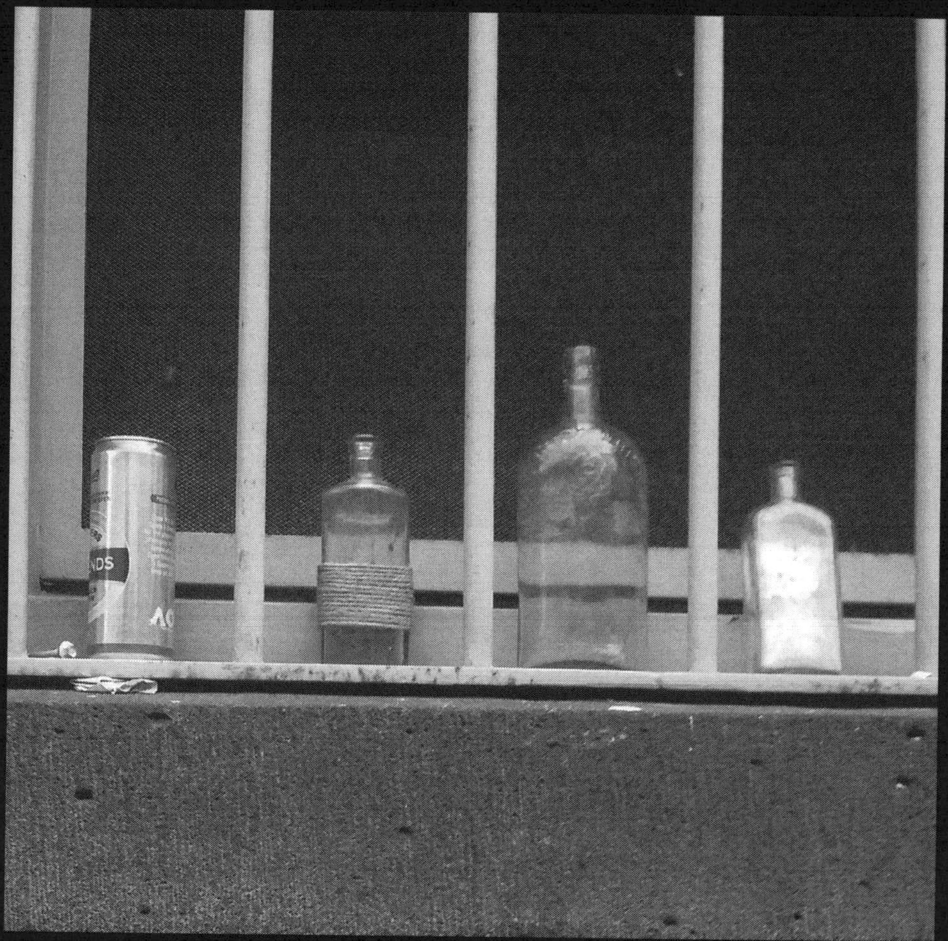

Fitzroy, Melbourne

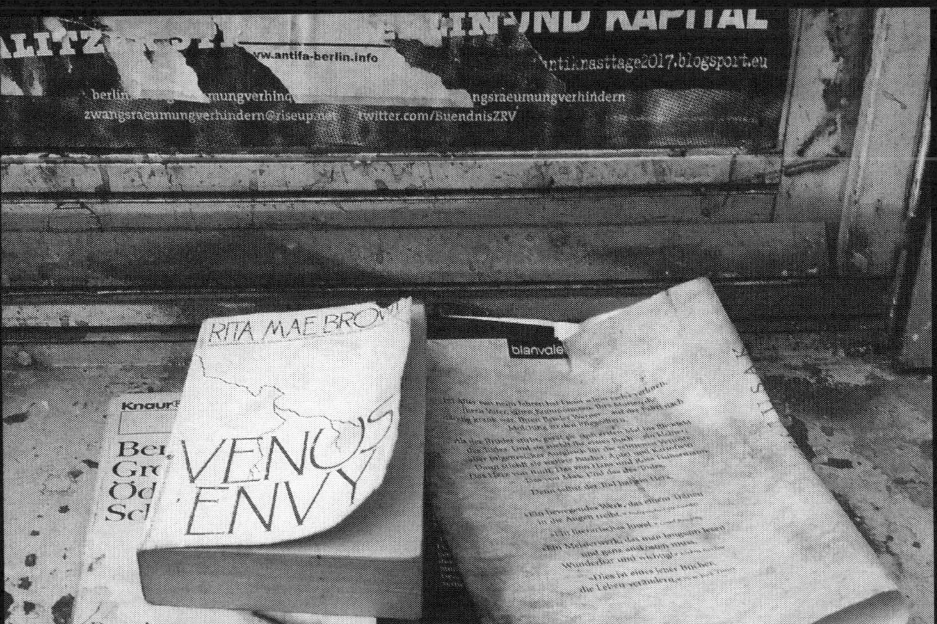

Kreuzburg, Berlin

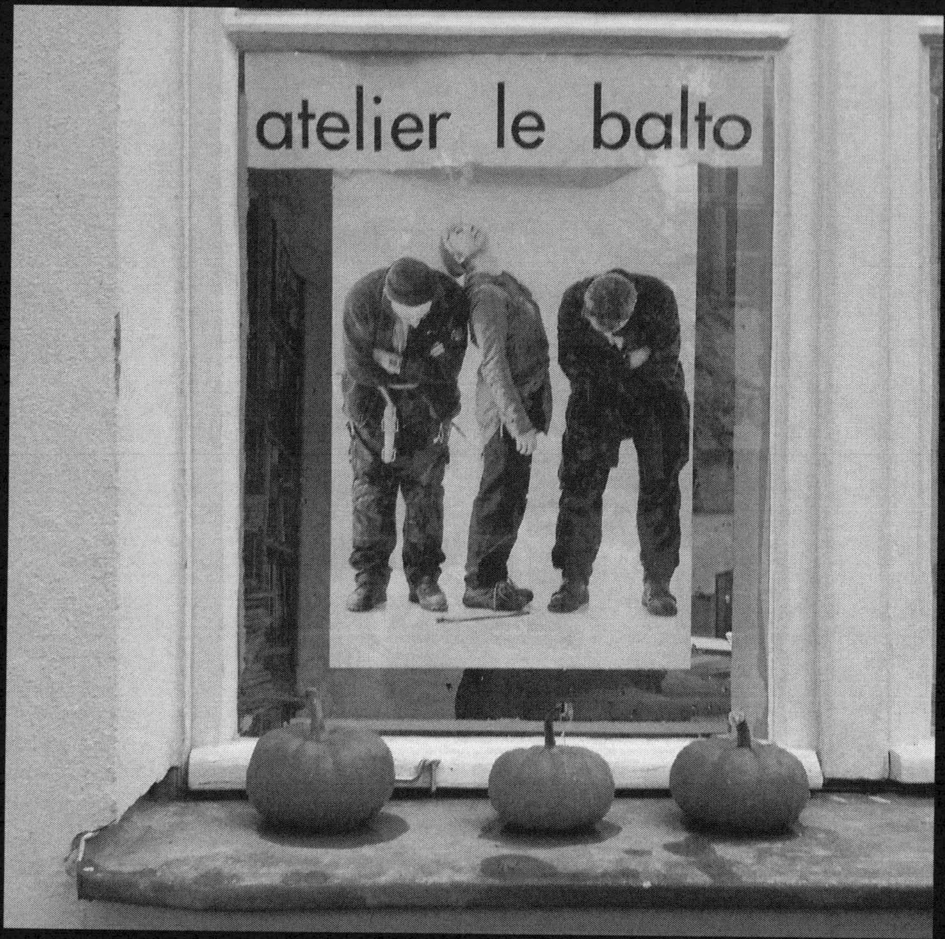

Mitte, Berlin

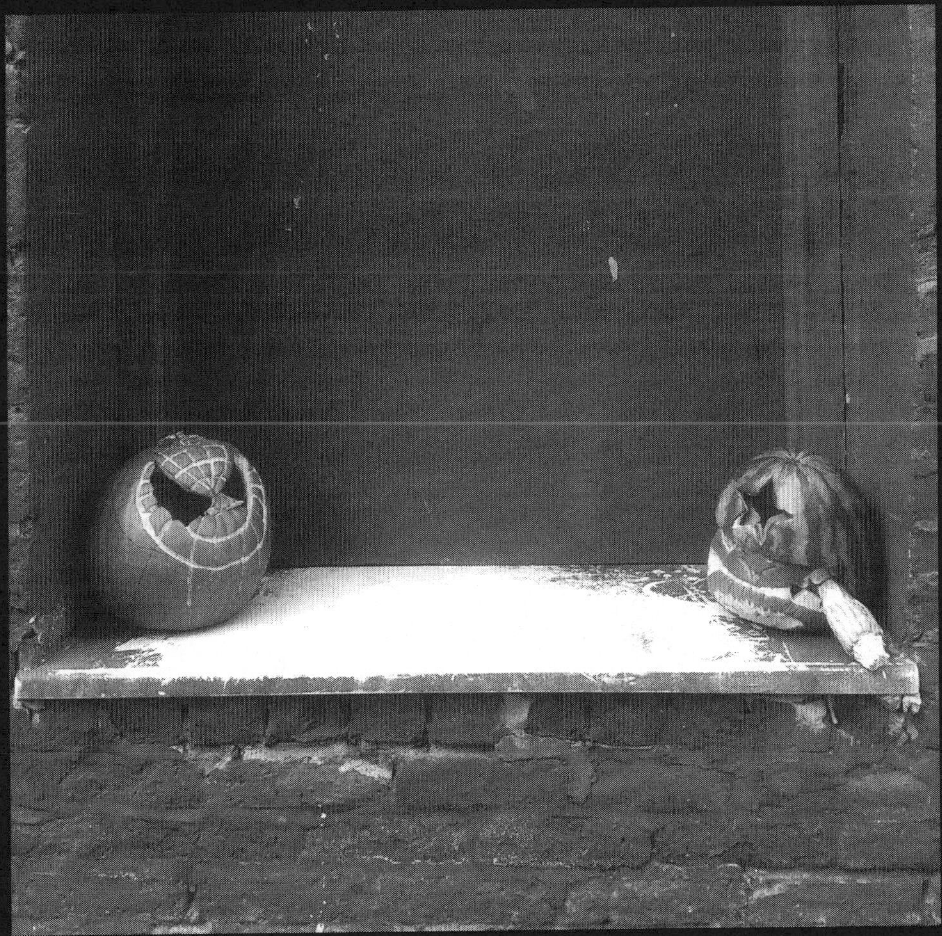

Williamsburg, New York

jeanette doyle

is a visual artist. Her practice encompasses the production of painterly objects alongside digital works and performative collaborations.

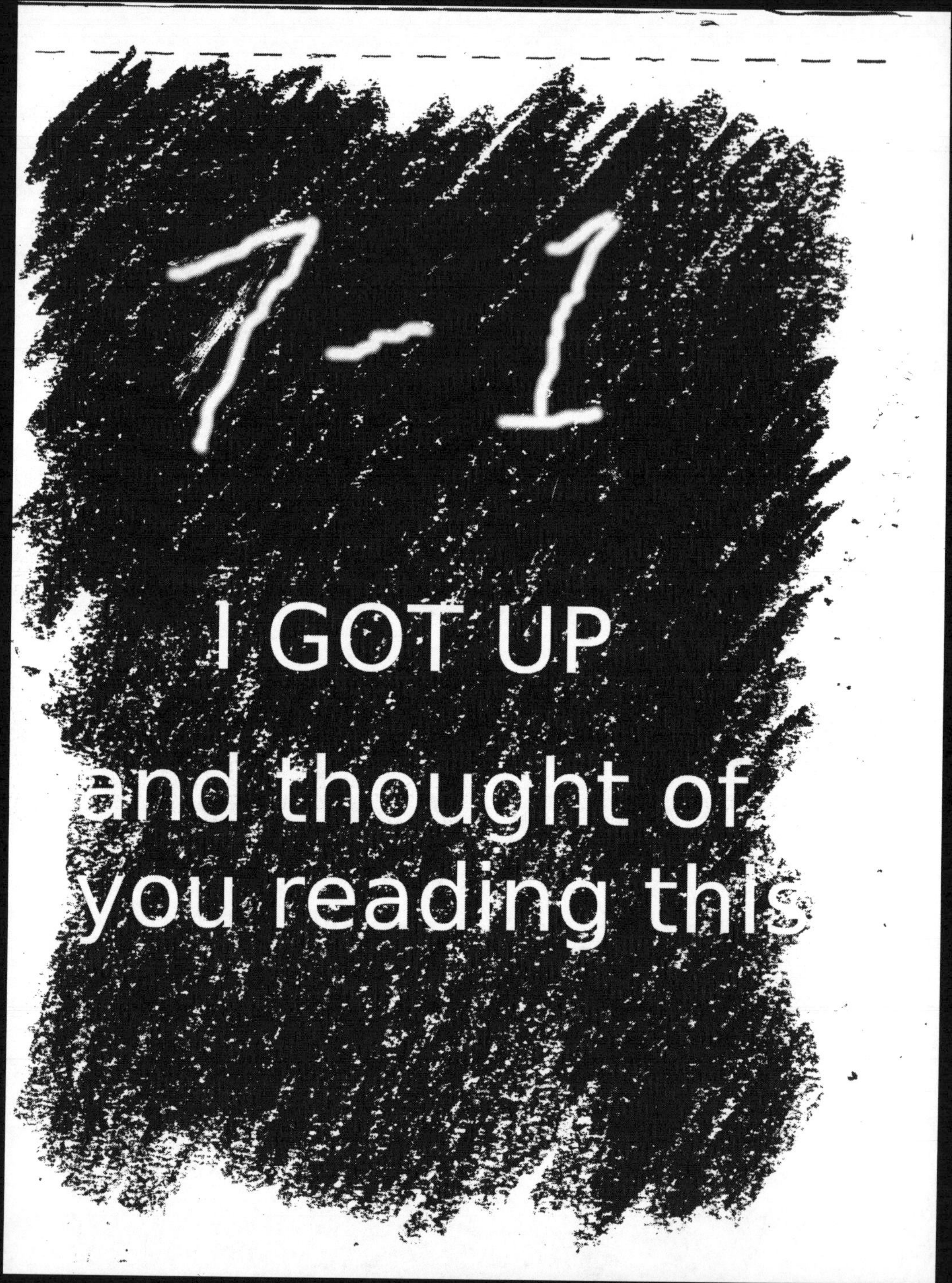
7-1
I GOT UP
and thought of
you reading this

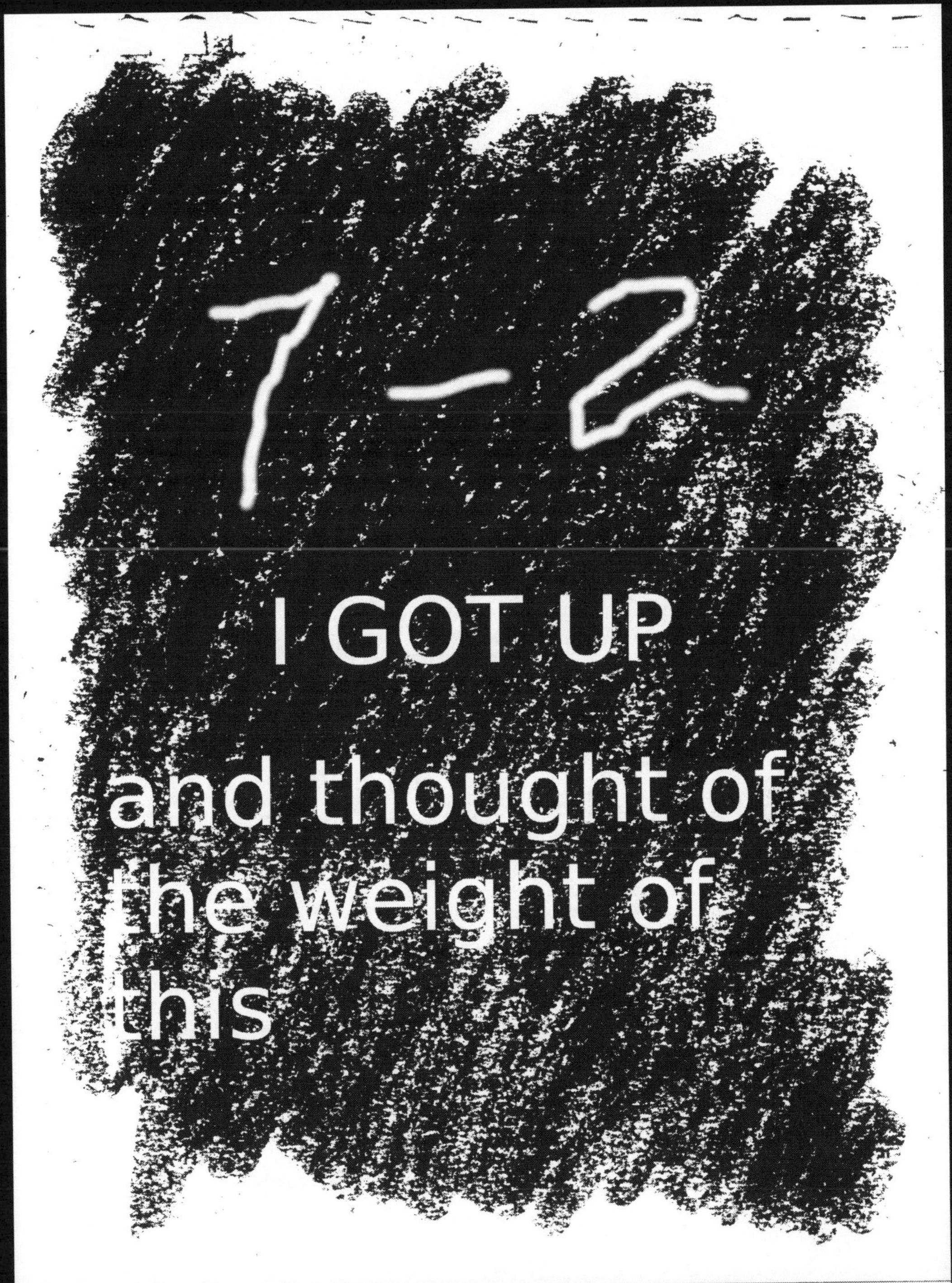
7-2
I GOT UP
and thought of
the weight of
this

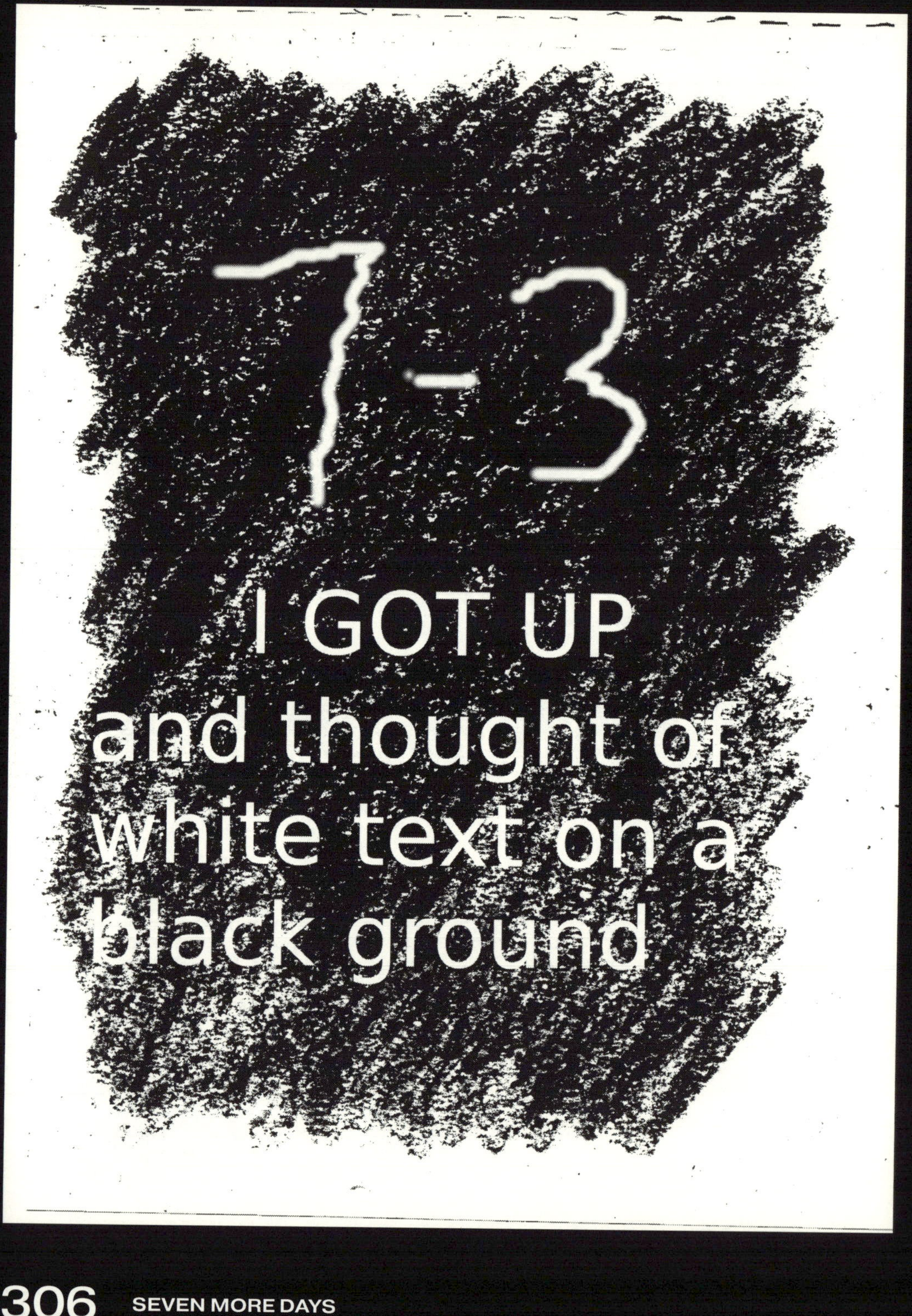
7-3
I GOT UP
and thought of
white text on a
black ground

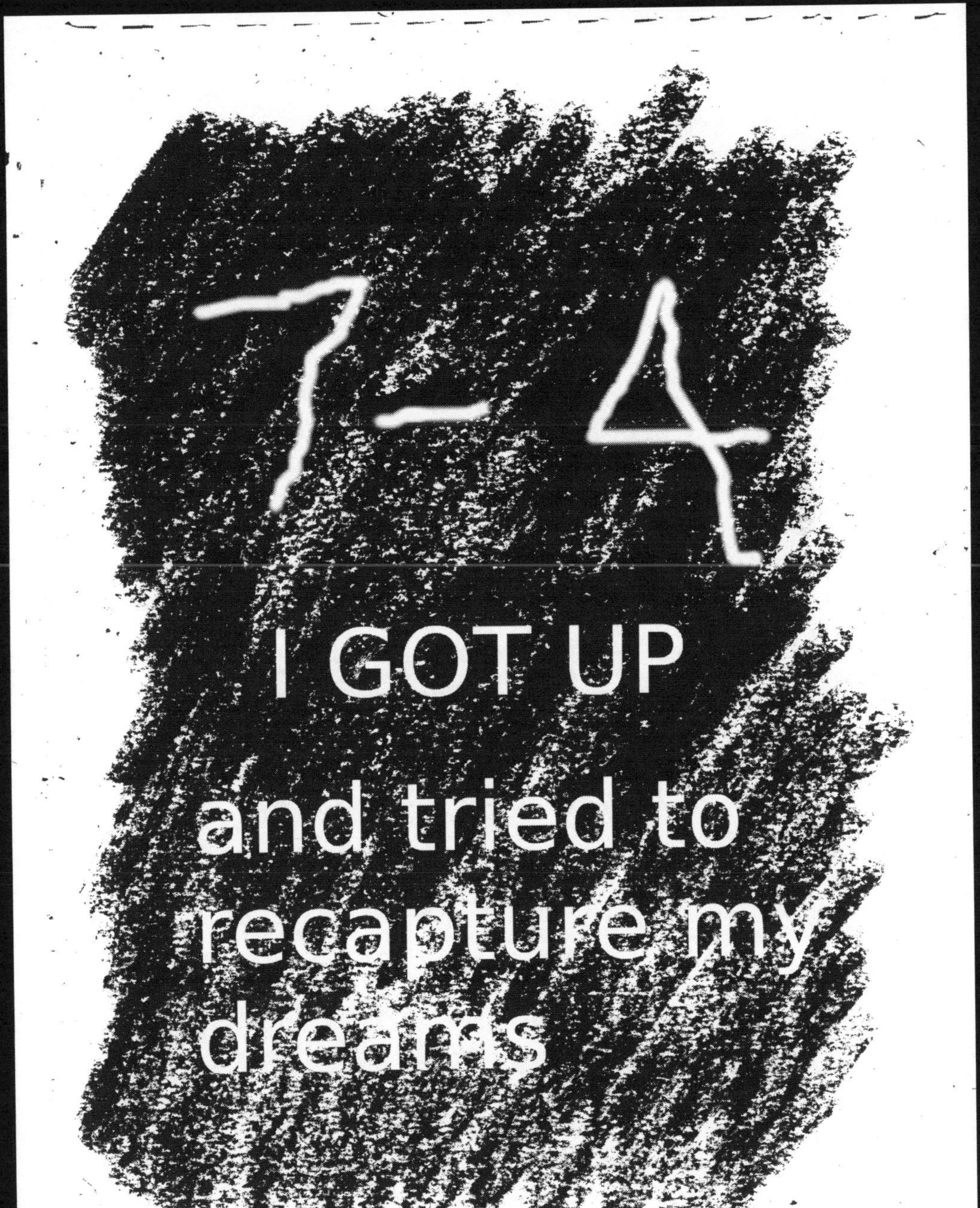
7-4
I GOT UP
and tried to
recapture my
dreams

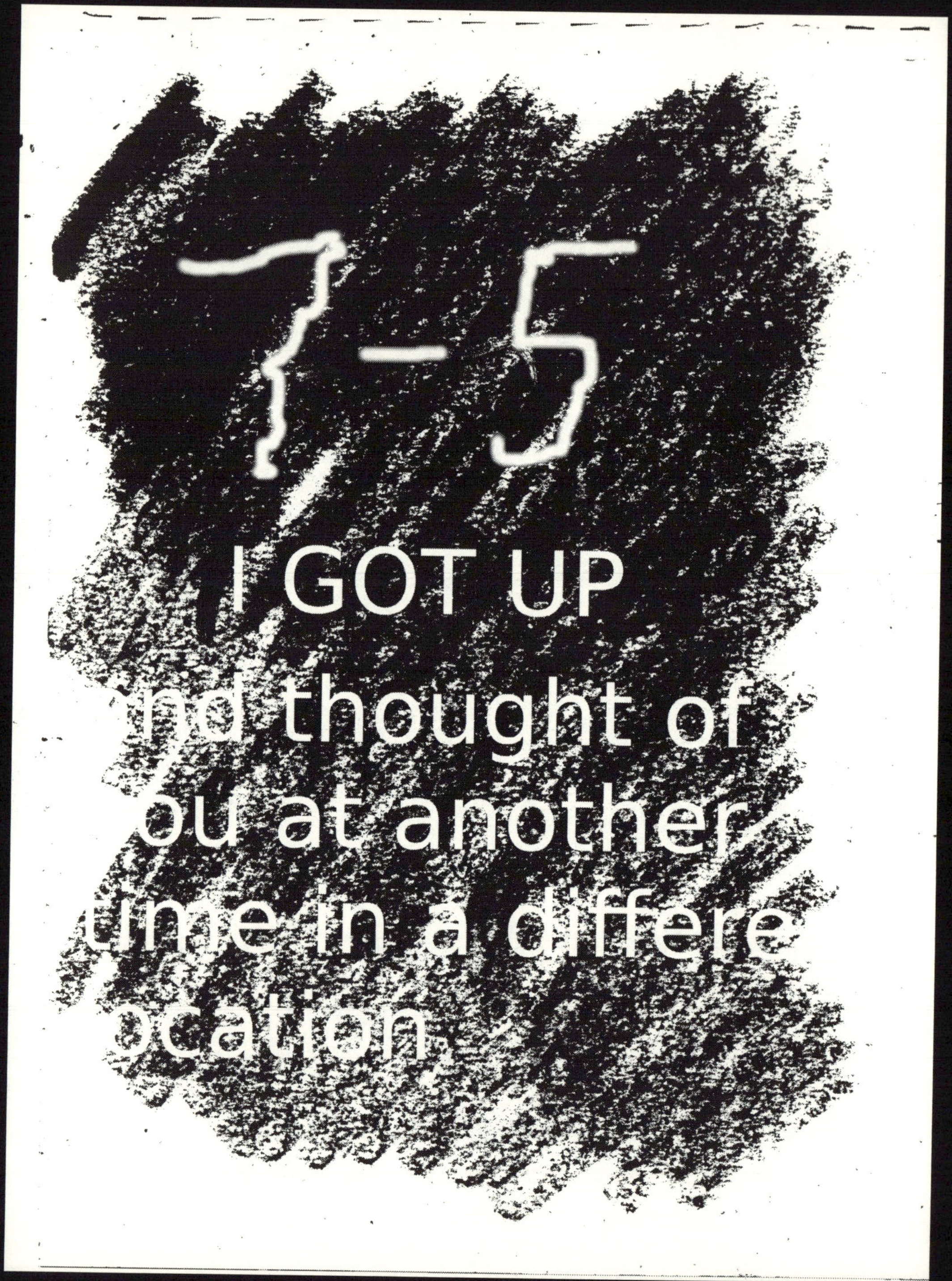
7-5
I GOT UP
nd thought of
ou at another
time in a differe
ocation

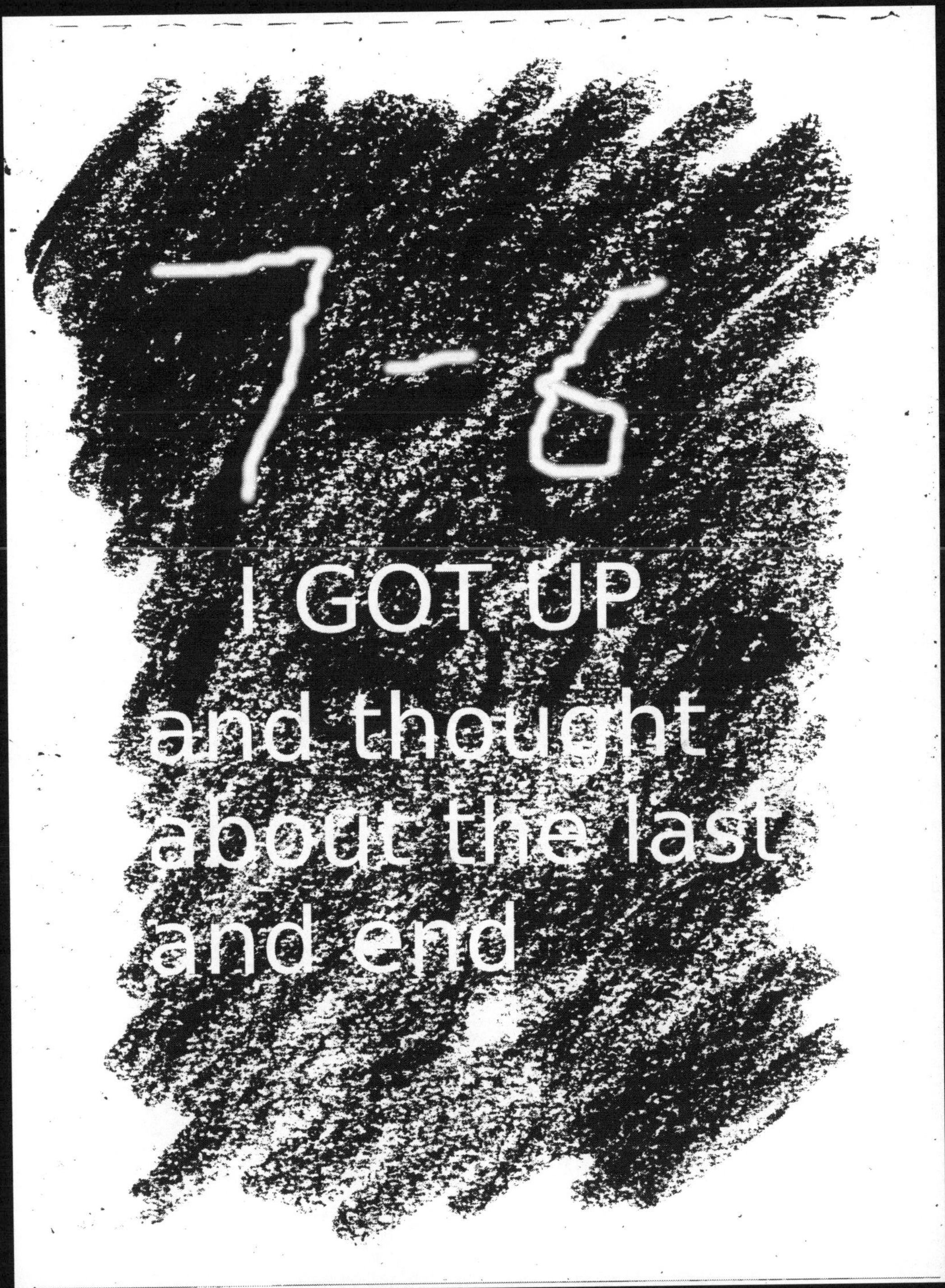
7-6
I GOT UP
and thought
about the last
and end

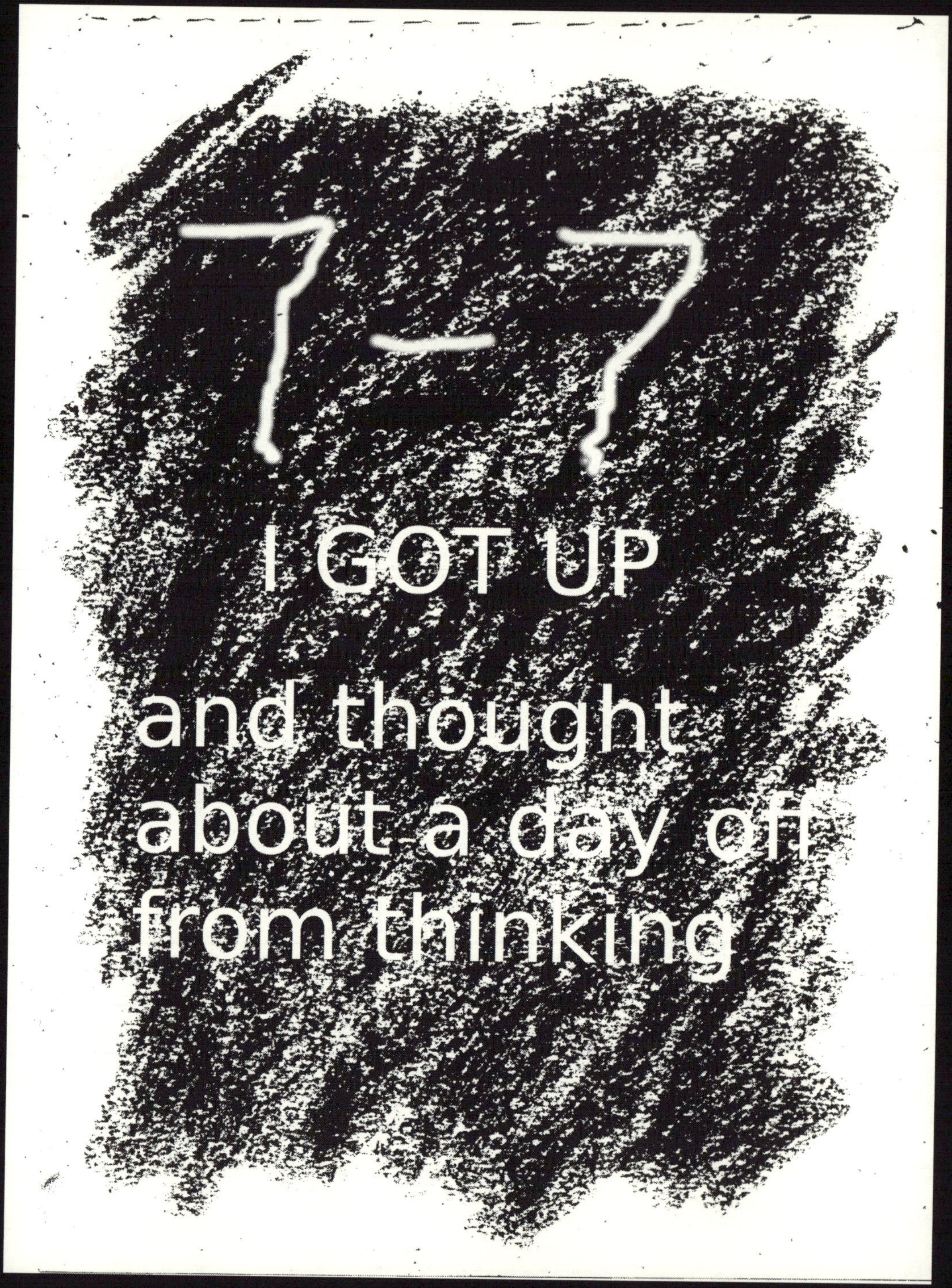
7-7
I GOT UP
and thought
about a day off
from thinking

dan cameron

is an American art curator based in New York. He is the Artistic Director at Open Spaces KC and was the Senior Curator at the New Museum BAM Art in Brooklyn.

40 years ago this week, I arrived in NYC with the dream of becoming a curator. I came in on an Adirondack Trailways bus (not Greyhound). A handful of high school and college friends had preceded me, and I had a tentative job, plus some contacts made from a couple of Bennington College work-study terms. There was no money or family connections, so I'd decided reluctantly that I couldn't afford grad school.

Looking back, it amazes me that a month later I was already living in the apartment I presently own, and that by September 1982 I'd finished my first New Museum exhibition, while working on 2 other museum shows. By September 1986 I was wrapping up my first big European museum exhibition, and co-organizing the Venice Biennale two years after that. This fairly rapid succession of events is arguably why, for me, this month always symbolizes a moment for new beginnings.

jonathon keats

is a conceptual artist, fabulist and critic residing in San Francisco and Northern Italy. Recently, he choreographed the first ballet for honeybees at Yerba Buena Center for the Arts. He has also exhibited extraterrestrial abstract artwork at the Judah L. Magnes Museum, unveiled a prototype Ouija voting booth for the 2008 election at the Berkeley Art Museum, and attempted to genetically engineer God in collaboration with scientists at the University of California, Berkeley. He is the recipient of fellowships from Yaddo and the MacDowell Colony, and is represented by Modernism Gallery, San Francisco, CA.

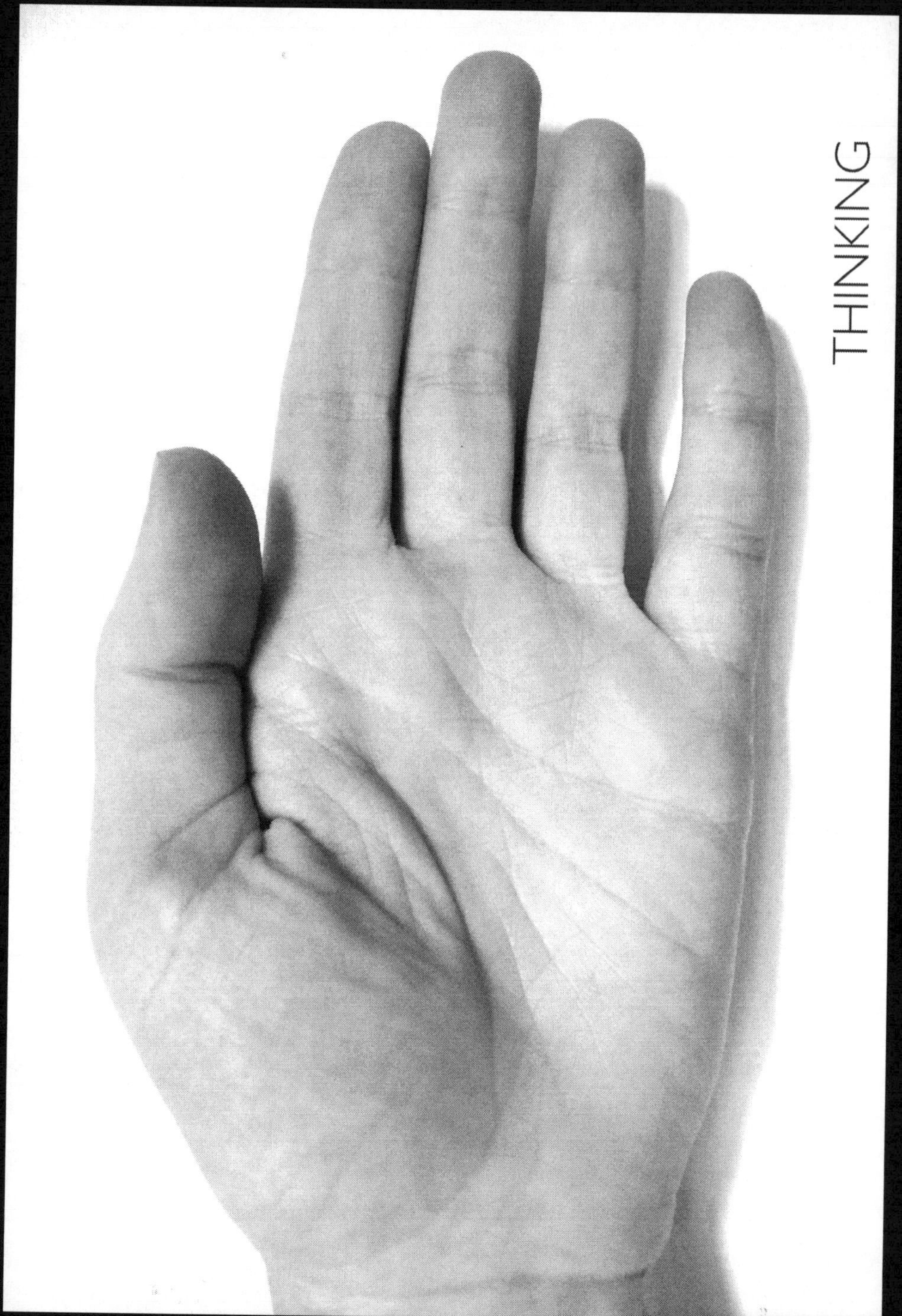
THINKING

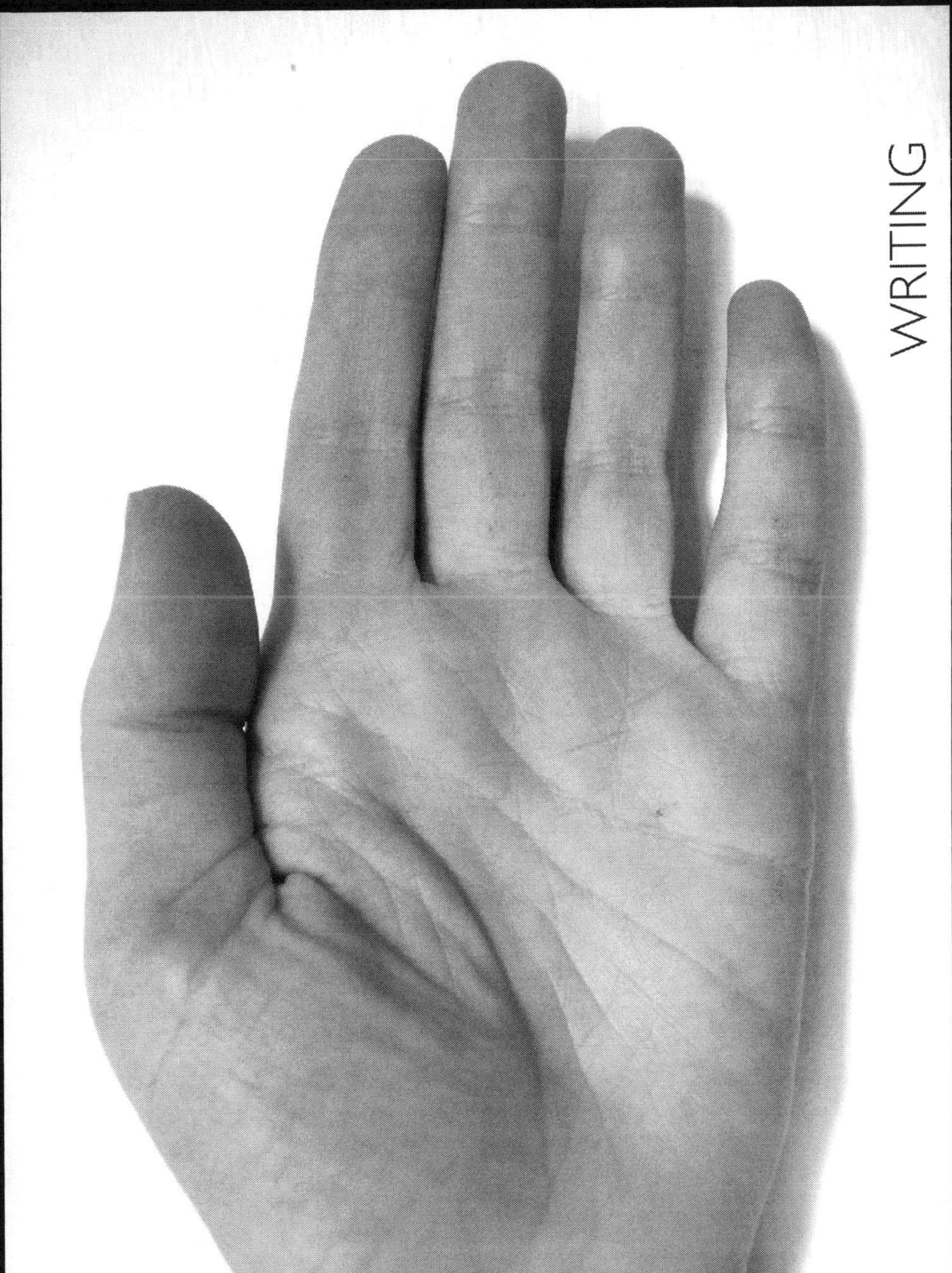
WRITING

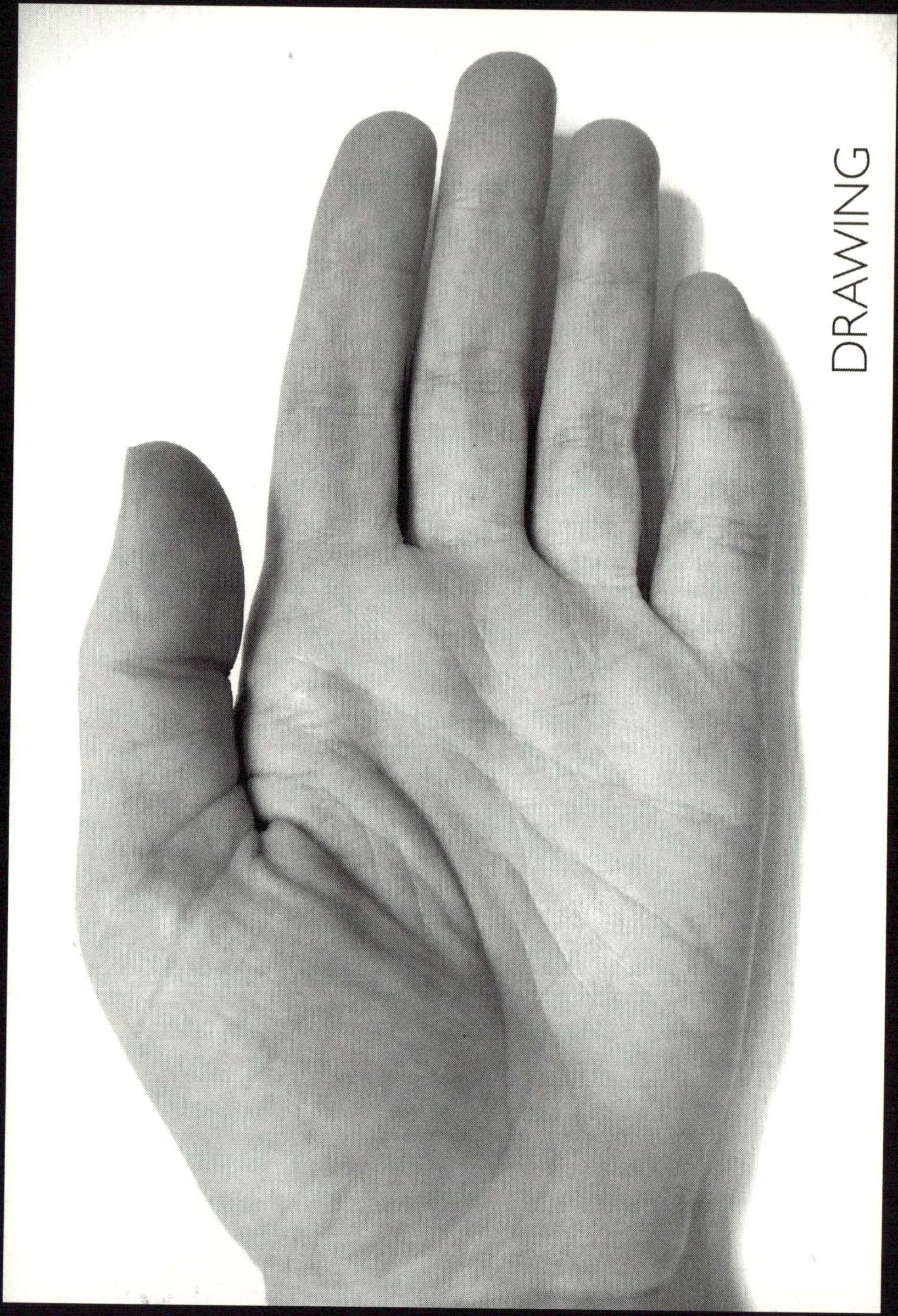
DRAWING

MEASURING

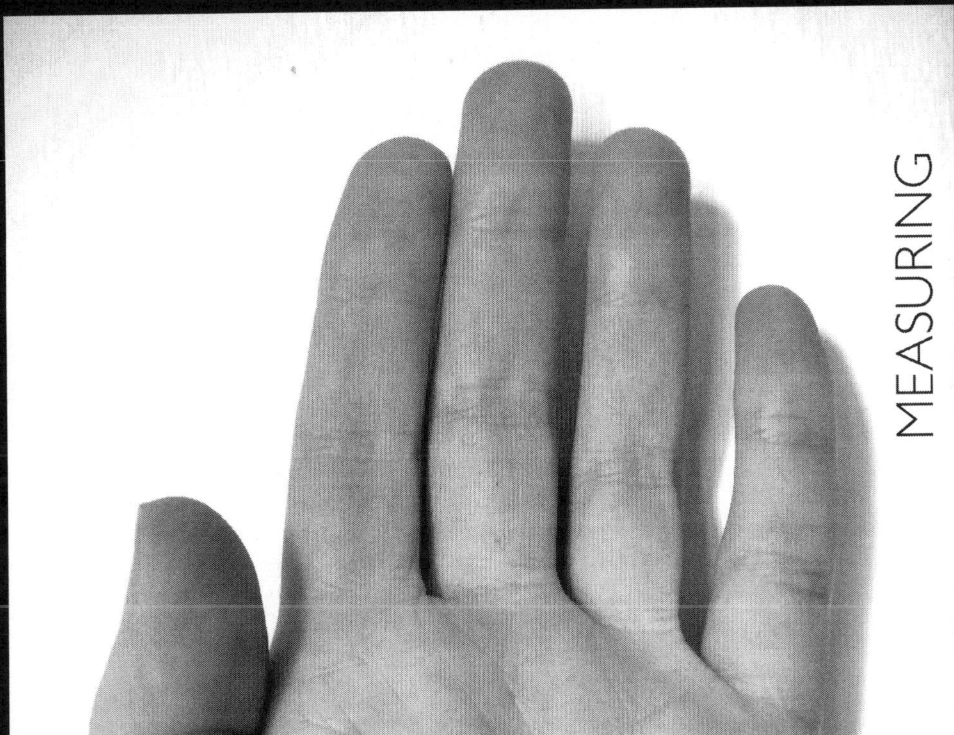

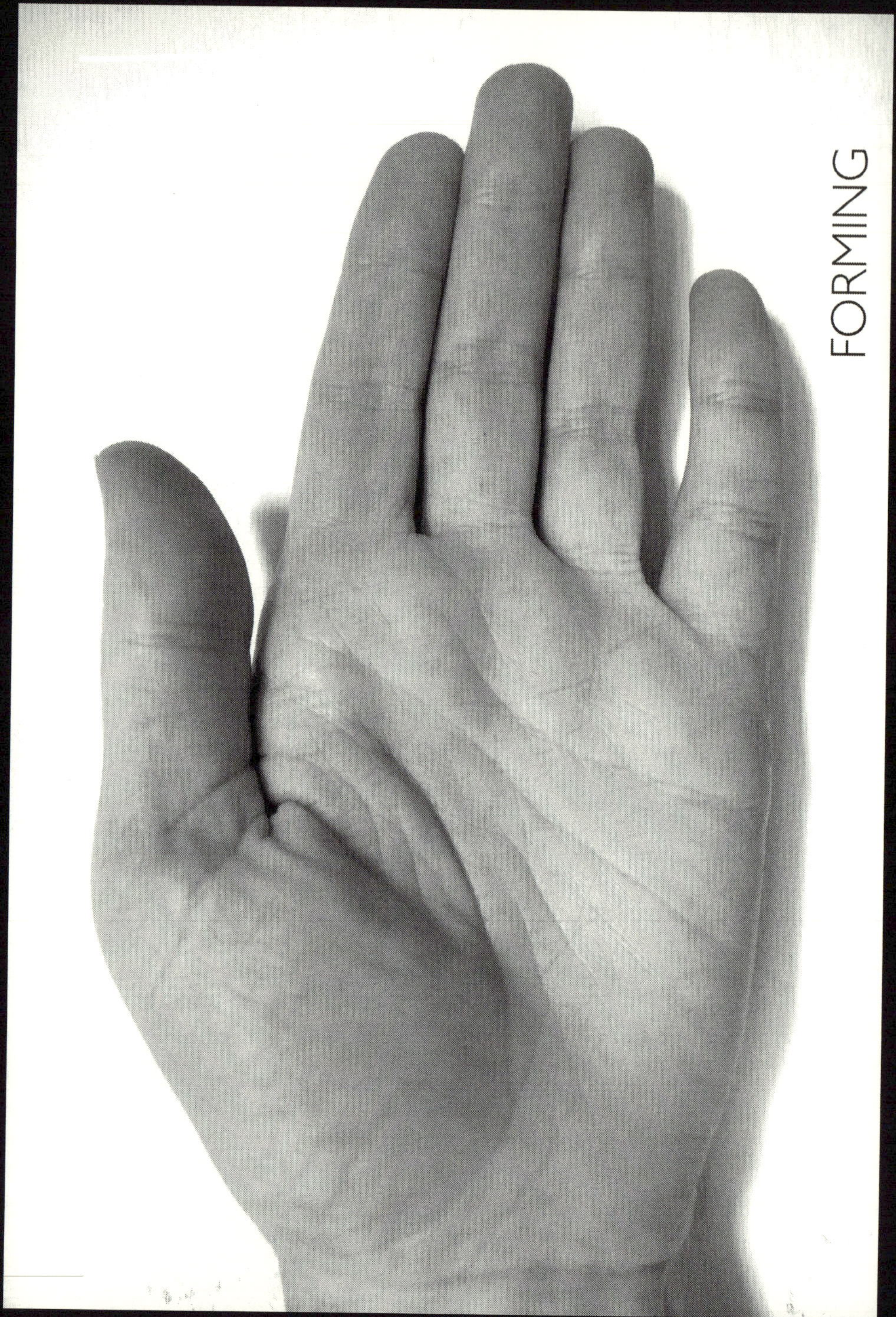
FORMING

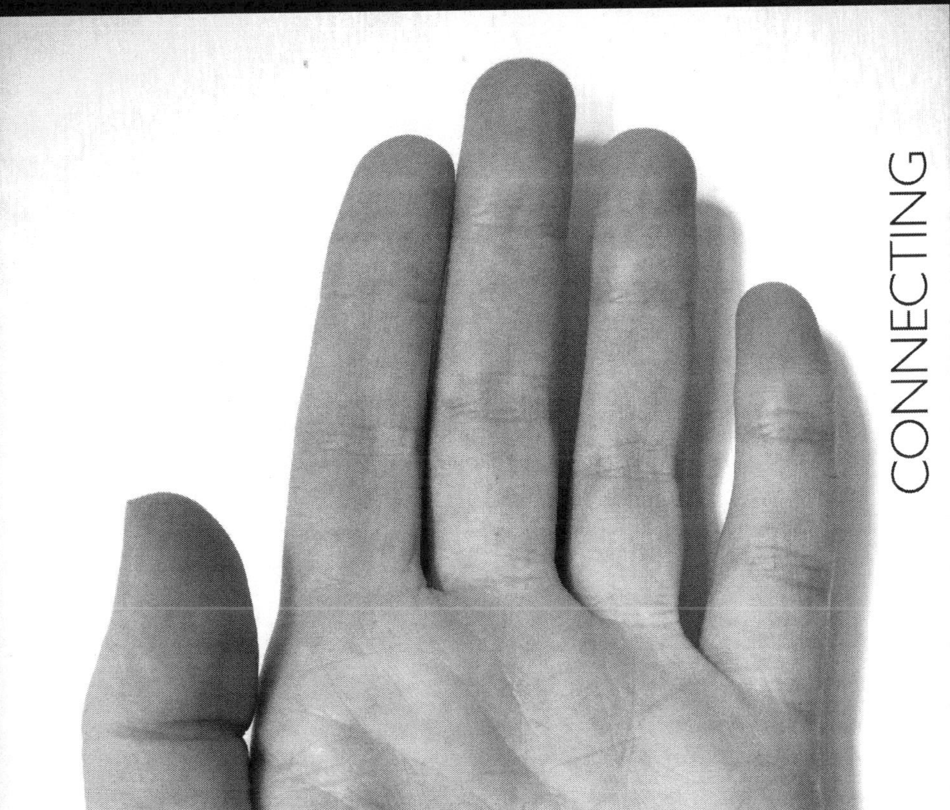
CONNECTING

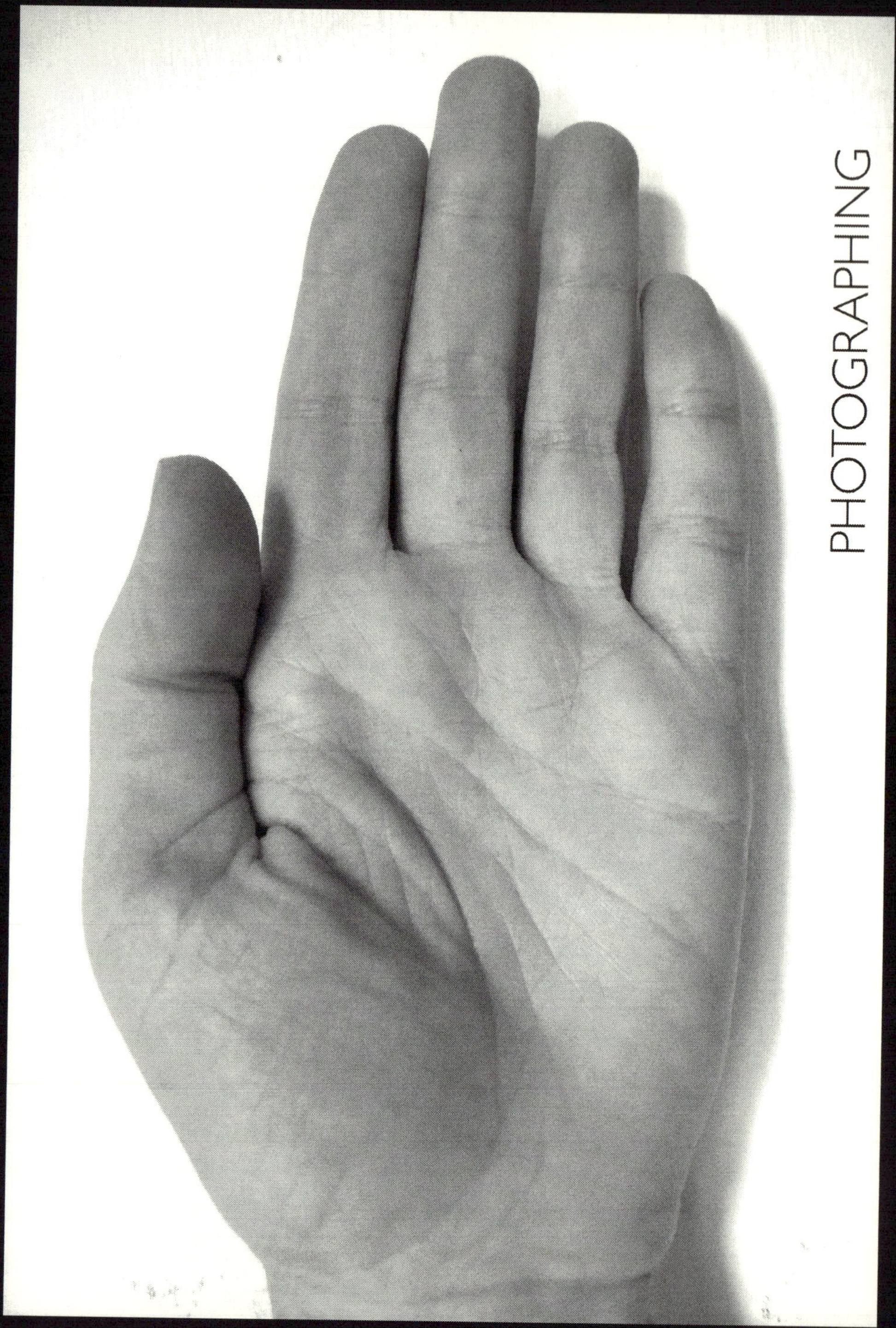

PHOTOGRAPHING